Language Arts Handbook

Level 6

A Division of The McGraw-Hill Companies

Columbus, Ohio

▶ **Consultants:**

Jean Wallace Gillet, Charles Temple, and James D. Williams

▶ **Acknowledgments:**

Grateful acknowledgment is given to the following publishers and copyright owners for permissions granted to reprint selections from their publications. All possible care has been taken to trace ownership and secure permission for each selection included. In case of any errors or omissions, the Publisher will be pleased to make suitable acknowledgments in future editions.

"Sweeping Pittsburgh Clean" from MAKING HEADLINES: A BIOGRAPHY OF NELLIE BLY by Kathy Lynn Emerson. Copyright © 1989 by Dillon Press. Used by permission of the author.

From SAVING THE PEREGRINE FALCON by Caroline Arnold. Text copyright © 1985 by Caroline Arnold. Published by Carolrhoda Books, Inc. a division of Lerner Publishing Group. Used by permission of the publisher. All rights reserved.

From ALEJANDRO'S GIFT text copyright © 1994 by Richard E. Albert. Reprinted with permission by Chronicle Books, San Francisco, California. All rights reserved.

From NATURAL FIRE: ITS ECOLOGY IN FORESTS reprinted by permission of Laurence Pringle. Copyright © 1979 by Laurence Pringle.

From The Nightingale by Hans Christian Andersen by Eva Le Gallienne. Text copyright © 1965 by Eva Le Gallienne. Selection reprinted by permission of International Creative Management.

"Amaroq, the Wolf" from JULIE OF THE WOLVES. TEXT COPYRIGHT © 1972 BY JEAN CRAIGHEAD GEORGE. Used by permission of HarperCollins Publishers.

"How Doth the Little Crocodile" from OWLS AND PUSSYCATS by Lewis Carroll © 1993 by permission of Oxford University Press.

From THE WRIGHT BROTHERS: HOW THEY INVENTED THE AIRPLANE by Russell Freedman. Copyright © 1991 by Russell Freedman. All rights reserved. Reprinted by permission of Holiday House, Inc.

From THE MOST BEAUTIFUL ROOF IN THE WORLD by Kathryn Lasky, text copyright © 1997 by Kathryn Lasky Knight, reprinted with permission of Harcourt, Inc.

From HATCHET by Gary Paulsen, reprinted with the permission of Simon & Schuster Books for Young Readers, an imprint of Simon & Schuster Children's Publishing Division. Copyright © 1987 by Gary Paulsen.

"The Search for Early Americans" reprinted with the permission of Margaret K. McElderry Books, an imprint of Simon & Schuster Children's Publishing Division from SEARCHES IN THE AMERICAN DESERT by Sheila Cowing. Copyright © 1989 Sheila Cowing.

From "I Have a Dream" reprinted by arrangement with the Heirs to the Estate of Martin Luther King, Jr., c/o Writers House, Inc. as agent for the proprietor. Copyright 1968 by Martin Luther King, Jr., copyright renewed 1991 by Coretta Scott King.

From SCHOOL SPIRIT by Johanna Hurwitz. TEXT COPYRIGHT © 1994 by JOHANNA HURWITZ. Used by permission of HarperCollins Publishers.

www.sra4kids.com

SRA/McGraw-Hill

A Division of The McGraw-Hill Companies

Send all inquiries to:
SRA/McGraw-Hill
8787 Orion Place
Columbus, Ohio 43240–4027

Printed in the United States of America

ISBN 0-07-569542-1

4 5 6 7 8 9 RRC 07 06 05 04 03 02

▶ Table of Contents

Rules for Writing: Grammar, Usage, and Mechanics

You Are a Writer

What's the key to being a good writer? There are many ways to answer this question, but "possessing a mysterious gift for knowing how to use words" is not one of them. Writing is not a mystery; it's a skill that *everyone* can learn. You've probably already learned a lot about writing. Think about the types of writing you've done in the past. Do any of the following sound familiar?

Common Types of Writing
▶ Book report
▶ Thank-you note to a family member
▶ Grocery list
▶ Made-up story
▶ Diary entry
▶ Letter to a long-distance friend
▶ Research report

The list above shows only a few of the many types of writing. Can you think of a type that isn't on the list? Do *news story, poem, science report,* or *advertisement* come to mind? With so many types of writing, it makes sense to learn the tools you need to improve your writing skills. Like other skills, writing takes practice. The more you write, and the more you learn about writing, the better your writing will be.

The Benefits of Writing

When you write, you get the satisfaction of sharing your thoughts, feelings, and opinions with others. That's just one of the ways in which writing can benefit you personally. Take a look at the following benefits of writing:

▶ **Writing helps you learn.** Writing allows you to explore ideas and learn new information. You get to know a topic or subject well by writing about it. For example, how much do you know about the American Revolution? If you research the topic and write about it, you'll increase your knowledge on that subject.

▶ **Writing makes you a discoverer.** Writing allows you to discover ideas and make unexpected connections among them. As you write, your thoughts develop and interconnect in new ways. These connections can lead to exciting new thoughts and discoveries.

▶ **Writing lets you express yourself.** Writing gives you a chance to express your unique personality and style through language.

▶ **Writing creates reading.** Once you finish a piece of writing, you have a permanent record of your ideas for others to read, enjoy, and consider.

Reasons for Writing

People write to accomplish different goals, but there are at least four common reasons for writing: to inform, to entertain, to persuade, and to explain. Every writer's most important reason for writing, though, is to connect with a reader. You are both a reader and a writer, so you already know what makes writing good. If you laugh while reading a funny story, then you know the writer has met his or her writing goal. At the same time, if you feel inspired and more knowledgeable after reading an essay about a specific topic, that writer has made a connection with you. How do you make that writer-reader connection? First, you have to think carefully about *task*, *audience*, and *purpose*. You will read more about *task*, *audience*, and *purpose* as you learn about the writing process in this handbook.

Try It

Can you identify the audience and the basic purpose for the writing mentioned in each example?

▶ *Maya writes to tell her classmates about the cat show she attended a week ago.*

▶ *Maya writes to convince members of the community to volunteer at their local animal shelter.*

The Traits of Good Writing

The secret is out! *All* good writing, ranging from made-up stories about Mars to factual brochures about taking care of your teeth, shares the same characteristics, or traits. The traits are ideas, organization, voice, word choice, sentence fluency, conventions, and presentation.

Ideas

A good piece of writing gives the reader something interesting and worthwhile to think about. Without strong ideas to support it, your writing loses its reader and, as a result, does not meet its goal, or accomplish its purpose. Writing that holds the reader's attention and interest has the following traits:

▶ A strong, focused message that leaves the reader with a clear impression of the subject

▶ Supporting details that effectively expand the main idea

▶ Specific details, visual images, descriptive words, or anecdotes (short, personal stories) that build the reader's interest and understanding as he or she reads your writing

In the following paragraph, the subject is focused, and the writer uses details to develop the main idea.

As recently as 20 years ago, people did much of their writing on typewriters. Today, people use computers to send letters, fax documents, and create artwork. They can analyze volumes of data or provide access to information from around the world. A modern desktop computer has more computing power than the huge computers of the early 1960s. Computers have changed our lives in ways we may not even realize.

Organization

Good ideas alone do not guarantee good writing. Your ideas need to fit into an overall design, or structure, that effectively presents your ideas to the reader. Good writing is organized so that one thought connects to the next in a way that makes sense. It is also designed to help your readers understand your main idea. Well-organized writing shares these qualities:

▶ The introduction is inviting, grabs the reader's interest, and sets up the main idea.

▶ Each supporting detail relates to the main idea *and* to the topic in each paragraph.

▶ Strong transitions help the reader make connections between sentences and paragraphs.

▶ The conclusion is satisfying and asks the reader to consider the most important point in a new way.

Take a Look

This well-organized paragraph appears in the story "Sweeping Pittsburgh Clean" by Kathy Lynn Emerson.

> All night long, Elizabeth worked on her article, writing and revising, scratching out passages and copying it over. At that time there were no word processors and no portable typewriters to make the work easier. Even in the newspaper offices, articles were composed with pen and ink. Despite the long, slow process, Elizabeth persisted until her story was just the way she wanted it. The next morning she returned to the *Dispatch* office with a final draft that was neat and easy to read. More importantly, the article said something. Mr. Madden was impressed and immediately agreed to publish the story.

Try It

Identify the successful organization strategies used in the paragraph above. How did the writer use transitions to make sure the reader doesn't get lost? Is it easy to tell what the writer's main point is? How does the first sentence grab and hold your attention? Does the last sentence "wrap up" the paragraph?

Voice

When your writing *speaks* to your readers by grabbing their attention and interest, it has a strong voice. In addition, the *tone*, or attitude, you express (serious, funny, angry, and so on) in good writing fits your intended purpose. Here are the qualities of voice and tone that are present in good writing:

▶ The reader can sense that you are interested in the topic.

▶ You, the writer, sound confident and knowledgeable about the topic.

▶ You connect with the reader.

▶ If your writing is a story or narrative, you sound truthful, open, and willing to share.

This example of voice in informative writing is an excerpt from the nonfiction book *Saving the Peregrine Falcon* by Caroline Arnold.

> Even though the peregrine chicks were cared for by people, it is important that they remain wild. During the first week or so, the chicks cannot see very well. Then it does not matter if people feed them directly. But as they get older, their contact with people must be limited.

This example of voice in narrative writing is an excerpt from the fiction book *Alejandro's Gift* by Richard E. Albert.

> Days passed and nothing happened. Still, Alejandro was confident. But the days turned to weeks, and it was still quiet at the water hole. Why, Alejandro wondered, weren't they coming? What could he have done wrong?

Try It

Can you hear the voice in each excerpt? Does the writer of the informative piece sound confident and knowledgeable? How does the writer of the narrative piece connect with the reader?

Word Choice

Words are the building blocks of language. They express emotion, present information, direct the reader's thoughts and attention, and paint vivid, memorable pictures. A good writer uses the power of words to create a strong piece of writing. You can learn to do it, too. Here are some characteristics of word choice in writing that excels:

▶ As the writer, you choose powerful, precise verbs that add energy and variety to writing.

▶ Words and phrases are original, memorable, and sometimes striking— they cause the reader to think and reflect.

▶ Words make your ideas clear and easy to understand.

▶ Words are precise and vivid without being *overly* descriptive or dramatic.

Take a Look

This excerpt from the nonfiction book *A Natural Force* by Laurence Pringle shows the energy and power that good word choice can bring to writing.

A lightning bolt flashes in the summer night. It sizzles and spirals down a tree trunk. Wisps of smoke rise from dead pine needles on the forest floor. Flames glow in the night, and a forest fire begins.

The fire spreads quickly. Flames leap up to the crowns of trees, which explode into fireballs. Overhead the fire leaps from tree to tree. A wall of flame moves through the woods, gaining speed. The forest fire seems like a terrible beast with a mind of its own. It roars; it changes direction. It hungrily sucks oxygen from the air and kills almost everything in its path.

Try It

Find the powerful verbs in the paragraphs above. How do they make the writing come to life? What other striking or memorable words or phrases does the writer use?

Sentence Fluency

Good writers pay attention to the sound of language. Sentences are *fluent* when they flow naturally—almost musically—from one to the next. Sentence fluency also refers to the way sentences are linked together logically. Take a look at the list of qualities that describe writing that flows.

▶ Sentences aren't all the same length, and the writing includes different *types* of sentences, especially ones that begin differently.

▶ Each new sentence connects to and builds on the one before it; transition words join sentences smoothly and logically.

▶ When spoken aloud, the writing sounds rhythmic and graceful.

Take a Look

This paragraph is from the story "The Nightingale" by Hans Christian Andersen.

> The music master wrote five-and-twenty tomes about the artificial bird, so long-winded and so learned and so full of the most complicated phrases that though everybody read them no one could understand a word; but of course they didn't dare admit it—they didn't want to appear stupid, for that would have meant having their stomachs punched, and they didn't like the thought of that!

Try It

Read the paragraph above out loud, and listen to the sound of the language. Can you hear how the repetition of words gives the language a rhythmic quality?

Conventions

A *convention* is "a general agreement about basic principles or procedures." In writing, conventions refer to the proper use of punctuation, grammar, words, spelling, capitalization, and paragraphing. Good writing is polished and ready to be published; it shares the following traits:

▶ Writing contains very few errors in grammar, usage, mechanics, and paragraphing.

▶ Writing looks neat, clean, and carefully edited/proofread.

▶ Sentences are easy to read—they are not distracting or confusing.

Try It

Look for the following errors in this paragraph: three misspellings, one run-on sentence, and two capitalization errors.

▶ *The cheerleading auditions were held in the school auditorrium last Friday, today principal Miller announced the names of the new cheerleaders. Only two members of the team are coming back this year. there names are Gretchen Peters and Jay Malone, and they're really exited for football season to start!*

Presentation

Good writing is presented well. It makes a good impression before even one word is read. It *looks* good. How can you, as a writer, do that? If a computer is available, you can add visual appeal to the text by using computer graphics or clip art and organizers such as bullets and subheadings. If your text is handwritten, you can write neatly and clearly with even margins. You can even include your own original artwork. As a rule, it's best to ask your teacher to find out how creative you can be in presenting your writing.

Reading Your Writing

These traits of good writing—*ideas, organization, voice, word choice, sentence fluency, conventions,* and *presentation*—apply to all types of writing.

The Writing Process

Writing is a process that is done in stages. Each stage is different and has its own characteristics. These stages are prewriting, drafting, revising, editing/proofreading, and publishing. You can go back and forth between the stages as often as you like until you are satisfied with what you have written. Using the writing process in this way will help you improve your writing.

The Writing Process

An Overview of the Writing Process

Good writing develops over time. Like any skill, it can't be learned overnight. It requires practice. The writing process is a way to help you improve your writing. From getting ideas right through producing a finished work, the writing process provides a framework that you can use to improve your writing skills. The writing process consists of the following five phases.

Prewriting

Prewriting is discovering what is worth writing about and making a plan of action based on the task, audience, and purpose for your writing. You think through an idea for a writing topic by brainstorming and researching, and you organize your ideas by grouping them together in a way that makes sense and will appeal to your audience. Prewriting takes time, but it may be the most important phase in the writing process.

Drafting

Drafting usually goes much faster than prewriting. When you draft, you quickly turn your prewriting notes into sentences and paragraphs. You create paragraphs by linking sentences that tell about the same thing or idea. You also create rough versions of an introduction, body, and conclusion. Once you have a draft of your paper, you can begin to carefully improve what you have written.

Revising

Revising comes from a word that means "to re-see." During this phase, you take another look at each part of your draft and think about ways to improve it. You work on making your ideas clearer for your reader, and you consider new ways to organize your paragraphs and sentences. You add, delete, consolidate, clarify, and rearrange words and ideas to suit your audience and purpose. Writers work hard at revising because they want to express their message clearly, completely, and effectively.

Editing/Proofreading

Editing/Proofreading means checking for correctness of grammar, spelling, punctuation, and mechanics. As you prepare to publish your work, you locate any errors and correct them. You may need to recopy your work if you have handwritten it. *Note*: Word processing programs for computers can *help* you edit/proofread your writing, but you should still check your work on your own to be sure it is correct.

Publishing

Publishing, the final phase of the writing process, involves sharing your work with your peers, friends, family members, or another audience. You may choose to display your writing in the classroom, post it on the Internet, send it to a newspaper or magazine, e-mail it to a friend, or invent your own original method of publishing.

Important Note: The five phases of the writing process do not always occur in a certain order. The phases may loop back and forth as each piece of writing develops. As you write, you repeat whichever phases you need to repeat to get the results you want. Remember, you're in charge. Make the writing process work for you.

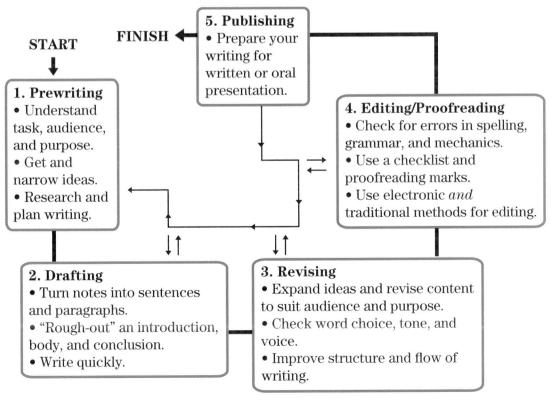

START

FINISH

5. Publishing
• Prepare your writing for written or oral presentation.

1. Prewriting
• Understand task, audience, and purpose.
• Get and narrow ideas.
• Research and plan writing.

4. Editing/Proofreading
• Check for errors in spelling, grammar, and mechanics.
• Use a checklist and proofreading marks.
• Use electronic *and* traditional methods for editing.

2. Drafting
• Turn notes into sentences and paragraphs.
• "Rough-out" an introduction, body, and conclusion.
• Write quickly.

3. Revising
• Expand ideas and revise content to suit audience and purpose.
• Check word choice, tone, and voice.
• Improve structure and flow of writing.

Prewriting

Inside the Writing Process: Prewriting

Prewriting is the thinking and planning you do before writing. An important part of prewriting is determining your task, audience, and purpose. Knowing those three things gets you started in the right direction.

Task

Task is easy to understand. It's the "what" of your writing project. Ask yourself these questions about your task:

▶ What *type* of writing am I preparing to write? A story? An essay?

▶ What is my topic? Is it assigned, or can I choose my own topic?

▶ Does my writing have to be a certain length? Do I have to follow any guidelines for formatting my final draft?

▶ Will I need to do research before I write?

▶ When is my writing due?

Read how a sixth-grade writer, Dante, answered the questions about task.

Dante: The assignment for my social studies class is to write a report on Benjamin Franklin. I plan on researching my topic at the library and on the Internet. My paper has to be six pages long and typed on a computer. It's due in two weeks.

Knowing the specifics about your task will help you plan the steps you need to take to accomplish your writing goal.

Audience

Audience refers to the people who will read or listen to your writing once it's ready to be published. One of your most important goals in writing is to connect with your audience. Knowing who your audience is will help you plan the best way to accomplish your purpose. Keep in mind that, when writing, you can never know too much about your audience.

Here are the questions you should ask about your audience for a piece of writing:

▶ Which people, or groups of people, will read or listen to my work?

▶ What does my audience already know about my topic?

▶ How can I organize and present my ideas in a way that interests my audience?

▶ Do I need to adjust my language or vocabulary for my audience?

Dante responded this way after thinking about his audience:

> I'm writing this report for my social studies class, so my audience will be my teacher and classmates. They already know some basic information about Benjamin Franklin, so I have to make sure I give them new information and ideas to consider. Overall, I need to sound as if I've done a lot of research and really know my subject.

Purpose

Purpose is your reason for writing. It's why you're sharing your ideas in writing with others. Your writing may have several different purposes, but it should have only one main purpose: to inform, entertain, persuade, or explain a topic. These questions will help you define your purpose:

▷ What is my goal with this piece of writing?

▷ What overall message do I want to send to my audience?

Here's how Dante wrote his purpose statement:

> The purpose of my report is to inform my audience about Ben Franklin's many careers, including inventor, scientist, diplomat, publisher, and writer. I hope my readers will be inspired to explore their own interests and accomplish great things.

Task, audience, and purpose work together to create a strong piece of writing. Make your writing just the right length for your audience, and design your purpose to appeal to your audience in the most effective way possible.

How and Where to Get Ideas for Writing

Some writing topics are assigned, and some you can choose on your own. In either case, there are several brainstorming strategies you can use to find ideas to develop in your writing.

Choosing Your Own Topic

When it's up to you to choose your own writing topic, you may not know where to start. On the other hand, you may have too many ideas, and you need a strategy for focusing in on a good topic. Asking questions such as the ones listed below is one technique for finding a topic.

▶ What do you feel strongly about? *people taking good care of their pets, friends not betraying each other, hating lima beans*

▶ What do you like to do? *play soccer, ride on rollercoasters, baby-sit my neighbor's son Zach, visit Mammoth Cave*

▶ What <u>don't</u> you like to do? *stay in hotels on vacation, wait in the doctor's office, put my clothes away*

▶ What are your hobbies and interests? *tropical fish, fossil hunting, making doll clothes, writing my own newspapers*

▶ Have you read any interesting books or articles lately? What ideas did they make you think about?

▶ Have you seen any fascinating films or TV shows recently? Did they introduce you to subjects you'd like to learn more about?

▶ What have you always wondered about? *how chewing gum is made, who named the stars, where trash goes*

Discussing writing ideas with people you know can also help you find a good topic. Ask a friend or family member to respond honestly and thoughtfully to the questions above or to your own questions.

Idea Books

Keeping an **idea book** is another way to discover writing topics. You can take notes in your idea book, or journal, about anything you observe, hear, think, read, discuss with others, or experience firsthand. You may even wish to include drawings or pictures in your idea book. On the next page, take a look at a few entries from a writer's idea book. Think about how the ideas could become topics for writing.

Sample Idea Book Entries

> Bus ride home – most people sit by
> themselves. Bus driver looks tired. I'm
> tired. Seats are that ugly green color. Two
> kids behind me always have headphones on.
> but I can hear their music anyway.
>
> We saw a real mummy at the art museum
> today. It was under a glass case. It's hard
> to believe that was a person thousands of
> years ago. Where did she live? Who was
> her family? What did she do every day?

How can these ideas become topics for writing? You might, for example, write an informative piece about the mummy at the art museum. A descriptive essay about the bus ride home is another option. Idea books should be full of ideas, which is just what you need when you begin to write.

Try It

Think about your experiences so far today. Which one or ones could you put in an idea book?

When Your Topic is Assigned

Often, you're given a writing topic and then asked to develop it on your own. How can you come up with ideas related to your topic? If your topic is broad, such as "the night sky," how can you make it more specific? You can try listing ideas or creating a web of ideas.

Listing and Webbing

Creating a list of ideas can help you remember what you know and find out what you don't know about a topic all at the same time. Start with your main topic and list as many related topics as you can, including any questions you have about the subject. It may help to categorize your ideas as you list them. To the left, the writer has grouped ideas into categories that reflect different parts of the night sky.

When you list ideas related to your topic, write down whatever words, ideas, or questions come to mind, whether you think they're good or bad. Your goal is simply to get your ideas flowing. Now take a look at the same list of ideas in web form:

Night Sky
Planets
 —Age
 —Climate
 —Other life forms?
Stars
 —Constellations—who named them?
 —Telescopes—sizes and locations
 —Life spans
Comets
 —Halley's Comet
 —How often do they return?
Asteroids & Meteors
 —Belts
 —Showers
 —Shooting stars
 —Danger to Earth?
The Moon
 —Beauty
  —Paintings
  —Poems
  —Songs

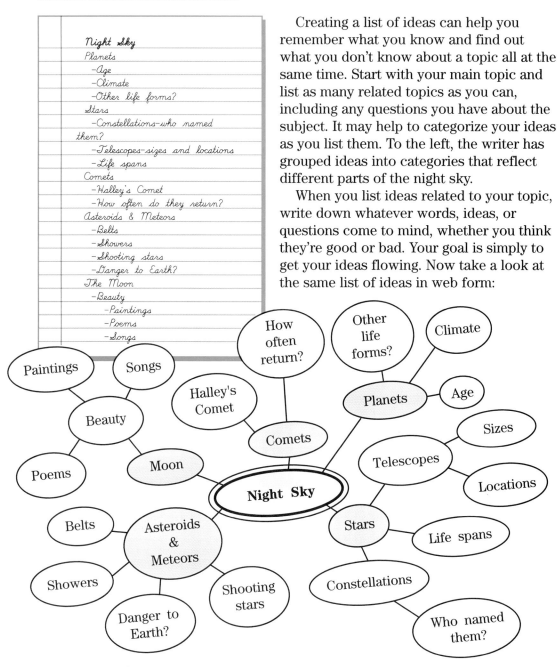

Webs are easy to create. Just place your main topic in the center circle, then add subtopics by circling and connecting them to the topics to which they relate. Notice that the first level of subtopics in the cluster about the night sky includes *planets, stars, asteroids and meteors, comets,* and the *moon.*

Freewriting

Freewriting is so called because it refers to letting ideas flow freely onto the page. It's different from listing or webbing because you don't have to categorize your ideas. Instead, you write them in the form of sentences. For freewriting to work effectively, try not to lift your pencil from the page (or your fingers from the keyboard) and just keep writing ideas about your topic as they freely pop into your mind.

Take a Look

Notice how the following sample of freewriting reveals what topic truly interests the writer.

We have to write about some aspect of the night sky for science class. Our teacher told us to look for topics by starting with "burning" questions we have about the subject. I guess I'd like to know more about the search for life on other planets. I don't know. Maybe I'm more interested in meteors. Can't meteors hit Earth and cause destruction? No, wait. I still want to know if we're the only life forms in the galaxy and what scientists are doing to find out if it's true or not.

Writers often change their minds during a freewriting exercise, as you can see in the example above. That's good because it helps them settle on a topic, or some part of a topic, that they really want to explore in writing.

Now that you know several ways to get ideas for writing—asking questions, keeping an idea book, listing, webbing, and freewriting—you can turn your attention to *focusing* your topic.

Focusing Your Topic

All of the writing topics in the following list are too broad, or general, to cover effectively in one piece of writing.

Music   *England*   *Holidays*
Airplanes   *Health*   *Animals*

A good writing topic is specific. It focuses on one part of a larger topic and brings the details of that topic to the reader's attention. Readers like specific images and facts. Notice how the following focused topics give the reader a clear picture of the writer's main idea.

General Topic		Focused Topic
Music → Jazz	→	Duke Ellington and His Jazz Trumpet
Animals → Endangered Species	→	Let's Save the Red Wolf!
Airplanes → Safety	→	Is Flying Safer Than Driving?
England → History of England	→	England During the Middle Ages

As you focus your topic, keep these hints in mind:

▶ Choose a topic you are curious about or like.

▶ Find out what topic would interest your audience.

▶ Consider what you already know and focus your topic based on that knowledge.

▶ Be sure you will be able to find enough information to support your focused topic and fulfill the goals of your writing project.

Try It

Choose one of the topics at the top of this page and make it more specific.

Reading Your Writing

Remember that whether your audience is small children, your classmates, or adults, readers prefer writing that has a strong, focused message—one that directs their thoughts toward a specific topic the entire time they are reading.

Where to Get Information (Details)

Researching a topic requires some detective work. It takes imagination and patience. When you conduct research, your goal is to come up with as many interesting, specific details as you can to support your purpose and make your writing come to life.

Imagine that your assignment for science class is to write an essay comparing and contrasting two related animals. You know that your audience will be your teacher and your class. You also know that your purpose is to inform readers about the similarities and differences between the two animals. After deciding to research lions and tigers, you set out to find facts and details about both.

To begin gathering supporting details, ask yourself this question: Where are ALL of the places I can find information about my topic?

Of course, the library and the Internet are excellent sources of information for any topic. However, you can gather useful ideas and information in other ways as well.

▶ Interview friends, family members, or other people you know.
▶ Take observation notes.
▶ Design and distribute a poll or survey to gather people's opinions on a subject.
▶ Search your own mind for more details about your life experiences or unique talents and abilities.

Choosing a Research Method

The research method you choose depends on the kind of information you need. Writers generally use library and online sources for information that is "official," such as facts or statistics that can be verified, or proven to be true. Here's an example of a fact that can be verified: *the longest recorded distance a tiger has swum is 29 kilometers, or 18 miles.* Obviously, you can't find that information by taking observation notes, surveying people for their opinions, thinking about your life experiences, or interviewing someone (unless that "someone" happens to be a known expert on tigers). On the other hand, searching for books at the library wouldn't help you write a news story about the recent student council election at your school—interviews and observation notes would be your best choice.

There are many research options, and choosing the right ones is a matter of planning and hands-on experience so you learn which sources are helpful and which ones are not for a specific writing project.

If you really were writing a compare/contrast essay about lions and tigers, where would you begin your research? It would make the most sense to check out the library, along with the Internet, for books and articles that provide facts about both animals. Here are some tips for conducting this kind of research.

Library/Internet Research Tips

▶ Every time you find a useful source of information, write down the title of the article or book, the author, and the Web address if you're using the Internet.

▶ Take careful, detailed notes as you read your sources for useful information; if you photocopy an article, take notes in the margins on either side of the text or on the back of the page.

▶ Don't hesitate to ask the librarian for help.

▶ Bring some coins (one or two dollars) in case you need to photocopy an article from a book, magazine, or Web site.

Organizing Information

Without a method for organizing the information you find while researching, your notes might end up scattered all over the page in no particular order. That won't help you when it's time to write your first draft. What you need is a *graphic organizer*. Graphic organizers help you visualize the main points you want to cover in your writing. There is a graphic organizer that is appropriate for any type of writing—it's up to you to choose the best one for your project. On the next few pages, you will be introduced to a variety of useful graphic organizers.

Venn Diagram

The **Venn Diagram** is a graphic organizer that is useful for comparing and contrasting two related subjects. For the essay about lions and tigers, you could transfer your research notes onto the diagram to help you visualize the similarities and differences between the two animals. Your diagram might look like this:

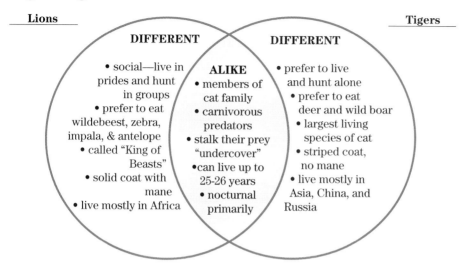

Lions

Tigers

DIFFERENT

- social—live in prides and hunt in groups
- prefer to eat wildebeest, zebra, impala, & antelope
- called "King of Beasts"
- solid coat with mane
- live mostly in Africa

ALIKE

- members of cat family
- carnivorous predators
- stalk their prey "undercover"
- can live up to 25-26 years
- nocturnal primarily

DIFFERENT

- prefer to live and hunt alone
- prefer to eat deer and wild boar
- largest living species of cat
- striped coat, no mane
- live mostly in Asia, China, and Russia

Story Map

A **story map** gives you a place to plan the different elements of a story and visualize how your story's plot will progress.

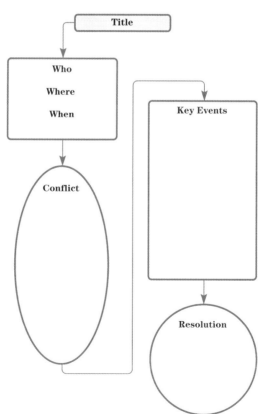

Title

Who
Where
When

Key Events

Conflict

Resolution

Cause/Effect Organizer

A **cause/effect organizer** helps you plan writing that explains the effects of a particular cause, such as air pollution, and proposes a solution to a problem.

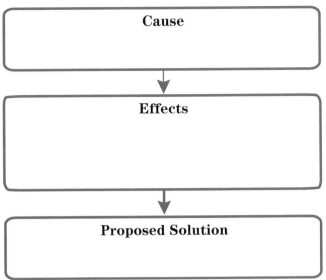

Informational Organizer

An **informational organizer** allows you to organize all of the subtopics and major points you plan on covering in an informational report.

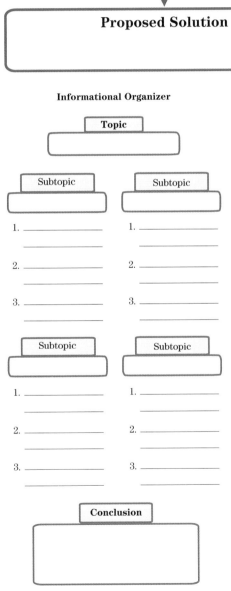

Time Line

A **time line** lets you visualize a sequence of chronological events, such as the events in a person's life or the major events during a historical period.

Subject of Time line: _____

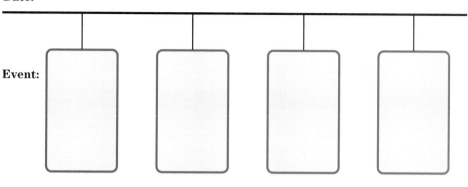

Date:

Event:

Try It

Which graphic organizers would you use to organize information for the following types of writing?

▶ *A report about the similarities and differences between lakes and oceans*

▶ *A biography of Harriet Tubman*

▶ *An essay explaining the reasons cardiovascular exercise is good for one's health*

▶ *A report outlining the evolution of rock 'n roll music in the United States*

Graphic organizers usually include *basic* points you wish to cover in your writing. Clearly, you can't fit *all* of your research notes onto one organizer. Once you have filled out a Venn diagram, a story map, a cause/effect organizer, an informational organizer, a time line, or perhaps a graphic organizer you designed yourself, you can work on drafting and building your paragraphs around the main points you have listed. The next section of the handbook will show you how to take all of your prewriting notes and turn them into a draft of your writing project.

Drafting

Inside the Writing Process: Drafting

One of the definitions of the word *draft* is "to draw the preliminary sketch, version, or plan of." Drafting, the second phase of the writing process, involves expanding your prewriting notes into the form of sentences and rough paragraphs. Remember that a first draft is only the first version of your writing project—not the last.

Eight Practical Approaches to Drafting

You should approach drafting with the understanding that much of what you first write will be changed by the time your writing is ready to be published. With this in mind, there are some practical steps you can take to make the drafting process proceed as smoothly and quickly as possible.

1. When writing a draft by hand, only use one side of the paper and skip lines so you can make notes in between each line. When drafting on a computer, double-space your text and set your margins no smaller than 1 inch on each side.

2. Write quickly and don't stop to think too long about spelling, punctuation, or grammar. Although these elements are important, they will only hold up your progress if you're concerned about editing/proofreading matters now. If you can't spell a word, write down the first few letters and leave the rest of the space blank or circle it. You can make corrections later.

3. Don't spend too much time worrying about word choice during the drafting stage of a project. Leave a space if you can't think of a word; you can choose the best word or phrase later.

4. Leave a blank space if you know you need to look up a fact or statistic that you can't remember while you're drafting.

5. Try using abbreviations for longer words to help you write faster. Don't forget what your abbreviations mean, though.

6. Don't start over and throw out what you've already written. You never know when your "rejected" words or ideas may fit perfectly into some other part of your writing. Simply cross out words or sections you don't like and may change. Avoid erasing parts of your draft.

7. Think about audience and purpose as you write. Without keeping in mind *why* you're writing and *who* will read your work, you won't accomplish your ultimate goal of connecting with your reader.

8. As you draft, think mainly about the content, or information, you are including in your writing. Remember that strong ideas are the backbone of a good piece of writing.

The key to drafting is to try your best without expecting a perfect piece of writing at this stage. You will have plenty of time to improve your work later when you revise.

Take a Look

Here's how one writer drafted the first paragraph of an essay comparing and contrasting lions and tigers.

Working title: Lions and Tigers: Are They That Different?

You may not think there are many differences between lions and tigers, but think again. Tigers are actually larger than lions. They have different appearances, habitats, social behavior, hunting behavior, diets, and life spans.

From Notes to Paragraphs

Before you transfer your prewriting notes into a draft that contains paragraphs, make sure you understand what a paragraph is and how it functions within a piece of writing.

A *paragraph* is a group of two or more related sentences that tells about the same thing or idea. Most paragraphs contain three basic elements: a topic sentence that expresses the main idea of the paragraph, supporting details that develop the main idea, and a concluding sentence that "wraps up" the ideas presented in the paragraph.

When you draft, you might think it makes sense to begin with the introductory paragraph, but writers sometimes find it easier to create the body paragraphs of their paper before they write an opening and a conclusion. Start with whichever section of your paper you feel most comfortable.

Tips for Writing Paragraphs

▶ Indent the beginning of each new paragraph.

▶ Introduce and develop only *one* main idea in each paragraph.

▶ Place most of your topic sentences at or near the beginning of each paragraph.

▶ Make sure the details in each paragraph support the main idea; take out sentences that seem out of place with the other supporting details.

How can you begin to organize your ideas into paragraphs? If you used a graphic organizer, your ideas will already be organized in some way. The graphic organizer for informational writing, for example, provides spaces for your main topic, subtopics, and several supporting details. In that case, you could easily build your paragraphs based on your subtopics.

If you completed a story map, you may choose to plan your paragraphs in the order in which information appears on your organizer. A sample plan might look like this:

Paragraph 1: Introduce characters, setting, and time period.
Paragraph 2: Introduce conflict.
Paragraph 3: Explain first key event.
Paragraph 4: Explain second key event.
Paragraph 5: Explain third key event (build suspense).
Paragraph 6: Show how conflict is resolved.

If you used a Venn diagram, you should already have entered general topics into the "alike" and "different" parts of the circles. Review the Venn diagram about lions and tigers on page 29 and take a look below at how one writer planned his paragraphs based on the organizer.

Lions and Tigers—Order of Paragraphs
Paragraph 1: Appearance
Paragraph 2: Habitat
Paragraph 3: Social Behavior
Paragraph 4: Hunting Behavior
Paragraph 5: Diet
Paragraph 6: Life Span

As a general rule, you should order your paragraphs in a way that makes sense, fits the purpose of your writing, and appeals to your intended audience. If you decide to organize your paragraphs differently when you are drafting, you can either circle the section to be moved and draw an arrow to the new location or rearrange your paragraphs later.

The next step, after you decide on an order for your paragraphs, is to select details from your research that support each subtopic.

Try It

How would you organize the paragraphs in an essay about what makes your family different from your friend's family?

The writer of the compare/contrast essay about lions and tigers grouped together details from his Venn diagram this way:

Appearance
—Lions: solid-color coat and tufts on tails
—Male lions have manes
—Tigers: striped coat and tail; no manes

Habitat
—Lions: found mainly in Africa south of the Sahara Desert
—Lions: grassy plains and open savanna
—Tigers: found mainly in southeast Asia, China, and Russian Far East
—Tigers: found in tropical forests, evergreen forests, woodlands near rivers, mangrove swamps, grasslands, savannas, and rocky country

Social Behavior
—Lions: only social cat; live in "prides"
—Tigers: live alone

Hunting Behavior
—Both are predators; must kill to live
—Both stalk their prey and rely on concealment
—Lions hunt in groups
—Tigers hunt alone

Diet
—Both are carnivorous; eat a variety of prey
—Lions eat wildebeest, zebra, impala, and antelope
—Tigers eat deer and wild boar
—Lions eat 10–15 lbs. of meat daily
—Tigers eat 33–40 lbs. of meat daily

Life Span
—Lions: 8–10 years
—Tigers: about 15 years
—Both can live up to 25 or 26 years in captivity

When you have mapped out a plan for your paragraphs, you can begin to write. Here are a few general tips for getting started:

▶ Write the "easiest" paragraphs first.

▶ Look for an unusual, creative, or fascinating word, phrase, or idea to present in your introduction to grab the reader's attention.

▶ Consider asking a question in the first sentence.

▶ Use transition words to join sentences or paragraphs.

As you read the first draft on the next page, note the way the writer transferred his notes into writing.

Revising: Can I think of a "catchier" title?

Revising: Does my introduction connect with my audience?

Revising: Does this paragraph have a topic sentence?

Revising: Should I combine these paragraphs?

Revising: Is this fact necessary to mention?

Revising: Can I make this conclusion more interesting?

Working title: Lions and Tigers: Are They That Different?

You may not think there are many differences between lions and tigers, but think again. Tigers are actually larger than lions. They have different appearances, habitats, social behavior, hunting behavior, diets, and life spans.

Lions and tigers are different ~~looking~~ in appearance. A lion can be recognized by its solid-colored coat and its mane. Another special feature of a lion is the tuft on the tip of its tail. Tigers have stripes all over their bodies. That also includes their tails.

Lions live south of the Sahara Desert in Africa. They love to bask in grassy plains or the open savanna. Tigers come mainly from southeast Asia, China, and the Russian Far East and they hang out in tropical forests, evergreen forests, woodlands near rivers, mangrove swamps, grasslands, savannas, and rocky country.

Tigers aren't very social. Unlike lions who are ~~actually~~ the only social cat. Lions live in groups called "prides." Tigers usually live alone.

Both animals are predators, meaning they kill to live. Prides of lions hunt together. Tigers hunt alone. Another (similaritie) is that they both stalk their prey and rely on concealment.

When lions and tigers eat, they eat a variety of prey. Lions prefer eating wildebeest, zebra, impala, and antelope, while tigers prefer to eat deer and wild boar. Even though it's hard to (beleive) tigers actually eat more every day than lions do. A lion's average daily consumption is 10–15 lbs. of meat, but a tiger's is 33–40 lbs.

Their life spans are about the same. Lions live about 8–10 years. Tigers live to be about 15. Both can live up to 25 or 26 years in captivity.

Lions and tigers are very different regardless of the fact that they seem like they're only different in physical appearance.

Reading Your Writing

Remember that the point of the drafting phase is to get all of your ideas and information down on paper. You can improve what you've written later in the revision phase of the writing process.

Revising

Inside the Writing Process: Revising

Your first draft of a writing project may be good, but experienced writers know that *all* drafts can be improved. The process of improving your writing by adding, deleting, consolidating, clarifying, or rearranging material is called *revising*. As you revise, you should also make sure your writing reflects the traits of good writing. (See pages 10–15.)

It's best to begin revising your work a day or two after you write your first draft. Then you can approach the task of revising with "new eyes" and a willingness to change any parts of your writing to better match your audience and purpose. Before you change one word, however, you should reread your draft with a few basic questions in mind.

Questions for the "First Read" of a Draft

▶ Do I have an introduction, body paragraphs, and a conclusion?

▶ Are my paragraphs long enough? Should any of them be combined?

▶ Is any part of my writing unfocused or uninteresting?

▶ Do I need to include topic sentences? How about transitions?

▶ Are my introduction and conclusion effective?

▶ Have I achieved my purpose? Have I reached my audience?

Writers often make notes on their drafts. Then they use their notes to make changes to their writing. The "first read" questions will help you begin to think of your writing project as a whole so you know the general areas you need to improve. There are more specific revising strategies you can follow, too.

Adding to Your Writing

When you revise by adding to your writing, review each sentence and paragraph to make sure you've included enough specific details or examples to support your subtopic. To say, "Tornadoes are dangerous storms," is not the same as saying, "Tornadoes are violent winds that spin in the shape of a funnel at speeds of 200–250 miles per hour or more." The second sentence is much more specific and detailed than the first one. The tricky part about adding material to a draft, however, is making sure that what you add supports the overall focus of your writing.

Original Paragraph

Lions and tigers are different in appearance. A lion can be recognized by its solid-colored coat and its mane. Another special feature of a lion is the tuft on the tip of its tail. Tigers have stripes all over their bodies. That also includes their tails.

Revised Paragraph with Added Material

Lions and tigers are different in appearance. A lion can be recognized by its solid-colored coat that comes in shades of yellow, orange, brown, and even gray. By contrast, tigers have stripes all over their bodies, and their coats can be red or white in addition to yellow and orange. Tigers lack a few of the lion's "fanciful" features such as its mane and the tuft on the tip of its tail. However, tigers do have one special feature—every animal has a unique pattern of stripes. Tigers actually weigh more than lions. Tigers have tipped the scales at 675 pounds, while lions don't weigh more than 500 pounds.

Deleting and Rearranging Material

Just as you must add material, you also need to delete, or remove, material that doesn't suit your audience or purpose. Good writing does not contain information that is disorganized or unnecessary. You may also need to change the position of words, sentences, or paragraphs to strengthen your message.

Look again at the draft of the compare/contrast essay on page 37. Are there any sentences or paragraphs that don't seem to fit with the purpose of the essay? Do any sentences or paragraphs seem out of order? In this case, the writer did a good job of planning the order of the paragraphs in advance, so that part of the essay does not need to be revised. Also, the writer talks about one topic in each paragraph, so the ideas within the paragraphs are not disorganized.

The only paragraph that looks out of place is the next-to-last one about life spans. There's very little to say about that topic—it's just a basic fact—so the writer doesn't need an entire paragraph to present that information. Because the fact doesn't fit neatly into any other paragraphs, and because it doesn't seem necessary for understanding the similarities and differences between the two animals, the writer can simply delete that detail from the essay.

Try It

Reread the paragraph below. Find the sentence that is out of place and should be deleted.

Lions and tigers are different in appearance. A lion can be recognized by its solid-colored coat that comes in shades of yellow, orange, brown, and even gray. By contrast, tigers have stripes all over their bodies, and their coats can be red or white in addition to yellow and orange. Tigers lack a few of the lion's "fanciful" features such as its mane and the tuft on the tip of its tail. However, tigers do have one special feature—every animal has a unique pattern of stripes. White-coated tigers are rare in the wild. Tigers actually weigh more than lions. Tigers have tipped the scales at 675 pounds, while lions don't weigh more than 500 pounds.

Clarifying Information

Clarifying your writing involves using specific words or phrases to make your meaning clearer to the reader. You can clarify your writing by adding modifiers like adjectives, adverbs, prepositional phrases, and participial phrases. You can also add transitions to help clarify the connection between ideas.

Take a Look

Compare these descriptions of lions. The words added for clarity are shown in the second paragraph.

Original Paragraph

Lions and tigers are different in appearance. You can recognize a lion by its solid-colored coat and its mane. Another special feature of a lion is the tuft on the tip of its tail. Tigers have stripes all over their bodies. That also includes their tails.

Paragraph Revised for Clarity

Lions and tigers are different in appearance. A lion can be recognized by its solid-colored coat **that comes in shades of yellow, orange, brown, and even gray**. **By contrast**, tigers have stripes all over their bodies, **and their coats can be red or white in addition to yellow and orange**. Tigers lack a few of the lion's "fanciful" features such as its mane and the tuft on the tip of its tail. **However**, tigers do have one special feature—**every animal has a unique pattern of stripes**. Tigers actually weigh more than lions. Tigers have tipped the scales at 675 pounds, while lions don't weigh more than 500 pounds.

The second paragraph is more specific. It lets the reader know exactly what lions and tigers look like and how they can be easily identified.

Consolidating Information

Consolidating, or combining, sentences improves your writing by helping it flow better. You can consolidate sentences by using coordinating and subordinating conjunctions and transitional words and phrases. You can also combine two paragraphs if they are short and closely related.

Take a Look

Notice how the writer has consolidated the following two paragraphs from the original draft shown on page 37.

Original Paragraphs

Tigers aren't very social. Unlike lions who are the only social cat. Lions live in groups called "prides." Tigers usually live alone.

Both animals are predators, meaning they kill to live. Prides of lions hunt together. Tigers hunt alone. Another similarity is that they both stalk their prey and rely on concealment.

Consolidated Paragraph

The two cats also have differences in their living and hunting habits. Tigers aren't very social. They prefer living alone and hunting on their own. Lions, on the other hand, live in groups called "prides," which hunt together. Both cats practice the same hunting techniques, though. They rely on concealment to stalk and kill their prey.

Peer Conferencing

After you've revised your writing on your own, you may wish to share it with fellow classmates. Called *peer conferencing*, these discussions can often give you new ideas to improve your writing. Listen carefully and take notes as your classmates comment on your work. When it's your turn to comment on someone else's writing, make sure that you start with the positive features of the writing, and then be specific about the areas you think could be improved. Peer conferencing gives you the opportunity to find out just what your audience thinks of your writing and then make changes based on their reactions.

Revising Checklist

The following checklist will help you revise your writing.

Ideas

▷ Do you have enough information?

▷ Have you deleted any unnecessary information?

▷ Do you use details that help develop, clarify, and support your main idea?

▷ Does your opening make the reader want to read on?

▷ Does your ending leave your reader with something to think about?

Organization

▶ Do you have a beginning, middle, and ending?

▶ Will the reader be able to easily make connections between sentences and paragraphs?

▶ Are your sentences and details in each paragraph focused around one main idea?

Sentence Fluency

▶ Have you used a variety of sentence types and lengths?

▶ Do parts of your writing sound rhythmic when read aloud?

Voice

▶ Does your voice match your purpose?

▶ Are you satisfied with the way your voice states your ideas?

▶ Does your writing show your own energy and enthusiasm for your subject?

▶ Is your tone appropriate for stating your ideas?

Word Choice

▷ Do you use precise nouns and verbs?

▷ Do you use vivid, descriptive adjectives and adverbs?

▷ Have you clarified any words the reader may have difficulty understanding?

Editing/Proofreading

Inside the Writing Process: Editing/Proofreading

Editing/proofreading your work will make your revised writing clearer, cleaner, and more accurate. It addresses *conventions*, one of the traits of good writing. In the editing/proofreading step, you evaluate the correctness and clarity of each sentence in your writing.

Many writers prefer to check for one type of error at a time. They may check for spelling first, then for punctuation, and after that for other types of grammatical errors. An editing/proofreading checklist can help you make sure that you don't forget to check for a specific type of error in your writing. A good habit to get into is to keep a list of the common errors you make in writing. What words do you frequently misspell? Do you tend to misuse commas in your writing? Have you followed the rules of capitalization? These are the kinds of items you should note on your personal editing/proofreading checklist.

Using Proofreading Marks

Whenever you edit your own or someone else's writing, you should use proofreading marks. Proofreading marks are a standard set of marks you can use to indicate exactly where a change needs to be made in a draft. When you use these marks, you avoid the awkward task of trying to interpret your own or someone else's handwriting. The proofreading marks are listed on the next page.

Mark	Meaning	Example
⌐F	Indent	⌐F Grandparents can teach you a lot.
∧	Add something	My gran^d^mother is eighty-six years old.
℘	Take out something	She grew up on a dairₚy farm.
∼	Transpose	The farm required a lot of ⁀work hard⁀.
☰	Make a capital letter	☰she milked cows every morning.
/	Make a small letter	She fed the chickens in the Ɓarnyard.
⬭ sp	Check spelling	Many chores are done ⟨automaticaly⟩ sp now.
⊃⊂	Close up space	The farm house is more like an office.
# ∧	Add space	Machines do a∧lot of the hard labor.
⊙ ∧	Add a period	Operating a farm still isn't easy⊙

In addition to using proofreading marks, there are a few other techniques you can use to effectively edit/proofread your writing. First, make sure a dictionary is available to you so you can check the spelling or the definition of a word. Second, you can read your writing out loud so you can hear the problems in addition to seeing them on the page. Finally, try pointing to each word as you read it out loud. That will ensure that you locate any missing words or letters, as well as any extra or repeating words.

Try It

Read each sentence out loud and point to each word. Can you find the errors?

▶ *I enjoy going the pool on hot summer days.*

▶ *It's impossible to know if if a tornado will strike a certain location.*

Editing/Proofreading Checklist

Use this checklist as a guide for editing/proofreading your written work.

Conventions

▶ Have I read over my writing carefully, pointing to each word?

▶ Have I used appropriate proofreading marks for my corrections?

▶ Are there any missing or repeated words in my sentences?

▶ Are all of my sentences complete, or do I have fragments?

▶ Have I checked for all other sentence problems, including run-ons, awkward sentences, and misplaced modifiers?

▶ Have I used punctuation marks correctly—including commas, colons, semicolons, quotation marks, parentheses, dashes, and hyphens?

▶ Is my grammar correct? Do the subjects and verbs in each of my sentences agree?

▶ Have I followed the rules of capitalization?

▶ Have I used a dictionary to check the spelling and definitions of words?

▶ Are my paragraphs the appropriate length?

▶ Are my paragraphs indented?

▶ Do I use a variety of words and sentence lengths?

▶ Am I certain that I have fulfilled the requirements of the writing assignment?

Important Note: A number of reference materials can help you edit/proofread your work. Dictionaries, handbooks or style guides, and thesauruses are good references to have available. However, be careful about using a thesaurus. A synonym from a thesaurus may not be a good substitute for a word due to the shades of meaning of many words.

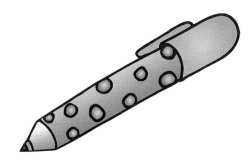

Editing on a Computer

The word-processing program on your computer should include features for editing and proofreading. Although these features are helpful, keep in mind that this software is not always able to identify the purpose of your writing. It may suggest corrections that don't make sense in certain sections of your work.

When you write on a computer, it is best to handwrite your corrections on a printed copy of your revised writing. After editing/proofreading your work, you can enter the changes on the computer. Save any changes you make on the computer, and make sure you keep your edited hard copy so you have a record of the changes that have been entered.

Some software programs can check your document for spelling errors as you go. These programs may automatically correct some misspelled words, like changing *teh* to *the*. You may also check for spelling errors after you have completed revising the work. Remember to proofread for spelling errors the conventional way as well.

Grammar check detects incorrect subject-verb agreement and some commonly confused words. Again, it's important to check your work after using the computer to be safe.

Reading Your Writing

Proofreading marks help you quickly and efficiently identify suggestions or corrections made by someone else because the marks are standard, meaning universal.

Publishing

The purpose of writing is to communicate a message to an audience for a reason. Without the *publishing* step, the writing process is not complete. This is where you present your work to the audience for whom you wrote your play, essay, poem, or other form of writing. Publishing involves designing, creating, and presenting—now that you're finished writing, it's time to provide an appealing background for your words.

Begin the publishing phase by deciding the following:

▶ What piece of writing you want to publish
▶ How you want to publish your work
▶ How to prepare your work to be published

Keeping a Portfolio—Deciding What to Publish

A *portfolio* contains a collection of the writing you've done over a period of time. It gives a picture of your progress as a writer. Photographers keep portfolios to show their customers samples of the different types of work they have done. They usually select the best photos from their collections to put in their portfolios.

Writers and artists also keep portfolios of their work. It allows them to display what they've done and highlight their wide range of skills. The contents of your portfolio will do the same thing for you. You and your teacher usually decide the content. There are different kinds of portfolios. Some include an example of each kind of writing you've done over a set period of time. Others show samples that illustrate your development of a specific writing skill. Once the purpose of your portfolio has been determined, remember to save your writing in a general folder for possible selection for your portfolio at a later date.

After you have completed several works, choose something for your portfolio. If it is your choice alone, choose a piece of writing that means something special to you. Then review the pieces you have selected for your portfolio to make sure that they are what you really want to include.

How to Publish Your Work

A few publishing options include reading your work aloud in class, submitting it to the school newspaper, giving it to a friend to read, or mailing it to a person or to a newspaper. Perhaps you would like to perform what you have written by dramatizing it. You can also bind your work as you would a book. Have you thought about using electronic mail, or e-mail, to publish your writing? What about making your own Web site and posting your writing there?

There are many ways to publish your work. Use as many of these as you can during the school year. You can mail it, perform it, post it, and/or bind it!

Mail It

You can mail your writing to a local newspaper, an organization, or a magazine. You can submit it to a writing contest. Perhaps your congressional representative may want to hear what you have to say about a topic. Editors at publishing companies or newspapers also accept writing from students. For a list of books or magazines that might publish your work, see *Literary Market Place*, which is published annually and can be found in most libraries.

A number of magazines hold contests or print young people's original stories, poems, opinions, artwork, photographs, and even jokes and riddles. Some of these are *Contact*, *Highlights for Children*, *Sports Illustrated for Kids*, *Stone Soup: The Magazine by Young Writers and Artists*, and *Zillions*.

Don't Forget. . .

▶ There is more than one way to mail your work! You can send it electronically over e-mail to a friend or a family member.

▶ When you mail your writing, make sure that the place where you are mailing it accepts that type of writing. For instance, a newspaper is usually interested in just essays or articles.

▶ Send your work to local publications first. They are more likely to publish it.

▶ Include a brief cover letter that includes the title, form, and length of your writing.

▶ Write your name on each page of your selection.

▶ Include a self-addressed stamped envelope if you want your work to be returned after it has been read. Make sure you include enough postage to have it returned.

Perform It

Performing your work involves sharing it with your classmates by reading it to them. You can give a dramatic performance of your work, or you can read it to other audiences, including another class. Tape–recording your writing as a class project gives you a way of performing your work. Videotaping a performance of your work or teleconferencing a performance is another way to perform it. You may also perform your work on stage.

Bind It

Bind your work to present it to the school librarian or to a literary group or magazine at school. Binding your writing can include making it presentable in a folder or special notebook, stapling it, or actually binding it with a spiral binding. You may choose to bind your work in a personalized writing portfolio.

Your bound portfolio could include these components:

▶ A decorative cover
▶ A table of contents
▶ A brief introduction to all of the selections
▶ Tabs to separate each selection
▶ An introduction to each individual piece of writing
▶ Artwork and illustrations for each piece
▶ Charts, diagrams, and/or tables to illustrate your writing
▶ Charts, graphs, photos, and clip art (if you use a computer)

Post It

One way to post your writing is to pin it onto the classroom, school, or library bulletin board. You can ask your doctor or dentist to post it in their waiting room. Sometimes posting it on the refrigerator at home gives your family and friends a chance to see it. Try your neighborhood recreation center. They may have a bulletin board or display case for you to share your work. Be sure to ask permission before you post your writing.

The public library often has a place where you can post your work. They may even have a time when you can perform your work for other young people.

Posting It On-Line

The Internet is another place for you to publish your writing. The Internet is a global network of interconnected computer networks. There are on-line publishing sites, including magazines and writing contests, that accept submissions from young people. Sometimes school systems have their own Internet site where students can post their work. Check with your school or teacher.

You can use your search engine to find places to publish, but be prepared to spend some time exploring. To shorten your search time, you might go to your Internet provider's home page to see if it lists a young people's site where you can post your work. In addition, you can send your provider an e-mail asking if they know of any sites. You may also consider making your own Web site by asking your Internet provider to help you get started.

Including Graphics and Illustrations

As you prepare to publish your work, plan how you will incorporate your illustrations into your text. You can illustrate your writing without a computer by using photographs, drawings, charts, or graphs. You can also use clip art if you are using word-processing software. As you arrange your text and your illustrations, think about your audience. Ask yourself if the format you've selected is best for the audience you want to reach.

A Publishing Checklist

Consider these questions when you are preparing to publish your work:

1. Did you decide what you wanted to publish and how you wanted to publish it?
2. Do you feel strongly about what you chose to publish? Does your writing show a passion and energy for your topic?
3. Does any part of your writing still need work? If so, finish it before publishing your work.
4. Have you saved all drafts of each writing project? You need to attach them to the final work if you are preparing a portfolio.
5. Is your presentation neat and clear? Is it organized well? Are the margins even? Does it make a good impression?

Additional Tips for Publishing

▶ Use pen and write on one side of the paper if you write by hand.
▶ Indent for paragraphs.
▶ Use an easy-to-read font if you use a computer.
▶ Make sure you use 1-inch margins around your page.
▶ Make sure that any graphics or illustrations are clear and suit the content of your writing.

Reading Your Writing

The publishing phase of the writing process is fun. It is your reward for putting so much hard work into your writing from start to finish. Congratulations!

Putting It Together

Now that we've explored each of the phases of the writing process, it's time to put this information to good use. This time, let's imagine that your class has been involved with a unit on government. You have been focusing on how the democratic government of the United States works for the people it represents. Your class assignment is to write an essay comparing and contrasting the national government with your school's student council.

Step I: Prewriting

Because you already know that your essay is to be in a compare/contrast format, you ask yourself some questions to get your paper started. What are some things that the student council and the United States government have in common? What is different about the two forms of government? Does either subject have any unique characteristics?

Focusing Your Topic

After considering these questions, you decide to create a Venn diagram to better organize your information.

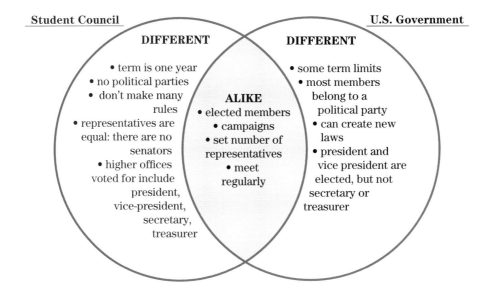

Student Council

DIFFERENT

- term is one year
- no political parties
- don't make many rules
- representatives are equal: there are no senators
- higher offices voted for include president, vice-president, secretary, treasurer

ALIKE

- elected members
- campaigns
- set number of representatives
- meet regularly

U.S. Government

DIFFERENT

- some term limits
- most members belong to a political party
- can create new laws
- president and vice president are elected, but not secretary or treasurer

Organizing Your Writing

The first thing you need to determine about your compare/contrast essay is how you will organize your writing. You can present your information topic by topic, whole subject by whole subject, or by likes and differences. After reviewing the information in your diagram, you decide to organize your compare/contrast essay in a topic-by-topic format. In this format, you introduce a topic, describe your two subjects, and explain how they relate to the topic and each other.

Introduction

Your first paragraph should prepare the reader for what you are going to discuss in the rest of the essay. It should introduce the subjects that you plan to compare and contrast.

Body

The most important part of your writing is the body, which is where you will actually compare and contrast your subjects. Use this space to describe how your subjects are similar or different in as much detail as possible. In a topic by topic compare/contrast essay, use one paragraph to cover each topic that you want to discuss.

Conclusion

In the last paragraph, summarize the information that you have compared and contrasted. Give the reader some way to remember what you have written by providing a conclusion that highlights the main theme of the entire essay.

Step 2: Drafting

The draft is the first full version of the essay. Its main purpose is to get the information you plan to use down on paper. The actual information and the order in which it appears may be changed later in the writing process.

Take a Look

Below and continuing on to page 57 is a draft of the compare/contrast essay about student council and the United States government.

Working title: Student Council vs. the Government

  Government leaders, decisions, and systems are popular topics of conversation. People always talk about the government. This essay compares and contrasts two systems of government. These are the United States government and the school student council. These two groups are alike in some ways but very different in others.
  First lets look at how they are elected. Canidates for student council and United States government positions have to campaign, or run for office. This lets voters know from whom they may choose. Many United States candidates are members of political parties. Student council candidates are not.

Student council members usually serve a Term of one year. United States government officials serve terms of different lengths of time. At the end of a term, most candidates may run for office again. A set number of members are elected to serve in both groups.

Once they are elected, both sets of representatives meet. U.S. representatives meet in Washington, D.C. The results of the meetings are recorded. The results are shared with the people the groups represent.

When U.S. government officials meet, they try to help people by writing new laws. Both groups meet to find ways to help the people they represent. Student council representatives don't make laws most school laws, or rules, are made by adults.

The last difference between student council and the United States government is how officers are chosen. Both groups elect a President and a Vice President. Student council also elects a secertary and a tresurer.

As you can see, student council and the United States government are similar in many ways regarding how their representatives are chosen. The roles they play in making rules are very different. The United States government has more ability to create laws that affect the people they represent.

Step 3: Revising

The first draft provides a starting point for the revising process. When you revise your own writing, make sure your changes improve the power of your writing. Don't make changes without a good reason. You may have written some information the best way the first time.

Take a Look

This is a revised copy of the same essay. Notice how the suggested changes strengthen the writer's message.

Student Council and the Government: Equal Powers?

Government leaders, decisions, and systems are popular topics of

Deleting ▶ conversation. ~~People always talk about the government.~~ This essay

Consolidating ▶ compares and contrasts two systems of government. ~~These are~~ the

United States government and the school student council. These two

groups are alike in some ways but very different in others.

members of each group are

Clarifying ▶ First lets look at how ~~they~~ are elected. Canidates for student council

and United States government positions have to campaign, or run for

office. This lets voters know from whom they may choose. Many

United States candidates are members of political parties.

Adding ▶ Student council candidates are not. Political parties are groups of people who share the same ideas about government.

Student council members usually serve a Term of one school year.

U.S. government officials serve terms of different lengths of time. At

Rearranging ▶ the end of their terms, most candidates may run for office again. A set

number of members are elected to serve in both groups.

Clarifying ▶

Deleting ▶

Consolidating ▶

Rearranging ▶

Clarifying ▶

Deleting ▶

of the United States government and the school student council hold meetings to get their work done.

Once they are elected, ~~both sets of~~ representatives meet. ~~U.S. representatives meet in Washington, D.C.~~ The results of the meetings are recorded. ~~The results are~~ and shared with the people the groups represent.

When U.S. government officials meet, they try to help people by writing new laws. Both groups meet to find ways to help the people they represent. Student council representatives don't make as many laws Most school laws, or rules, are made by ~~adults~~. teachers and the principal.

The last difference between student council and the United States government is how officers are chosen. Both groups elect a President and a Vice President. Student council also elects a secertary and a tresurer.

As you can see, student council and the United States government are similar in ~~many ways regarding~~ how their representatives are chosen. The roles they play inmaking rules are very different. The United States government has more ability to create laws that affect the people they represent..

Try It

Before moving on, read the letter again and look carefully for editing/proofreading errors.

Step 4: Editing/Proofreading

During the editing phase of the writing process, you make minor corrections that "fine-tune" your writing. These include corrections in spelling, punctuation, capitalization, and any other changes that still need to be made.

Take a Look

Consider the revising performed on the first draft. Search for the proofreading marks. What other corrections would you make?

Student Council and the United States Government: Equal Powers?

Government leaders, decisions, and systems are popular topics of conversation. This essay compares and contrasts two systems of government: the United States government and the school student council. These two groups are alike in some ways but very different in others.

First let's look at how members of each group are elected. Canidates [sp] for student council and United States government positions have to campaign, or run for office. This lets voters know from whom they may choose. Many United States candidates are members of political parties. Student council candidates are not. Political parties are groups of people who share the same ideas about government.

A set number of members are elected to serve in both groups. Student council members usually serve a Term of one school year. U.S. [spell out] government officials serve terms of different lengths of time. At the end of their terms, most candidates may run for office again.

Once they are elected, representatives of the United States government and the school student council hold meetings to get their work done. The results of the meetings are recorded and shared with the people the groups represent.

Both groups meet to find ways to help the people they represent. When spell out (U.S.) government officials meet, they try to help people by writing new laws. Student council representatives don't make as many laws. Most school laws, or rules, are made by teachers and the principal.

The last difference between student council and the United States government is how officers are chosen. Both groups elect a President and a Vice President. Student council also elects a secertary and a tresurer. As you can see, student council and the United States government are similar in how their representatives are chosen. The roles they play inmaking rules are very different. The United States government has more ability to create laws that affect the people they represent...

Now read the essay with all of the corrections made. Compare this version to the original draft. In what ways is this version improved?

Student Council and the Government: Equal Powers?

Government leaders, decisions, and systems are popular topics of conversation. This essay compares and contrasts two systems of government: the United States government and the school student council. These two groups are alike in some ways but very different in others.

First let's look at how members of each group are elected. Candidates for student council and United States government positions have to campaign, or run for office. This lets voters know from whom they may choose. Many United States candidates are members of political parties, but student council candidates are not. Political parties are groups of people who share the same ideas about government.

A set number of members are elected to serve in both groups. Student council members usually serve a term of one school year. United States government officials serve terms of different lengths of time. At the end of their terms, most candidates may run for office again.

Once they are elected, representatives of the United States government and the school student council hold meetings to get their work done. The results of the meetings are recorded and shared with the people the groups represent.

Both groups meet to find ways to help the people they represent. When United States government officials meet, they try to help people by writing new laws. Student council representatives don't make as many laws. Most school laws, or rules, are made by teachers and the principal.

The last difference between student council and the United States government is how officers are chosen. Both groups elect a president and a vice president. Student council also elects a secretary and a treasurer.

As you can see, student council and the United States government are similar in how their representatives are chosen. The roles they play in making rules are very different. The United States government has more ability to create laws that affect the people they represent.

Thanks to the *Writing Process*, this essay has smoothly grown from an undeveloped idea into a clearly organized and detailed piece of writing.

Reading Your Writing

Your essay can be truly informative only if it is obvious that great time and care was spent in its planning and writing. Don't rush it.

Forms of Writing

The purpose of writing is to communicate a message. When you write, it's important to choose a form of writing that fits the message you want to convey.

Sometimes the message is very simple. For example, you want to thank a friend for a gift. You write a thank-you note. At other times, the message is more complex. You want to communicate to your classmates your concern about the need for more recycling. You have some choices about how to communicate that message. You might write a poem. You might write a story in which the events of the plot and the actions of the characters reflect your message. You might prepare an informational report. These are just a few of your choices. There are many others.

In this unit you will learn about the different forms of writing: personal, expository, narrative, descriptive, persuasive, and poetry. Think about how and when to use them when you write.

Personal Writing

Do you write notes to your friends? Do you make lists to remind yourself to do things? Do you write in a journal? These are all examples of personal writing. In these kinds of writing, you can express yourself in a more personal, or individual, way.

Some kinds of personal writing, such as lists and notes, are very practical. Others, such as journals, are more reflective. Think about how you can use each of them.

► Journals

A **journal** is a personal record of a writer's thoughts, feelings, observations, and ideas. *Personal* is the key word in journal writing because *you* may be the only person who will read your journal. Sometimes, a teacher might ask you to keep a journal for class and then check your entries to make sure they are thoughtful and complete. In general, though, a journal is a place to freely explore ideas or subjects (or even try your hand at some fiction writing!) Rereading your journal entries is a great way to get ideas for writing, too.

Keeping a Journal

When you write in a journal, you can write freely without worrying about mistakes. Try to get into a writing routine with your journal. Here are some ideas that might help:

► Decide if you will use a **notebook** or a **computer** for your journal. If you prefer to use a notebook, choose one that you like and keep it in the same place all the time so it is easy to find. If you keep your journal on a computer, put all of your journal entries in the same computer folder. You might even want to print them and keep them in a binder.

► **Set a schedule.** Do you find it easier to write in the morning, evening, or afternoon? Choose one time of the day and get into the habit of writing every day at that time. You can always change your scheduled writing time later if you want. It's also a good idea to decide how long you will write each day. Try starting out with five or ten minutes of daily writing.

► **Get organized.** Start each entry by recording the date, perhaps even the time. Do you want to start a new page every time, or would you prefer to just start a new line? You might even use alternating color pens to easily see where a new entry starts.

Take a Look

Here is a journal entry written by Karen Li. She writes every morning when she wakes up. She starts each entry on a new page.

October 15

This morning the air is crisp and cool and the sky is clear. The sun isn't completely up yet, but the new morning light is sparkling off the yellow and orange leaves. Autumn is my favorite season. I love the smells, the sounds, and the colors.

This afternoon, my best friend and I are going apple picking and I can't wait! Apples are my favorite fruit. There's just something about picking your own that makes the fruit taste even better.

Yesterday we had a meeting at school to plan for this year's Fall Festival. I volunteered to be in charge of decorations. We raised a little money at the rummage sale, so I can buy some of the decorations. That means I have to find people to help me make the rest of them. Maybe I can plan an "art party" to make it more fun for everyone. My mom will probably make her famous hot cider, and we can have pumpkin bread. I'll ask her today.

Karen's journal is a **personal journal** because she uses it for personal reflection. Personal journals can provide many topics and ideas for writing. For example, Karen could use her journal entry as a starting point for writing a descriptive essay about the fall season.

Try It

What other writing ideas can you find in Karen's journal entry?

Special Types of Journals

There are other types of journals that you can use for specific purposes. Some of the most common types are learning logs, literature response journals, dialogue journals, and travel logs.

Learning Log

A **learning log** is a place to "log" what you are learning, usually for a class. "Logging" involves recording notes and ideas about a subject, as well as questions you have about that subject. In a learning log, you can write your reactions to experiments, class discussions, or ideas you discovered while reading.

Keep in mind that the purpose of a learning log is to reflect on and review information about a subject—not simply to take notes. As with all journals, you should write freely in your learning log.

Take a Look

Health Science   The Circulatory System
Parts: heart, arteries, veins, capillaries, blood

<u>Blood</u> <u>brings food and oxygen</u> to all parts of the body.
The <u>heart</u> <u>pumps blood</u>.
The blood coming away <u>from</u> the heart is carried by <u>arteries</u>.
The blood going <u>back to</u> the heart is carried by <u>veins</u>.
   Today we learned about how the circulatory system works. It is amazing the way capillaries release food and oxygen to the body's cells and carry carbon dioxide and waste products back to the right side of the heart. I'd like to know more about what capillaries do.
<u>Questions</u>
– Can eating the right foods help you live longer?
– What are the best and worst foods to eat?

You can respond to anything you read—including books, magazine articles, and poems—in your **literature response journal.** *Any* thought or question that you have about what you are reading can be entered in this type of journal. It is a place to write what you like or dislike about a character or what you would change if *you* had written the piece. You may write about an event in your life that the story made you remember. You may respond to an idea, theme, or topic in the literature.

There are no set rules for a literature response journal. However, you may wish to develop your own "rules" to help you stay organized.

▶ Decide ahead of time **how often** you'll write in the journal. Will you write a certain number of entries per book? Will you write each day?

▶ You might keep a list of possible **kinds of entries.** Your list might look something like this: reaction to a character; how the literature relates to my life; how I would write the story; response to an idea, theme, or topic; poem about the story.

▶ It is a good idea to put a **date** on your entries and write the **title** of the book, magazine, or other reading material to which you are responding.

Take a Look

Dec. 20 How <u>School Spirit</u> by Johanna Hurwitz Relates to My Life

Maybe the kids at our school need more school spirit and togetherness. Our building is pretty old, and it has that "nice old-school smell" just like the one in the story. I like our school, but some kids complain about it because it doesn't have a big swimming pool or a new cafeteria. Maybe we can make T-shirts or organize an art project to show our school spirit!

Try It

What are some good writing topics in the entry above?

A **dialogue journal** is a place to carry on a conversation in writing with another person. In this unique type of journal, two writers can talk about a specific topic, learn more about each other, share a common interest, or give advice about an assignment. The people can be teacher and student, two friends or classmates, or parent and child.

Take a Look

March 12

Dear Ben,

I'm at the point in my story where I don't know what to do. Remember how I told you that the alien was chasing the two main characters? Well, I can't decide whether to let them get away or to have them get captured. What do you think?

—Jared

Dear Jared,

If the characters get away, that would end the story. You could extend the chase, having them almost get caught a couple of times. I think I'd rather have them get kidnapped, because then you could describe the alien ship (or planet) the way they see it. They could even plan a big escape.

—Ben

A dialogue journal can help you ask questions that you might otherwise forget to ask. It also makes it easier for each person to think through what he or she has to say before saying it.

Going on a trip? While you're "on the road," record your observations in a **travel log.** Write down what you do each day of your trip and reflect or comment on the day's activities. When you return home, you can use your travel log entries as a starting point for further writing.

Tips for Writing in Your Travel Log

▶ At the top of each entry, write the date, location, and, if you want to, the exact time. You may wish to title each entry.

▶ Describe your surroundings and the people you see—that will help you understand the culture of the place you are visiting.

▶ Write freely. Be honest about your observations. In your travel log, be specific about why you like or dislike a place.

Take a Look

Below is the second entry from Beth's travel log for her winter vacation. In the first entry, she complained about being in cold Cincinnati, Ohio, when she'd rather be in Florida. Notice how this second entry shows that she has changed her mind.

> Day 2 – Ocean-less Fun in Cincinnati – 12/21
> I didn't think this trip could get better, but it has. It snowed last night, and now it looks like tiny diamonds are scattered all over Aunt Martha's lawn. Today we went ice-skating at the zoo, where they're having a winter festival of lights. I drank some hot chocolate and ate a soft pretzel, my favorite. Everyone was laughing and having fun, even Uncle Ray, who always acts so serious. I guess I can wait <u>a little</u> longer for a suntan.

Try It

What are some possible writing topics in the travel log entry above?

Notes and Cards

Notes and cards are good ways to keep in touch with people. Most of the time, notes and cards are informal, but there are a few rules you can follow.

Phone Messages

A phone message should include each of the following pieces of information.

Date: the day and date that you received the call
Time: the time that you received the call
To: the name of the person the caller wishes to reach
From: the full name of the caller
Phone: the phone number of the caller
Message: what the caller asks you to tell the person
Initials/Name: your name, so the recipient knows who took the call

Take a Look

Date: *Friday, 9/22*
Time: *4:35 p.m.*
To: *Dad*
From: *Suzanne Gardner, our neighbor*
Phone: *555-9821*
Message: *She wants to know if we have anything to sell at their garage sale next weekend. Please call her and let her know ASAP.*
Initials/Name: *Jake*

Thank-You Notes

You write a thank-you note when you want to let someone know that you appreciate a gift, card, or thoughtful action. The parts of a thank-you note include the **date,** a **salutation,** a **message,** a **closing,** and a **signature.** The message part should include the following:

▶ the words "thank you" or a similar phrase that expresses your gratitude (for example, "I really appreciate . . .")

▶ why you are thanking the person

▶ what the gift/card/action meant to you—or, if it's a gift, be sure to say what the gift was so the giver knows that you received it. Also, you can mention how you plan to use it.

Take a Look

November 17, 2003

Dear Aunt Regina
and Uncle Jerome,

Thank you so much for your birthday card and the money that you sent. I was so excited to hear from you on my birthday! I plan on buying a new mountain bike soon, and with the money you sent, I finally have enough saved to buy the one I want! I'll send you pictures of it as soon as I get it. Thank you again.

With love,
Leigh

Birthday Cards

How often have you simply written the date, a salutation ("Dear Sam,"), a closing ("Your friend,"), and your signature on a birthday card? You probably did this because the card you chose had a message already printed on the inside. Whether or not there's a printed message inside the card, though, you can write your own unique birthday greeting that gives the card a more personal touch. In your message, you may want to mention one or more of the following:

▶ how much you appreciate that person's friendship

▶ special memories of time you have spent with that person

▶ common interests you share

▶ an inspiring or thought-provoking quote you know that person would enjoy reading

Of course, any birthday message should include the words "happy birthday" or a similar phrase. Birthday messages are usually short, so three to five sentences is an acceptable length.

Fun Fact

How do you say "Happy Birthday" in Greek? "Chronia Polla!"

Take a Look

August 13, 2003

Dear Brandi,

Happy 12th birthday! I'm so glad we're friends. Who would've thought we'd have so much in common when we met on the bus last September? Here's to another year of sketching trees in your backyard, riding our bikes, and trying to make homemade ice cream! Have a wonderful day!

Your friend,
Heather

Get-Well Cards

You can send a **get-well card** when someone you know is sick, hurt, or just feeling sad. Like other cards, get-well cards should include the date, a salutation, a closing, and a signature. If you use a card that does not have a printed message inside, your written message should include the words "get well soon," "feel better," or a similar phrase. Here are some tips that will help you write a thoughtful get-well card:

▶ Focus on the recipient's feelings and not your own—remember that your letter is meant to let someone know that you care about his or her well-being.

▶ Consider offering to help in some way. For example, you could offer to take notes in class for a friend who is ill.

▶ Be positive and encouraging instead of talking about the discomfort and negative effects of an illness.

▶ Sending your letter sooner rather than later will show how much you care.

Take a Look

March 3, 2003

Dear Laura,

I am sorry to hear that you have been sick lately. I, for one, am very excited about seeing you back at school soon! I bet you'll even feel better by the time you get this card. Well, you take good care of yourself and get well soon. Tell your mom that I'm counting on her to make her fabulous chicken soup for you.

Take care,
Yuki

Congratulatory Cards

Congratulatory cards congratulate someone for having achieved something. As with all cards, you should include the date, a salutation, a closing, and a signature. To write a special congratulatory message, follow these tips:

▶ You may wish to tell how you heard the good news.

▶ Be specific about why the person is receiving your congratulations— mention what he or she accomplished.

▶ Don't delay in sending your card. If you do send it late, apologize briefly for not writing sooner.

Take a Look

May 10, 2003

Dear Dao,

Congratulations! Your father told us that your artwork has been selected for the student art exhibit at the local museum. That is very exciting! We are also glad to hear that you are doing so well in school. Your grandpa and I will be coming to visit next week because we want to see your work and spend some time with you. We are very, very proud of you.

Love,
Grandma

Personalize It

When you want to add a personal touch, you can make your own cards and notes. There are several different ways to do this. You can draw, color, or paint your own artwork and do your own fancy hand lettering. Another fun way to make your own cards and notes is by using a computer to either create the artwork, design the card, or both!

E-mail

E-mail, also called *electronic mail,* is a way to write and send messages on a computer. Fill out the "to" line at the top of the e-mail message, using an exact e-mail address. Fill out the "subject" line, too, so the recipient knows the general topic of your message.

Take a Look

A friendly, informal e-mail message may or may not include a salutation and a closing. Either way, it is a good idea to type your name at the end of every e-mail message you send. It is not necessary to use your full name, however.

[to] myfriend@greatfriends.com

[from] yourfriend@greatfriends.com

[subject] After Soccer Practice

Brian,

Do you want to go to that new movie after soccer practice on Saturday?

My parents said that they'd take us. Ask your parents and let me know.

Andrew

Friendly Letters

A **friendly letter** is an informal letter you write to someone you know personally. The style and tone you use should be warm, natural, and conversational, not formal and businesslike. Friendly letters differ from business letters in their tone, style, audience, and purpose.

Why write friendly letters? Letters are a good way to keep in touch with people who are important to you to show them that you care. Letters are also fun—and, chances are, if you send letters, you'll get some in return!

To whom do you write friendly letters? Friends who live far away, pen pals, and relatives all appreciate getting letters. You can even write to friends and relatives who **don't** live so far away. Maybe you want to keep in touch with a teacher or babysitter that you don't see anymore. Maybe you have a friend who goes to a different school. Most everyone likes to get mail, so you can write to anyone that you care about and know.

Parts of a Friendly Letter

Heading	sender's address, date of letter
Salutation	greeting including recipient's name
Body	the message(s) that you want to say to the recipient
Closing	closing phrase such as "Your friend," "Love," or "Sincerely"
Signature	your handwritten name (first name is fine, if the person knows you very well)
Postscript	written as "P.S."—this can be used to add something that you forgot to say in the main part of your letter

Here's a friendly letter written by Kerri to her friend Ramona.

Heading ▶ 230 Kinzie Avenue
Superior, Wisconsin 53216
August 29, 2003

Salutation ▶ Dear Ramona,

Body ▶ You're not going to believe this, but I'm writing this letter on the computer at school—for class! I will actually get class credit for it. Isn't that funny? We have to practice writing a friendly letter for English class, and of course I thought of writing to you.

After I got home from camp, my family went to Winona, Minnesota, to visit my Aunt Cheryl and Uncle Jack for a week. I like Winona. My aunt took us on a little tour and told us some of the history of the city. A long time ago, when the railroad tracks were first being laid, people couldn't decide whether to make Winona or Chicago, Illinois, the major "hub" of the Midwest. It's hard to imagine that the little city of Winona could actually have grown to be as large as Chicago is today!

My uncle took my brother and me canoeing in the backwaters of the Mississippi River. That was a lot of fun, but I'm kind of glad that he didn't take us out on the river. I found out that my brother is not very good at canoeing. Since you and I got so good at canoeing at camp the past two years, I'd forgotten what it was like to tip over. Boy, was that a shock! We all laughed about it later, though.

Closing ▶ Well, now it's your turn to write to me. What did you do after camp? How's your first week of school going? I can't wait to see a picture of your purple bedroom. Your parents were so great to paint it for you while you were gone.

Your friend,

Signature ▶ *Kerri*

Postscript ▶ P.S. How do you like this picture of us on the last day of camp? I think it turned out great!

Friendly Letters ▲ Personal Writing **81**

Using E-mail to Send a Friendly Letter

Snail mail (regular mail) isn't the only way you can send a friendly letter. E-mail, or *electronic mail*, is another option. When you send a friendly letter over e-mail, you can choose whether or not to include a salutation and a closing. Also, you don't need to include your e-mail address and the date because they should automatically appear with your sent message. Make sure you type your name (usually just your first name) at the end of the message, give your message a subject, and double-check the recipient's e-mail address for accuracy.

Student Model—"E-mail Letter"
Sean decided to send an "e-mail letter" to his cousin Kayla.

[to] myfriend@mailbox.com
[from] yourfriend@mailbox.com
[subject] My Crazy Week

Hi Kayla,

I thought I'd drop you a line since I haven't talked to you for a while. I've been *so* busy lately.

Did I tell you that I had a swim meet on Saturday? Well, I actually won **all three** of my events: backstroke, freestyle, and butterfly. The first one was the backstroke, and I thought I had touched the wall second. So when I saw the results, I was totally surprised! I could have gone home then and been perfectly happy, but I had to substitute for Mike, one of my teammates, in the freestyle event (he hurt his shoulder at practice last week). I wasn't really prepared, but I guess none of the other swimmers were either because I won anyway. Then I beat my own record during the butterfly event—I couldn't believe my luck.

Tuesday at school, I got a test back in my science class and did much better than the last test, so that made my day. The cafeteria even served good pizza for a change.

Oops. It's getting late. Write back soon and tell me what's going on in your life.

Your cousin,
Sean

Tips for Writing A Friendly Letter

Prewriting   Make a Plan

▷ Think about why you are writing. Do you want to tell something specific, or are you just writing to keep in touch?

▷ List the events and details you want to tell about in your letter.

Drafting   Get Your Thoughts on Paper

▶ Remember to keep the tone of your letter conversational.

▶ If you have a specific reason for writing, you might want to write that part first so that you don't forget to include it later.

Revising   Be Sure It Makes Sense

▶ **Ideas** Will the letter keep the reader interested?

▶ **Voice** Does the letter read the way you would talk to that person?

▶ **Organization** Make sure you don't skip around too much. Friendly letters don't need to follow a specific format, but they shouldn't be confusing to read.

Editing/Proofreading   Look Closely at the Details

▶ **Conventions** Check your spelling and punctuation. This will make it easier to read the letter.

Publishing   Get Your Letter Ready to Mail

▷ Check the address and make sure you copy it correctly onto the envelope. See page 88 for help with sending your letter.

▷ Be sure to include the correct postage.

▷ **Presentation** Design your letter on a computer and experiment with different backgrounds and graphics, or write your letter on designer stationery.

Business Letters

A **business letter** is a formal letter you write to a professional person or organization for a specific reason. In most cases, you do not know the recipient personally, so the tone of your business letter should be formal, polite, and direct. All of these characteristics make business letters very different from friendly letters, especially in terms of purpose and audience. Here are three common types of business letters:

▶ **Letter of Request**—asks for information
▶ **Letter of Complaint**—complains about a product, service, or policy
▶ **Letter of Concern**—expresses concern about an issue or problem

How to Write a Business Letter

Even though there are different types of business letters, there are rules that all business letters follow.

Parts of a Business Letter

Heading.	sender's address, date of letter
Inside Address	recipient's name or title (if known), department name (if known), company name or organization, recipient's address
Salutation	greeting including person's name (if known), followed by a colon
Body	clear, specific, brief message—stating purpose, giving short background or additional information, ending on a polite note
Closing	formal but short complimentary closing phrase such as "Yours truly" or "Sincerely yours"
Typed Name	the typed, full name of the sender (possibly sender's job title/position on the following line)
Signature.	sender signs his or her name between the closing and the typed name

Form: Business letters can be written in *block form* or in *modified block form.* Modified block form is shown in the example on the next page. The heading, closing, and typed name are placed near the right side of the page. Each paragraph of the body is indented. A business letter written in block form has nothing indented and all parts start at the left margin. There is an example on page 86.

4-7 lines between heading and address ▶

589 West Brompton Ave #23
Chicago, Illinois 60657
April 16, 2003

Summer Festivals Coordinator
Mayor's Office of Special Events
121 North LaSalle Street, Room 703
Chicago, Illinois 60602

1 line between inside address and salutation ▶

Dear Sir or Madam:

colon after salutation

1 line between salutation and body

Please send me information about the process of planning Chicago's summer festivals. I am writing a report for school about different functions of the city government. I realize that planning these outdoor festivals must be a large project for your office each year.

My questions are as follows:
1. How are the festivals chosen each year?
2. How are the dates for each festival decided?
3. What kind of planning is necessary for these events?
4. Are there any special traffic or safety issues that must be addressed?
5. Is your office involved in the actual running of the festival?

I would also appreciate any other information that might help me better understand what goes into making these events happen. Thank you very much for your time and cooperation.

1 line between body and closing ▶

Yours sincerely,

comma after closing

Maria Garcia

4 lines between closing and typed name ▶

Maria Garcia

Note: This letter is written in block form.

6315 Roselawn Avenue
Reynoldsburg, Ohio 43068
August 2, 2003

4-7 lines between heading and inside address ▶

Tabitha King
General Manager
Blue Sky Shoe Store
1001 East Main Street
Reynoldsburg, Ohio 43068

1 line between inside address and salutation ▶

Dear Ms. King:

1 line between salutation and body ▶

I purchased a pair of Forest Trek boots from your store two weeks ago. I have enclosed the receipt for these boots. As you can see, the cost of the boots was $68. The next day, I happened to be near the Blue Sky store in downtown Columbus and saw the same boots selling for $45. You can imagine my surprise at the difference in price.

I went into the downtown store and found out that they were not having a special sale. In fact, the salesperson at that store told me that $45 was the regular retail price for these boots. I then checked the Forest Trek Web site, and it also says the retail price is $45.

I would like your store to refund me the difference ($23) for the boots. I would also like to see that the prices in your store change to match the other Blue Sky stores.

Thank you for your cooperation.

1 line between body and closing ▶

Yours sincerely,

4 lines between closing and typed name ▶

Mark Petretti

Mark Petretti
shows that something else (the receipt) was sent in the same envelope ▶ Enclosure

Note: This letter is written in block form.

125 South Broad Street
Lake City, Florida 32056
January 23, 2003

Heading ▶ Public Relations Manager
Columbia County Historical Museum
P.O. Box 3276
Lake City, Florida 32056

Salutation ▶ Dear Sir or Madam:

Body ▶ It seems that there has been some miscommunication with the public regarding the museum's hours of operation. The local paper stated, in a recent article, that the museum is open 1–5 p.m. on Mondays. The sign on your door says that the museum is closed on Mondays. When I called the museum last week, the person who answered the phone stated that it is open 12–2 p.m. on Mondays. As you can imagine, this is very confusing for the public.

I enjoy going to your museum to learn about our country's impressive history, and Monday afternoon is an excellent time for me to do research. Could you please clarify all of your hours of operation for me so that I may arrange my time appropriately?

I would also appreciate it if you could look into this miscommunication and correct it. I'm sure others will be grateful for your attention to this, as well. Thank you for your time and cooperation.

Closing ▶ Yours sincerely,

Signature ▶ *Nick Eisenman*

Typed name ▶ Nick Eisenman

Try It

What type of business letter would you write for each of these?

▶ *You think your town should have a curfew for teenagers.*

▶ *You need to find out how many people drive with invalid driver's licenses each year.*

▶ *A store refuses to refund your money for a scratched CD.*

Sending Your Letter

Folding Your Letter: Long envelopes are commonly used for business letters. Follow these instructions to fold your letter so it fits properly into a business-size envelope.

1. The envelope should be 4 1/8 by 9 1/2 inches.
2. Looking at the front of your letter, fold the bottom third up.
3. Then fold slightly less than the top third down.
4. Insert the folded letter into the envelope so that the top third of the letter (the second fold above) is on top and shows when the recipient opens the envelope.

Addressing the Envelope

There are two ways to address an envelope. Both are acceptable. Look closely to see the differences between them. Sample 2 is preferred by the U.S. Post Office.

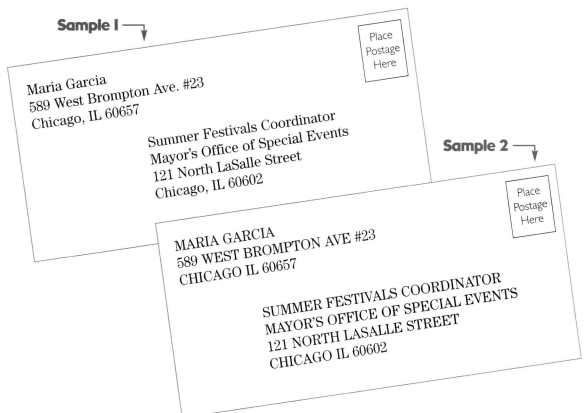

Sample 1

Place Postage Here

Maria Garcia
589 West Brompton Ave. #23
Chicago, IL 60657

Summer Festivals Coordinator
Mayor's Office of Special Events
121 North LaSalle Street
Chicago, IL 60602

Sample 2

Place Postage Here

MARIA GARCIA
589 WEST BROMPTON AVE #23
CHICAGO IL 60657

SUMMER FESTIVALS COORDINATOR
MAYOR'S OFFICE OF SPECIAL EVENTS
121 NORTH LASALLE STREET
CHICAGO IL 60602

Tips for Writing A Business Letter

Prewriting — Make a Plan

▷ Do some research. Try to find out the name of the person you need to contact.

▷ Think about the specific purpose of your letter and jot down phrases that you may use. Think about clear and concise ways to make your point.

▷ Organize your thoughts. What should come first, second, and last?

Drafting — Get Your Thoughts on Paper

▶ As you write, remember that your tone should be polite and professional without sounding conversational.

▶ Keep it short, but don't leave out necessary information.

Revising — Be Sure It Makes Sense

▶ **Ideas** Make sure your important points support the purpose of your letter (to request, complain, or express concern).

▶ **Organization** The first sentence should clearly state the purpose of the letter.

▶ **Voice** Does the letter sound respectful and formal?

▶ **Sentence Fluency** Is the letter easy to read? Does it flow smoothly from one sentence to the next?

Editing/Proofreading — Look Closely at the Details

▶ **Conventions** Make sure you've correctly spelled the name of the contact person and the company or organization.

▶ **Conventions** Check to see that you've used a colon after the greeting.

Publishing — Get Your Letter Ready to Mail

▶ **Presentation** Fold your letter lightly at first until you know you've gotten the folds right. Then crease the folds more firmly.

Note: If you have a computer, you may have software that automatically formats business letters. Ask your teacher to help you with this.

Writing a Memo

The word *memorandum*, often shortened to *memo*, means "a written reminder." A memo is basically a short, businesslike letter you send to an individual or a group, except it includes only two parts: a **heading** and a **body.** The purpose of a memo is to present information or ask a question as concisely as possible so that your reader can quickly get the "gist" of your message and know what action, if any, he or she needs to take. One of the most common reasons for writing a memo is to remind your audience of an important date or event.

In the body of a memo, you write what you have to communicate. The heading is made of four parts, shown below.

Take a Look

To: Grant Hill
From: Martha Stein
Date: September 15, 2004
Subject: Math Lesson

◄ Handwrite your initials next to your name before sending

◄ Sometimes the date is placed first

I would just like to remind you that we made an appointment to meet tomorrow for your math lesson.

Please bring your math book, homework, and any questions you have. I will meet you in the media center at 2:30. Also bring your most recent test. I would like to go over the problems you missed and have us work them out together.

I look forward to working with you for the next few weeks. Believe it or not, we can have fun and learn math at the same time!

Tips for Writing A Memo

Prewriting Make a Plan

▷ Write a sentence that clearly states your main message in as few words as possible. Use this statement as a base for writing your memo.

▷ Make a short list of the points you need to cover so you don't forget any of them.

Drafting Get Your Thoughts on Paper

▶ Keep your memo brief, and only include information that your audience needs to know.

Revising Be Sure It Makes Sense

▶ **Ideas** Make sure your important points are accurate, clear, and stated briefly. Ask yourself if the reader will immediately know what you are trying to say.

▶ **Sentence Fluency** Is the memo easy to read? Does the order of your sentences make sense?

▶ **Voice** Does your memo sound businesslike? Your tone should be friendly, but not too conversational.

Editing/Proofreading Look Closely at the Details

▶ **Conventions** Have you spelled the recipients' names correctly?

▶ **Conventions** Have you capitalized all of the important words in the subject line of your heading?

Publishing Send Your Memo

▷ Be sure you make enough copies of your memo for everyone who is to receive it. Don't forget to keep a copy for yourself.

▷ **Presentation** Type your memo on a computer to make it look more professional.

Writing Minutes

Minutes are the official notes for a meeting. They are written to keep an organized record of the people present and the issues discussed. Student councils, neighborhood cleanup committees, clubs, and other groups often keep minutes of their meetings.

Here are the parts to include in meeting minutes.

▶ **Group Name:** *official name of the group or organization*

▶ **Date of Meeting:** *date and time of the meeting*

▶ **Members in Attendance:** *names (and titles) of the members at the meeting; include absent members*

▶ **Old Business:** *issues that are discussed again*

▶ **New Business:** *any issues discussed for the first time*

▶ **Next Meeting:** *the date and time as well as any issues that will be discussed then*

Take a Look

Group name ▶ Jacksonville Community Theatre Group

Date and time of meeting ▶ 4:30 p.m. – January 12, 2003

Also note members absent ▶ **Attendance:** Leo Glover, president; Jessica Wilson, vice president; Alexis Weaver, artist in residence; Mitchell Sprague, secretary; Siobahn Harrigan, Nadia Hahn, Ben Define, actors. Absent: Mark Weigand.

Old business ▶ **Old Business:** The minutes from the December 15, 2002, meeting were read. The group officers elected last meeting were acknowledged.

New business ▶ **New Business:** Discussion of the 2004-05 season. Members in attendance decided to hold a vote at the Jan. 19, 2003, meeting to determine shows for 2004-05.

Alexis presented a motion for developing a schedule of acting classes for the public. All members agreed. The motion was passed. Alexis will present a schedule for the group to review at the next meeting.

Next meeting ▶ **Next Meeting:** 4:30 p.m. – January 19, 2003
Main issue to be discussed will be 2004-05 season.

Tips for Writing Minutes

Prewriting   Make a Plan

▷ Be ready when you come to the meeting. Have some pens, pencils, and paper or a computer available.

▷ Write down the date and the names of all the people at the meeting.

▷ Listen and take notes carefully.

Drafting   Get Your Thoughts on Paper

▶ Use your notes to write out minutes in the proper format.

▶ Avoid including too many details, but don't omit important information.

▶ Draft as soon as possible so that you don't forget any important points.

Revising   Be Sure It Makes Sense

▶ **Word Choice** Reread the minutes to decide if there are any simpler, clearer words you can use to say the same things.

▶ **Sentence Fluency** Are the minutes easy to read?

Editing/Proofreading   Look Closely at the Details

▶ **Conventions** Does your page look clean and organized? Does it follow the proper format?

▶ **Conventions** Be sure that each person's name is included and spelled correctly.

Publishing   Get Your Minutes Ready to Present

▷ Remember to include your name at the bottom, telling everyone who wrote the minutes.

▷ Make enough copies of the minutes for everyone who attended the meeting. Don't forget to keep a copy for yourself.

Expository Writing

Expository writing does two things. It explains how to do something, or it presents information about something. The steps in the explanation are arranged in a logical way so that the reader can follow the procedure or repeat the activity. When information is presented, it is clear, correct, complete, and well organized.

Much of the writing you do for school is expository. Some of the lessons in this unit can help you improve your reports and book reviews. You can use the others to try types of expository writing that may be new to you.

Writing a Summary

You're studying for a huge test, and you just can't seem to get a handle on the subject. What can you do? You can write a summary! Summarizing gives you a better understanding of what you are reading. It sharpens your understanding of the important ideas in a piece of writing.

A **summary** is a shortened version of another piece of writing. It includes only the main idea and most important details. Writing a summary involves more than just pulling out a few sentences from the original and stringing them together. The trick is to use your own words but keep the *meaning* of the original piece of writing. That way you are creating a new piece of writing that can stand on its own.

Read the original article about habitat exhibits below. Then read Luis's summary of the article on the next page.

Take a Look The following excerpt is from *Windows on Wildlife* by Ginny Johnston and Judy Cutchins.

What Are Habitat Exhibits?

The excitement of watching an animal in the wild is unforgettable. What a thrill it is to hear gorillas growl and hoot or watch them care for their young. But few people get a chance to venture into African forests where the great apes live. Many of the world's most fascinating creatures live in habitats too far away or too difficult to visit. However, most people can watch them by visiting a zoo or aquarium.

Until recently, animals in such places were usually caged behind bars, and people walked by to stare at them. The visit held none of the excitement of seeing animals in the wild.

Today, modern zoos, aquariums, and wildlife parks are showing plants and animals in natural-habitat exhibits. These exhibits duplicate a part of an animal's true environment as closely as possible. Because many animals are endangered in their native lands, habitat exhibits may be the only places they can survive....

These modern exhibits are much more expensive than cages with bars, but it is worth the money to provide the best possible environment for captive species. The well-being of the plants and animals is the number-one goal. Scientists believe that zoo animals live longer and have more babies in naturalistic settings. Raising more young, especially if a species is rare or endangered, will prevent the species from becoming extinct. American zoos no longer take rare animals from the wild for exhibits, so raising these babies is extremely important.

Here is Luis's summary of the article.

Natural-habitat exhibits give visitors a sense of seeing animals in the wild. They also provide the only place some endangered animals can survive. Because these zoo exhibits try to copy an animal's natural habitat, they cost more to build than cages. They're worth the extra money because zoo animals in these exhibits live longer and have more babies. This is especially important in keeping the species from becoming extinct.

Steps in Writing a Summary

The first step in writing a summary is to read carefully the piece of writing that you are going to summarize. Then identify main ideas and important details in each paragraph. Pay attention to topic sentences and boldface headings; they often reveal key points.

Based on what you underlined, write the central idea of the piece you are summarizing. Think of this as the topic sentence of your summary. Look at the first sentence of Luis's summary as an example. Keep your topic sentence in mind as you write the rest of your summary.

Next, decide how you want to organize the summary. In Luis's summary, he simply followed the logical organization of the writer. Decide which points to leave in and which to cut. Delete details that don't support your topic sentence. Combine and shorten sentences in the original, but be careful to always use your own words. At the same time, don't add your own opinion or comments on the subject.

Writing a Paraphrase

Like summarizing, paraphrasing also gives you a deeper understanding of the words you're reading. Paraphrasing is different from summarizing, though, because when you paraphrase, you restate in your own words *all* of the ideas of the original—not just the main ones. This means that you don't try to shorten the original when you paraphrase, as you do in a summary. A paraphrase is usually about the same length as the original; a summary is much shorter. Notice the difference between the paraphrase and the summary of the same piece of text below.

Original Text

Visitors may see more in natural-habitat exhibits than they would see in nature. Windows, for example, allow people to remain warm and dry while watching penguins "fly" under icy water or waddle across snow-covered tracks. Naturalistic exhibits are not only more fun for visitors but healthier and more comfortable for captive wildlife.

Paraphrase

Naturalistic exhibits allow visitors to observe animals more closely than they could in nature. Without the benefit of windows, how else could people easily and comfortably watch penguins behave normally in their wet, icy environments? These realistic exhibits make going to zoos more fun for visitors, and they also help the captive wildlife live in healthier and more comfortable surroundings.

Summary

Naturalistic exhibits allow visitors to observe animals' behavior more closely than they could in nature and are a better environment for captive wildlife.

Reading Your Writing

Both paraphrasing and summarizing mean restating another's ideas in your own words. It might be tempting to copy someone else's sentences—especially the good ones! However, when you do this, you are plagiarizing. This means that you're not summarizing or adding to your understanding of the writing—you're simply copying words from one place to another.

Tips for Writing a Summary

Prewriting Study and Plan

▷ Study the piece of writing you are summarizing.
▷ Figure out what the main idea is.
▷ Identify and organize points that support this idea.

Drafting Restate and Combine

▶ Combine sentences or phrases in the original that make the same or similar points, then rewrite them in your own words.
▶ To help you use your own words, put away the original, and write the draft based on what you remember.
▶ Leave out any opinions of your own.

Revising Compare and Clarify

▶ **Ideas** Compare your summary to the original. Are any important ideas left out? Add them. Are any not-so-important ideas left in? Cut them.
▶ **Word Choice** Change any phrases that are too similar to those in the original.
▶ **Organization** Does your topic sentence restate the central idea of the original piece?
▶ Check the length of your summary. If it is more than one-third the size of the original, shorten it.

Editing/Proofreading Double-Check the Details

▶ **Conventions** Check against the original for the spelling and capitalization of any proper names or specialized words.
▶ **Conventions** Proofread the summary for mistakes in grammar and punctuation.

Revising Make It Useful

▷ Write out neatly or type your summary.
▷ **Presentation** Consider keeping your summary in a notebook with other summaries that you write to help you study.

Analyzing Fiction

Have you ever enjoyed reading a book so much that you couldn't put it down? Maybe you were drawn in by a fascinating setting, a suspenseful plot, or interesting characters. All of these things—characters, setting, and plot—are key elements in any piece of fiction. By analyzing each one, you can deepen your understanding of the text in different ways. You can also explain to others *why* you liked or didn't like a piece of fiction.

Character Analysis

One way to analyze a character is to use a character web that lists examples from the text about the character.

The following details could appear in a web based on Miyax, the main character in "Amaroq, the Wolf," by Jean Craighead George.

Miyax

Actions ran away into frozen tundra all by herself; built her own shelter; ate grass blades and lichens; studied and interacted with the wolves, even the fearsome leader

Thoughts knew she needed help to survive; knew that talking to the wolves would help her survive; thought she could work her way to San Francisco as a laundress or dishwasher; began to doubt her reasoning

Words "Wolves do not eat people. That's gussak talk. Kapugen said wolves are gentle brothers."
"I never dreamed I could get lost, Amaroq...."
"Amaroq, I understand what you said.... I'm hungry...."
"Please bring me some meat."

Feelings was more afraid of her predicament than of the wolves; frightened of her husband Daniel; stomach ached from no food; afraid of Amaroq but had courage

Reactions of Others ignored by Amaroq at first but has courage; Amaroq made her one of the pack after she acted like a pup; pups wagged their tails at her, obeyed the "wolf command" she learned

Physical Characteristics classic Eskimo beauty; short, compact limbs for efficiency in cold climate

Here is a character analysis about Miyax. When you write a character analysis, use the notes on your character web to decide what to say about the character's personal traits. For example, Miyax is described as self-reliant, confident, and proud, among other qualities, in the analysis below.

Miyax, a Deserving Wolf

Miyax, the main character in "Amaroq, the Wolf" by Jean Craighead George, faces great challenges as she struggles to survive on the barren North Slope of Alaska. Her frightening experience forces her to use all of her strengths and discover new ones she didn't even know that she had.

Although she wants to be a part of the wolf pack, Miyax is fiercely independent. She ran away from her comfortable home to escape from her husband, Daniel. She had planned to walk by herself across the frozen tundra to a faraway port, where she thought she could wash dishes to earn her fare to San Francisco.

She is also self-reliant and confident in her own abilities. She builds her own house and relies on her own knowledge of the local area to find her way. She eats grasses and lichens to survive. She uses her knowledge of wolves to become friends with them.

Miyax changes as a result of her situation. Before she got lost, she was very confident and proud. She tells Amaroq that she never dreamed she could get lost. Her confidence and pride fade a little when she realizes her bad situation: she is afraid and very hungry. She learns that she is not able to take care of herself and that she will have to ask for help.

In trying to get the wolves to help her, Miyax shows perseverance and courage. For days, she studies the wolves to figure out how they communicate with each other. She is afraid of Amaroq, but she continues to try to talk to him and finds the courage to pat his chin.

Miyax will be a good member of the wolf pack. In befriending the wolves, she has shown that she is brave, observant, knowledgeable of her surroundings, and self-sufficient. She is aware of her place in the pack and shows respect to the leader, Amaroq.

Try It

Think of one of your favorite characters in a book you've read recently. What kinds of things would you list in a character web for that character?

Analyzing Plot

The **plot** is what happens in a story. It is the series of events that take place over the course of the story. First, a problem is introduced near the *beginning*. The **problem** usually involves a character against another character, against society, against nature, or against a supernatural force.

In the *middle* of the story, as the characters work to deal with the problem, they go through a conflict or conflicts. A **conflict** is an internal or external struggle to resolve a problem. When the problem is about to be resolved, the story reaches its **climax,** or turning point. The story's **conclusion** tells how the problem is solved.

Plot Analysis

One way to analyze the plot is to fill out a chain-of-events map like this one for "Amaroq, the Wolf." Notice how the map below includes basic elements of the plot but leaves out minor details.

Chain of Events in *"Amaroq, the Wolf"*

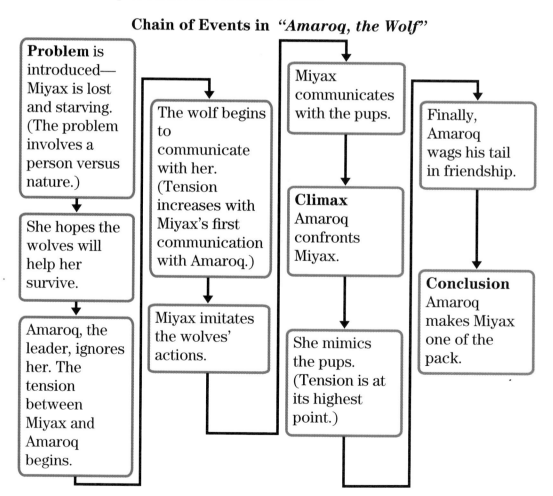

Problem is introduced— Miyax is lost and starving. (The problem involves a person versus nature.)

She hopes the wolves will help her survive.

Amaroq, the leader, ignores her. The tension between Miyax and Amaroq begins.

The wolf begins to communicate with her. (Tension increases with Miyax's first communication with Amaroq.)

Miyax imitates the wolves' actions.

Miyax communicates with the pups.

Climax Amaroq confronts Miyax.

She mimics the pups. (Tension is at its highest point.)

Finally, Amaroq wags his tail in friendship.

Conclusion Amaroq makes Miyax one of the pack.

Read the plot analysis below. Notice how the writer uses some details to explain the major parts of the plot.

A Suspenseful Plot

When Miyax finds herself lost in the Alaskan tundra, she knows she must befriend the pack of wolves or die. Relying on stories of her father's experience with wolves, she observes the wolves and communicates with them. First, she earns the trust of the pups. However, she knows that to become one of the pack, she must win over Amaroq, the leader. This is the main problem of the plot and the story's source of tension.

Each scene with Amaroq is tenser than the last, building suspense as the story goes on. Miyax's scenes with the pups, on the other hand, have a happy, light-hearted feeling. They let the reader relax a little, easing some of the tension. Just when Miyax is feeling happy about her meeting with the pups, though, a scary Amaroq arrives on the scene, causing the tensest moment in the story. We hold our breaths to see what Miyax will do next. Miyax mimics the playful pups and pats Amaroq under the chin, and Amaroq accepts her into the pack. We can breathe a sigh of relief as the tension disappears and the problem is resolved.

Try It

Think about a story you like. What events take place in the story? In what order do they occur? How do these events work to build suspense? What problem is presented at the beginning? How is it solved at the end? What is the turning point, or climax, of the story?

Reading Your Writing

A well-written plot analysis shows the writer's understanding of the plot and how it works. It examines the problem, the conflict or conflicts a character faces while attempting to solve the problem, the climax, and the conclusion of the story.

Analyzing Setting

Do you go sledding in the winter where you live? Do buses and cars speed down your street? Is your neighborhood different today from how it was fifty years ago? All of these questions have to do with **setting,** which is when and where a story takes place. A story's setting also includes a description of the values and beliefs of the characters who live in it. It's important to keep in mind that the setting often influences how the characters think and act.

The setting may change many times in a story, or it may remain the same. A setting may be a very general place and time, such as Paris in the 1990s. On the other hand, it may be very specific, such as a certain street in Paris in April of 1994.

Setting Analysis

A good first step to understanding a story's setting is to make a chart. List some examples and clues from the text that tell about the setting. Sometimes, small details that don't seem important tell you a lot about the setting.

Setting of "Amaroq, the Wolf"

Time	Place	Ideas, Values
• mention of TV, buildings, traffic lights—must be at least 1950s	• North Slope of Alaska—barren slope that stretches for 300 miles one way, 800 miles another way; every direction looks the same • lichen-speckled frost heave in the midst of the bleak tundra; soil permanently frozen—no trees, only a few plants; grass everywhere • wolves and caribou roam; the sun will not set for a month—no North Star	• instincts of Eskimos are very important • Miyax calls the pup wealthy because he is fearless and smart; a man with intelligence, fearlessness, and love was considered wealthy by some Eskimos • Miyax, her father, and others believe they can communicate with wolves

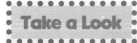

The Importance of the Alaskan Tundra in "Amaroq the Wolf"

The setting in "Amaroq, the Wolf" causes the main character Miyax to take action. One part of the setting in "Amaroq, the Wolf" is the place—the frozen Alaskan tundra. It is a dangerous place for a person to be in, even someone as capable and knowledgeable as Miyax. There is little food to be found, and although there are animals, they can be hunted only with a weapon, which Miyax does not have. In the current season, the sun does not set, so she can't even use the North Star as a compass. Because of the harsh place in which she finds herself, Miyax is forced to befriend the wolves so that they will help her or she will most likely die. In this way, the setting influences the actions she takes. The setting also emphasizes Miyax's courage and strong will to survive.

Another part of the setting also plays a role in the story—the ideas and values of the Inuit culture of the time. It was considered all right to marry at age thirteen, so Miyax, who does not want to be married, reacts to this part of the setting by leaving her home. Once again, the setting pushes a character to action. Also, it is because of another Inuit belief—that Inuit can communicate with wolves—that Miyax tries to befriend the wolves.

Try It
Read this story beginning. What does the description tell you about the setting and how it might affect the characters?
▶ *Lucy sat on the front stoop of her old brick apartment building waiting for her best friend, Amelia. The front lawn was mostly weeds, and garbage littered the gutter. Cars whizzed and screeched by, and fumes from big trucks hung in the humid air.*

Reading Your Writing
Analyzing how the setting affects the characters in a story can help you know what to include when you describe the setting in a story that you write.

Tips for Analyzing Literature

Prewriting Decide on a Topic

▷ If you are writing a character analysis, use a character web to explore the character's actions, thoughts, words, feelings, physical characteristics, and so on.

▷ If you are writing a plot analysis, use a chain-of-events map to help you understand the basic elements of the plot.

▷ If you are writing a setting analysis, create a chart to help you understand how these elements of the setting—time, place, and ideas and values—affect the characters' actions.

Drafting Get Your Thoughts on Paper

▶ Get the reader's attention in the first paragraph.

▶ Try starting with a quote from the literature you're writing about that relates to your subject:

> "Amaroq," she whispered. "I am lost and the sun will not set for a month. There is no North Star to guide me." This is Miyax's situation in the story "Amaroq, the Wolf." She is lost in the frozen Alaskan tundra, the setting of the story, a setting so harsh that it forces her to take action.

▶ Another way to get the reader's attention is to ask a question to which the reader can relate:

> Do you act one way at school with your friends and act another way at home with your family? If so, this is because school and home are two different *settings*. The different settings you live in affect your actions. The same is true for the setting in which Miyax finds herself in "Amaroq, the Wolf."

Drafting, continued

▶ In the last paragraph, summarize the points you have made and show how they support your focus. End on a thought-provoking note.

> The two main settings presented in the story persuade Miyax to take action. How does the world in which you live force you to do, or not do, certain things?

Revising · Make it Clear

▶ **Organization** Make sure your first paragraph clearly explains the main point you want to make about the plot, setting, or character.
▶ **Organization** Check your paragraphs—do they have clear topic sentences?
▶ **Ideas** Decide whether you have used too many, too few, or just enough details from the text to support your ideas.
▶ Does your title capture the essence of your analysis and grab your reader's interest?

Editing/Proofreading · Fine-Tune

▶ **Conventions** Check your plot, character, or setting analysis. Did you use the same tense throughout?
▶ **Conventions** Check the names of characters and place names. Are they spelled and capitalized correctly?
▶ **Conventions** If you used quotes, make sure that you used the correct punctuation around them.

Publishing · Get Your Analysis Ready for Readers

▶ **Presentation** You may wish to add a cover with art that relates to your topic.
▶ **Presentation** For a plot analysis, consider transferring your chain-of-events map onto a poster to display in class.

Analyzing Nonfiction

One reason for reading nonfiction is to learn something about a subject that interests you. Writing a nonfiction analysis helps you explain the main point and important supporting points in a piece of nonfiction. In it, you tell what the author's message is and how the author organizes the information in the text. Some organizational strategies include compare/contrast, chronological sequence, and cause-effect. To help you understand the author's main idea, choose a graphic organizer that matches the way the text is organized. If you can't determine which graphic organizer to use, just list the main ideas and supporting details on a sheet of paper.

The following T-chart shows how the ideas are organized in "A Natural Force" by Laurence Pringle.

Main Idea: Many people think that all forest fires are bad; in reality, most are good.

Benefits to Trees and Other Plants	**Benefits to Animals**
▶ Fire has been a natural, beneficial force for millions of years	▶ Elk and deer depend on fires because the shrubs they eat depend on fire to sprout and grow
▶ Some trees have reacted to fires by becoming more fire-resistant	▶ Fires rarely kill wildlife; most escape unharmed
▶ For some trees, fire damage causes more growth; in fact, they depend on high temperatures that the fire creates to sprout and to release seeds onto the ground	▶ Fire brings plentiful food and provides nutrients for the soil
▶ Without fire, ponderosa pines grow too thickly; they depend on fire to thin them out	▶ Fire causes more varieties of plants to grow
▶ Fire controls the insect population and the growth of damaging fungi	

Here's Keisha's analysis of the nonfiction article "A Natural Force." Notice how she begins her analysis with a surprising twist and then states the author's main message in the first paragraph.

Fire: Friend or Foe?

A fire rages through a forest, killing everything it touches, causing permanent, untold damage. A forest fire is a very bad thing. Right? According to Laurence Pringle in the article "A Natural Force," forest fires are almost always <u>good</u> things. Here are the reasons.

Many trees actually <u>depend</u> on fires to grow and thrive. Some trees have become fire-resistant. This means that they have adapted to live through a fire, and they also depend on fire to survive. Some trees have thick barks that withstand fire's heat. Others grow new sprouts after a fire sweeps through a forest. The high temperatures of the fire cause seeds to be released, generating new growth. In addition, the smoke produced by a fire controls the growth of fungi and insect populations that can cause damage to trees and plants.

Animals also benefit from forest fires. Elk and deer depend on fires because the shrubs they eat need fire to sprout and grow. Because the fire eventually makes the soil richer, plant-eating animals feed on a wider variety of plants that are more nutritious. Finally, you may be surprised to know that although some animals do die in a forest fire, most escape unharmed.

Fires have blazed across Earth for millions of years, a natural, mostly beneficial force in our environment. So the next time you hear about a forest fire, don't automatically assume it's a bad thing—it's just a "natural force."

Try It

This article could also be analyzed using a cause-effect graphic organizer: fire would be listed as the cause, and what it does would be listed as the effects. What might the graphic organizer look like?

Analyzing the Nonfiction Analysis

Keisha used a chart to organize the information from the nonfiction article and write her analysis. On the chart, she listed supporting details in two categories because a good deal of the article simply includes details that support the main idea—"fire is a good thing."

In her analysis, Keisha uses the same technique that the author uses to hook the reader. First, she presents the commonly held belief about forest fires—that they are bad. Then, just as the author does, she tells the reader that the *opposite* is true. The reader is curious and wants to read on.

Next, Keisha begins to list the details that support this main idea. She organizes the details according to the two categories she used to complete her graphic organizer: *How Fire Benefits Trees and Other Plants; How Fire Benefits Animals.* Keisha then devotes one paragraph to each one of these categories. She supports the main idea of each paragraph with several details from her organizer.

Finally, she ends her analysis by adding a new piece of information that also supports the main idea. The reader comes away from the analysis with a new and interesting piece of information to consider.

Fun Fact

Early Native Americans recognized the benefits of forest fires: they regularly burned select areas so that new plants would grow and attract game animals.

Reading Your Writing

By analyzing nonfiction, you do more than add a list of facts to your memory; you gain a deeper understanding of the topic presented, and you improve your own writing skills by studying and analyzing the writing of others.

Tips for Analyzing Nonfiction

Prewriting Get to Know the Text

▷ Read and reread the nonfiction piece that you are analyzing to make sure that you understand what the author is saying.

▷ Figure out how the author has organized the information.

▷ Take notes using a chart or graphic organizer that fits the way the author has organized the information or that best fits how you want to analyze the writing.

Drafting Get Your Thoughts on Paper

▶ Use a few direct quotes from the piece of writing to add emphasis or to better illustrate an idea you have.

▶ Use the author's exact words only when you include a direct quote. Otherwise, restate the author's ideas in your *own* words.

▶ End your analysis by stating in a different way the idea you introduced at the beginning—or add a question or a new piece of information to make your reader think.

Revising Check for Accuracy and Clarity

▶ **Ideas** Read your analysis, and then compare it to the original piece of nonfiction. Are there any parts that disagree? Did you forget to put in an important point that the author makes?

▶ **Organization** Study the organization. Does it make your writing easier to follow?

Editing/Proofreading Look Closely at the Details

▶ **Conventions** Double-check your use of quotation marks if you've included direct quotes from the text.

▶ **Conventions** Are there any proper nouns from the text that you misspelled?

Publishing

▶ **Presentation** Add a graphic or other illustration to your final version to make it more interesting.

Writing a Book Review

A **book review** tells about the book's plot and characters, the message the author is sending, and what the person reviewing the book liked or didn't like about it. After reading a book review, you should be able to decide whether or not you would like to read the book.

Reading a book review is easy. Writing one is a little more involved. What exactly should you include in a book review? First, it depends on what kind of book it is—fiction or nonfiction.

Review of a Fiction Book

Use the following steps to help you organize the information for a review of a fiction book.

First

Introduce the book by identifying the book's title, author, illustrator (if there is one), and copyright date. Then briefly describe the main characters and setting.

Second

Summarize the book's **plot,** or chain of events. What are the important things that happen in the book? How are the characters and setting involved in these events? Use a graphic organizer, such as a chain-of-events map, to help you summarize the book's plot.

Third

Give your opinion of or reaction to the book. Did you like the book? Why or why not? Did you identify with the main characters? Did you like the author's style of writing? Was the plot especially interesting? Does the book begin or end in an unusual way?

Fourth

What point do you think the author is trying to make through his or her writing? What message is he or she trying to send? How does this message apply to your own life or to today's society in general?

Book Review of <u>Summer of the Swans</u>

<u>Summer of the Swans</u>, by Betsy Byars, was published in 1970. It takes place in a small West Virginia town. The main character is 14-year-old Sara Godfrey, who takes care of her brother Charlie. As a result of a severe illness, Charlie is mentally challenged and does not speak.

One day during the summer, Sara takes Charlie to see some swans that have just arrived at the lake near their house. Charlie likes them so much that he gets up in the middle of the night to find them, but he gets lost in the woods. The next morning, everyone is panicked when they discover that Charlie is missing. Sara's aunt calls the police, but a worried Sara decides to search for Charlie herself. She meets up with Joe Melby, a boy she thinks stole Charlie's watch. She finds out that he had taken the watch from other boys who stole it from Charlie and then he returned it to Charlie. She forgives him, and together they continue a tense search for Charlie.

I liked this book because the characters seemed like real people. I cared about what happened to them. I also liked the way Sara acted with her brother Charlie. You could tell that she really loved him, and she treated him like a regular person—she didn't talk down to him and she didn't pity him. The book was very suspenseful, too.

I think that the author sent several different messages through her story. One was that mentally challenged people have feelings like the rest of us and that they should be treated with dignity. Another was that you shouldn't jump to conclusions; you should first learn the facts before assuming that something is true.

Try It

Think of a book you know well—maybe one you've read over and over. What do you think the author's message was? Was there more than one message?

Review of a Nonfiction Book

Reviewing a nonfiction book is a little different from reviewing a fiction book. Fiction books have made-up plots and characters, whereas nonfiction books present information about real subjects such as people, events, processes, wildlife, and so on.

The following steps will help you organize your nonfiction book review.

First

Introduce the book by identifying the book's title, author, illustrator (if there is one), and copyright date. Then describe the main subject of the book. If it's about a person, what part of the person's life does it cover? How much detail does it go into about its subject? Does the author concentrate on one or two major elements of the subject?

Use a web such as the following to help you explain the subject of the book. The web shown includes only the major subtopics.

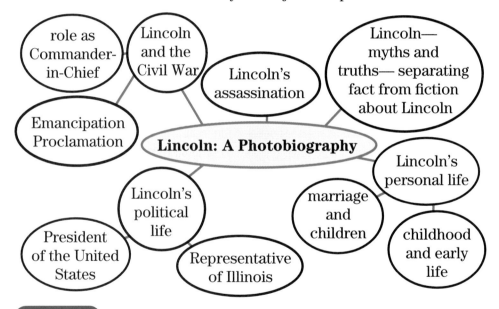

Second

Give your opinion of or reaction to the book. Did you like the book? Why or why not? How was the information presented? Was it organized in a way that was easy to understand and follow? Did the author give enough details? Too few? Was there a certain part of the book that you liked in particular?

Third

What point do you think the author is trying to make? If you could ask the author why he or she wrote this book, what do you think he or she would say?

Here is a nonfiction book review written by Marion.

Book Review of Lincoln, a Photobiography

Lincoln, a Photobiography, by Russell Freedman, tells the story of Abraham Lincoln's life. The book, published in 1989, first looks at the myths and facts about Lincoln. Then it discusses his early childhood in Kentucky, where he really was born in a log cabin. It describes his rise in politics as a young lawyer, as well as his marriage to Mary Ann Todd, and his home life with her and their four sons.

I enjoyed reading this book because the author gives information about Lincoln as a person, as well as about Lincoln as a politician, and how his personality and beliefs influenced his views on politics. The author tells about Lincoln's awkward teenage years and how he witnessed slavery at an early age. He also lets us in on Lincoln's family life with the First Lady and his sons. Small details make the book more interesting—for example, Lincoln signed the Emancipation Proclamation with his full signature, although he usually signed documents "A. Lincoln."

I also liked the samples of Lincoln's writing and speeches because they helped me understand his thoughts and feelings better. I especially enjoyed the many photos and illustrations of Lincoln and the people and places that surrounded his life.

I think the main message that the author is sending is that there is more to Lincoln than just the myths we hear. He wants to let the reader know that Lincoln was a real human being with real feelings and real struggles.

Reading Your Writing

Writing a book review is a way to deepen your understanding of a book, as well as to sharpen your critical-thinking and writing skills.

Tips for Writing a Fiction Review

Prewriting Choose a Book

▶ Choose a book you have just read or one that you especially liked.

▶ Try to choose a book to which you reacted strongly.

▶ Jot down some thoughts about the book, including why you chose to write about *this* book. Include a description of the main characters and a summary of the plot. Use a web to help develop your thoughts.

Drafting Get Your Response on Paper

▶ At the beginning, identify the book's title and author, as well as the important characters and the setting.

▶ Describe the plot, but don't give away the ending or details that will take away from the reader's enjoyment of the book.

▶ Include a short quote from the book, as well as descriptions, that support your opinion.

▶ To end the review, tell what message you think the author is sending.

Revising Be Sure It Makes Sense

▶ **Ideas** Check your ideas against the book. Do they correctly tell what happens?

▶ **Organization** Make sure your ideas are clear and well organized. Add transitions to move smoothly from one idea to the next.

▶ **Word Choice** Make sure you've used the present tense to write the plot summary.

Editing/Proofreading Look Closely at the Details

▶ **Conventions** Remember to underline or italicize the title of the book.

Publishing Get Ready to Share Your Response

▶ **Presentation** Have a copy of the book you reviewed on hand so that your audience can skim through it.

Tips for Writing a Nonfiction Review

Prewriting Choose a Book

▷ Choose a nonfiction book you just read for a class or one you chose to read for pleasure. Pick one that has a subject that interests you.

▷ Don't try to review a textbook or other reference book.

▷ Describe the book's main subject and use a web or an outline to help you gather ideas.

Drafting Get Your Response on Paper

▶ Identify the book's title, author, and subject matter.

▶ Introduce the subject of your book review in an interesting and different way, such as asking the reader a question.

▶ When you give your opinion of the book, use a few details from the text to back up your opinion.

▶ Discuss the book's organization—does it make reading easier or harder? If the book includes charts, photos, illustrations, or other visual aids, tell how these affected your opinion as well.

Revising Be Sure It Makes Sense

▶ **Ideas** Did you clearly state what the main subject of the book is? Do the details you provide support your opinion?

▶ **Voice** Did you use the pronoun *I* and confidently state your opinion of the book?

▶ **Organization** Did you remember to include your thoughts on the book's overall message?

Editing/Proofreading Look Closely at the Details

▶ **Conventions** Have you spelled the author's name correctly?

▶ **Conventions** Underline or italicize book titles. Use quotes to indicate chapters.

Publishing Get Ready to Share Your Response

▶ **Presentation** Create a collage that illustrates the main message of the book.

Explaining a Process and Giving Directions

The point of explaining a **process** or giving directions is to pass along information to a reader. That's why these two practical types of writing are classified as expository writing.

Explaining a Process

When you explain a process, such as how to make a chef's salad or how photosynthesis occurs, it's very important to include *every step in the process*, describe the steps in the *right order*, and make sure each step is *accurate*. You also need to consider your audience. What do they already know about the process you are explaining? Do you need to define any scientific or technical terms for them? How can you get them interested in the process you are explaining if they're not already interested?

How to Write a Process Essay

First, pick a title that clearly states what the process is and what the reader will learn: **How to Wash a Car.**

Next, tell the purpose of the process, and introduce any terms you think your readers will need to know. Then organize the steps in the process. Use numbers for each step. Be sure that you list the steps separately—do not include more than one main step for each number. Start each step with a verb: 1. **Move** the car into the shade.

If you are teaching the reader how to do something, include any other information he or she needs to know in each step. Why do this step now? What will happen after you complete this step? You can put this kind of information in parentheses: 1. Move the car into the shade. (This will keep the soap from drying on the car before you rinse.)

Use a graphic organizer to help you organize the steps you wish to include. Include transition, or signal, words that tell the audience when something happens in relation to something else. Here are some examples of transition words: *first, next, then, finally, now, while,* and *after.*

Student Model

Take a look at Trey's explanation of the process of washing a car.

How to Wash a Car

Here are some instructions for washing a car. You'll need some carwash soap and a hose with a nozzle.

1. First, have someone move the car so that it is in the shade. (This way, the soap won't dry before you have had a chance to rinse.)
2. Next, rinse the entire car with water from a hose, using a nozzle.
3. Next, put some carwash soap into a bucket that holds five gallons or more. (Read the instructions on the bottle to tell how much soap to put in.)
4. Next, spray water from a hose into the bucket until it is about two-thirds full. (The soap and water should make thick, soapy bubbles.)
5. Place a large, clean sponge deep into the water in the bucket and squeeze it so that it absorbs the water and soap. (The sponge should be dripping when you take it out of the bucket.)
6. While the car is still wet from the rinse-off, begin washing the car, using large, circular movements. (Start with the top of the car, then do the sides, the front, and the back.)
7. After the whole car has been scrubbed, rinse off the soap. (Again, start at the top of the car, rinse it until it is free of soap, and then do the sides, the front, and the back.)
8. Finally, dry the car. (Use a soft cloth that won't leave fibers on the car. Use the same circular motion.)
   Your family member, friend, or paying customer now has a sparkling clean car at considerably less than the cost of a professional car wash!

Reading Your Writing

When explaining a process, avoid writing every single detail in every single step. Make sure you include only details that your audience needs to know in order to perform or understand the process.

Giving Directions

If you're having a party, you don't want your guests to get lost on the way there. Writing clear, accurate directions will help avoid creating that kind of confusing, frustrating situation.

Writing Directions to a Place

First make sure that *you* already know the directions yourself. If you aren't sure, consult a map, or even draw the map yourself to see if it makes sense. If you are writing directions for how to get from one store to another in a mall, for example, go to the mall to walk the route yourself. Take notes along the way.

In your title, clearly tell what the directions are for: *Getting from Our School to My House for My New Year's Eve Party.*

Then write a short introduction that gives your audience an idea of how long it will take to get from Point A to Point B. You could also give your audience a clue about how easy or difficult it will be to find the way.

Next, write the actual directions. Here are some tips to follow to help your readers find their way:

▶ Use directions words—*north, south, east, west, left, right, through, around,* and so on—to tell them which way to go. "As you leave the school, go *south* on Maynard Avenue for two blocks."

Some road signs don't have any words. That's because they were created a long time ago, when the majority of the population could not read.

▶ Include *landmarks*—specific buildings, water towers, billboards, bodies of water, and so on—that the readers can look for while following your directions. When they see a landmark that you have included, it reassures them that they are on the right course.

▶ Alert your audience to any parts that might be confusing or tricky. For example, if people coming to your house sometimes miss an important street sign because it is hard to see, warn your readers about it.

▶ Include a map if you think that the path is difficult to follow.

▶ Be careful not to tell *too much*. Only mention important street names and landmarks—not *every* street your audience will pass along the way.

▶ Tell the readers when they have arrived at the right place. Also include any information they need to know about the place once they get there, such as where to park.

Student Model

Here are some directions from Mai's school to her house, where she has invited some classmates for the first meeting of an after-school computer club.

How to Get to Computer Club Headquarters (Mai's House)

Here are directions to get to my house from school. It should take only about five minutes by car. You'll get there faster than you can log on to the Internet! E-mail me if you need any more information!

From the school parking lot, turn left (or south) onto Keyboard Drive. Drive south six blocks until you reach Gates Boulevard. You'll see a big We-R-Computers store on the left. Make a left onto Gates. Continue past Hard Drive Park. Two blocks after you pass the park, you'll come to Memory Street. Be careful, because it's a small street and a tree partially covers the street sign. Turn right onto it. (This is the only way you can  turn, because Memory is on only one side of Gates Boulevard.) Drive for two blocks until you reach Monitor Circle, and turn left onto it. Just as the name suggests, this street forms a circle. My house is about halfway around the circle. The address is 12 Monitor Circle. Look for the mailbox that is shaped like a computer monitor! Your parents can just drop you off at the walkway and continue around the circle. See you soon! :)

Reading Your Writing

Make sure you include accurate details in your directions. After you write your directions, test them out yourself. Follow them exactly as you have written them. If you take a wrong turn, you know you need to revise them! Your audience will appreciate your extra effort.

Tips for Writing About a Process

Prewriting Find a Subject That Works

▶ Think of a few processes with which you are familiar or ones you have read about or that interest you.

▶ List general steps for each one. Do some research to find out more details if necessary.

Drafting Get Down the Main Steps on Paper

▶ Use your notes and write all of the steps of the process.

▶ As you write, keep in mind what your audience already knows and *needs* to know about the process.

▶ In the introduction, include a list of materials needed to carry out the process (if applicable) and define terms your audience might not understand.

Revising Be Sure It Makes Sense

▶ **Organization** Are the steps in the correct order?

▶ **Ideas** Make sure that the audience knows exactly what process you are describing and what the end product (if any) should be.

▶ **Ideas** Did you include explanations for steps that are a little bit hard to follow?

▶ **Word Choice** Did you use transition words to help the reader follow the steps?

▶ **Ideas** Are all of the necessary steps included to explain the process?

Editing/Proofreading Check the Details

▶ **Conventions** Make sure the steps are numbered correctly.

▶ **Conventions** Look up any technical (or other) terms if you are unsure of their spellings.

Publishing Get Ready to Share Your Response

▶ Make a neatly typed copy or handwritten final copy.

▶ **Presentation** Include a diagram or illustrations that will attract the reader's interest and help explain the process.

Tips for Writing Directions

Prewriting Figure Out a Set of Directions

▶ Think of a few different trips that you make every day or every week.

▶ Choose the trip with which you are most comfortable. It may be the trip you take the most often (such as from home to school) or the trip that is the easiest to explain.

▶ List some of the streets and landmarks you see on the route you take. Think about how long it takes you to make the trip.

Drafting Write Down the Main Steps

▶ Write the directions for the route you chose. Use your notes and draw a rough map if you're having trouble with some of the directions.

▶ Keep your audience in mind as you write. If they aren't familiar with the area on your route, add more details.

Revising Be Sure It Makes Sense

▶ **Organization** Are the directions in the correct order?

▶ **Ideas** Make sure that the audience knows what your directions are for, where they will end up, and about how long it will take them to arrive there.

▶ **Word Choice** Include direction words and landmarks to keep your readers on the right route. Make sure that the direction words are the *correct* ones—don't tell your readers to turn right when they should turn left.

▶ **Ideas** Include only the directions your audience *needs*—not too many or too few.

Editing/Proofreading Check the Details

▶ **Conventions** Check the spelling of street names and landmarks. Misspellings can confuse readers who are looking for words spelled a certain way.

Publishing

▶ Make a neatly typed copy or handwritten final copy.

▶ **Presentation** Include a map for a route that is especially tricky.

Writing a News Story

What is news? According to the dictionary, *news* is "a report of information about a recent event or development, especially when important or unusual." The key words here are *important* and *unusual*. For example, your tour of the White House may not be newsworthy because families tour the White House every day. On the other hand, if the President toured *your* house, *that* would certainly be newsworthy!

In addition to being important or unusual, a **straight news story** should be about a real event that has taken place *recently*. It should also be something about which your audience cares and will want to read. For example, "School Gets New Computers" is a newsworthy story, but "Classroom Gets New Pencil Sharpener" is not.

A news story should answer the five *Ws*—*who, what, when, where,* and *why*—as well as *how*. It should also be *accurate*. If you get any part of the facts or details wrong, you're relaying incorrect information to your readers. Also, people involved in the story may be hurt or inconvenienced by your reporting of inaccurate information.

Collecting Information for News Stories

Interviewing people involved in the event is a common way to collect information for a news story.

Interviewing Tips

1. First, do some research on the person you are interviewing, as well as on the subject of your news story. This will help you figure out what questions you want to ask the interviewee.

2. Based on your research, write down questions to ask during the interview.

3. Contact the interviewee and set up a time for the interview. Be polite and professional.

4. Ask the interviewee the questions you wrote down. *Listen* carefully to the responses, and ask follow-up questions to clear up any confusing points.

5. Take quick notes or tape-record the conversation, with the permission of your interviewee. Let the person talk, but try to keep him or her from getting too far off the subject. Remember that you don't have to ask each question in the exact order you wrote it down.

6. If you are unsure of the spellings of proper names, ask the person to spell them out.

7. Thank your interviewee for taking the time to be interviewed. Let him or her know when and where your article will be published.

Researching and Observing

In addition to doing interviews, you can do *research* to find information for your news story. You can look up topics on the Internet, use the library's books and other resources, consult city records, and so on. Another option is to simply *observe* the world around you to collect information. For example, if someone is picketing outside a store or other facility, you may simply watch and listen to the people picketing. Keep in mind that for most kinds of news stories you write, you'll probably need to use a combination of the different methods of collecting information to make your story more in-depth and believable.

Kinds of News Stories

One kind of news story that is especially suited to the interview is the feature article. It is different from a straight news story. A **straight news story** tells only the facts, without using creative language or trying to make the audience feel a certain way. A **feature article** tells a story that focuses on a person's unique skills or experiences or on one aspect of a current event, trend, or other subject, such as how cell phones and pagers have changed school life. Still another kind of newspaper article is the editorial. In an **editorial,** you introduce a topic and then give your opinion about it, using information you've gathered to support your ideas. An article about why your school should do away with school uniforms is an example of an editorial.

Try It

Tell what kind of story each of the following is: straight news, feature article, or editorial.

▶ *A story about a man who repairs old bicycles and gives them to kids who need them*

▶ *A story about why the cafeteria food should be improved*

▶ *A story about the damage done to the school gym by a flood*

Parts of a News Story

Headline

The **headline** tells the reader what event the news article covers. Keep headlines short and to the point.

School Carwash Raises Record Amount of Money

Byline

This is the name of the reporter who wrote the news article. It is usually printed at the beginning of the article, under the headline.

Lead Paragraph

The first, or *lead*, paragraph should include all of the main and important facts about the event. *Who, what, when, where, why,* and *how* should be answered here. Two or three sentences is a good length.

Body

The body of the story fills in the information presented in the lead. The information should be arranged from the most important to the least important. This way, the editor can cut text at the end of the story to save space if necessary.

Quotes

A good quote from someone involved in the event makes the article come alive:

> *"The kids worked really hard," said Coach Pryor, coach of the girls' team. "I know they'll work just as hard in their games, and they'll rack up a lot of points on their new scoreboard!"*

Photo Caption

A photo caption appears under or next to a photo. It names the people who appear in the photo (in the correct order) and tells what they are doing in the photo.

Ending

The ending presents the last bits of information about the story's topic. A not-so-important quote or small details are good things to put in the last paragraph. Again, if the article is too long, to save space, the editor simply cuts the last paragraph or two.

Here's a news story about the sports department's annual car wash.

Headline ——▶ **School Car Wash Raises Record Amount of Money**

Byline ——▶ *by Miriam Chung*

Lead Paragraph ——▶ The Washington Wildcats basketball teams washed their way to a school record on Saturday. About twenty-five students and coaches raised more than $600 during their annual car wash in the school parking lot.

Photo Caption ——▶ *Athletes scrub with suds at the athletic department's annual Wash for the Wildcats sports fundraiser.*

The money will help pay for badly needed equipment, including new nets for the basketball hoops and a new scoreboard. The old scoreboard broke during the last game of the boys' season last year.

Body ——▶

"The kids worked really hard," said Coach Pryor, coach of the girls' team. "I know they'll work just as hard in their games, and they'll rack up a lot of points on their new scoreboard!"

Ending ——▶

The students and coaches credited the perfect weather for boosting sales past last year's record of $550. It was 75 degrees and sunny, without a cloud in the sky.

The cost of a car wash was $5. Next year, the teams plan to add a "deluxe" car wash that includes cleaning the outside and inside.

Susan Jackson, the starting center, grinned as she said, "This is the most fun I've had earning money." Then she squirted guard Janelle Watkins with the hose.

Reading Your Writing

Remember to keep your audience in mind as you write your news story. For example, an article about a school event for the community newspaper will probably include details that are different from those in an article about the same event for the school newspaper. Make sure you include details that the audience wants to know, and leave out those that wouldn't interest them.

Writing Good Leads

The lead paragraph in a straight news story should
- ▶ grab the reader's attention
- ▶ include most of the important facts about the story's topic to give the reader a quick overview of the story's contents
- ▶ use action verbs and descriptive words.

Notice the difference between the bad lead paragraph and its improved version.

Bad Lead

▶ The school's cook is making different meals. She has changed the menu. She worked with a nutritionist to plan the menu. There are new smells in the cafeteria now, and you can try them on Monday.

Better Lead

▶ There's something different in the air in the school's cafeteria! That's because, thanks to a new cook and consulting nutritionist, the cafeteria has a brand-new and improved menu. Students will get their first taste of the new dishes on Monday.

In the bad lead, most of the five *Ws* and *how* are answered, but the lead is not interesting. So what if the cook is making different meals? The ideas are disjointed, and the reader has a hard time figuring out the main point.

In the better lead, all of the five *Ws* and *how* are answered. Also, the first sentence captures the reader's attention. The writer uses a play on the words "something in the air," which can mean "there's something new about to happen," or, in the context of cooking, that there are new smells in the air. Also, the sentences flow more smoothly, and the ideas are organized in a logical, easy-to-follow order.

Fun Fact

E. W. Scripps, newspaperman and pioneer of American journalism, once said:"A good newspaper is one that will sell." Do you agree?

Tips for Writing a News Story

Prewriting Form a Story Idea

▷ Choose a subject that is newsworthy.

▷ Collect ideas from interviews, observations, and research.

Drafting Get the Story Across

▶ Write your lead paragraph. Include the most important details first. Try to answer *who, what, when, where, why,* and *how* in this paragraph. Make it interesting.

▶ Write the body of the news story. Include details that fill out the ideas in the lead paragraph.

▶ Include only one main idea in each paragraph. Keep paragraphs short. Only include information that directly relates to your topic.

▶ Include quotes where appropriate.

Revising Check Your Information

▶ **Ideas** Have you answered all of the important questions?

▶ **Ideas** Is your information accurate? If you are unsure of a fact, do more research or interviews until you are sure. Double-check the accuracy of direct quotes.

▶ **Organization** Check your headline. Does it tell the main focus of the article?

▶ Paragraphs shouldn't be more than three or four sentences long. Cut those that are too long.

Editing/Proofreading Closely Check the Details

▶ **Conventions** Make sure the dates and times are accurate.

▶ **Conventions** Check the spelling of proper nouns. Pay close attention to those you name in photo captions. Are the names in the right order?

▶ **Conventions** Include the titles or occupations of people related to the topic, if these are important.

Publishing Get Ready to Share Your Story

▷ **Presentation** If possible, use a desktop publishing program to present your article in newspaper-type columns.

▷ **Presentation** Add photos if you have them; include captions.

Expository Essay

An **expository essay** presents information about a specific subject. To write an expository essay, you need to do research on your subject and then organize the information in a clear, easy-to-understand way. An expository essay is different from a research report because it presents the information in a less formal way. It can be more conversational, and it includes the writer's personal observations and thoughts about the subject.

You can organize an expository essay in a variety of ways, including the compare/contrast format. Be sure, though, that the things you are comparing really can be compared. For example, two dinosaurs can be compared because they are two types of the same thing—*dinosaurs*. You couldn't compare an allosaurus to a dinosaur, however, because an allosaurus is a *type* of dinosaur. You also can't compare two things that are different types of things—an allosaurus and a cactus, for example. One is an animal, and one is a plant, so there are no points of comparison.

Try It

Think of some subjects that interest you, such as two types of music (jazz and rap), or two places you like to visit (two amusement parks, for example). What would your points of comparison and contrast be between the two subjects?

Venn Diagram

After you have chosen the subjects to compare and contrast, your next step is to collect research about them. Then organize some of the basic facts you have found into a chart such as a Venn diagram or T-chart.

Venn Diagram That Compares and Contrasts the Brachiosaurus and the Allosaurus

Brachiosaurus
one of Earth's tallest and largest creatures; 90 to 100 feet long, weighed as much as 80 tons • fossils found in Europe • was a sauropod—a huge, four-legged plant eater • name means "lizard arm" • teeth shaped like chisels for eating treetops; nostrils high up on nose • its large size was its main defense against predators

Similarities
lived during the same period of time • large in size • belong to a group of dinosaurs called *saurischian* • fossils found in U.S. and Africa

Allosaurus
up to 30 feet long, weighed at least 2 tons • fossils found in South America, Asia, and Australia • was a theropod—a two-legged meat eater • deadly hunter and scavenger, like Tyrannosaurus • name means "different lizard" • good parent to young • may have hunted in packs • massive head, filled with razor-sharp teeth, long legs and powerful arms; three fingers with sharp claws; bony ridges above and in front of eyes

Use your diagram to write the essay. Include an introduction; a body, which includes the points of comparison and contrast; and a conclusion.

Here's a compare/contrast essay about two types of dinosaurs.

The Big and the Deadly

If you have ever seen the movie *Dinosaur* or *Jurassic Park,* you probably rooted for the huge, peace-loving brachiosaurus (BRACK-ee-uh-SAW-rus) and *against* the crafty and deadly allosaurus (al-uh-SAW-rus). These two dinosaurs lived side by side. Were they really as different as they seemed?

Both the brachiosaurus and allosaurus are *saurischian* dinosaurs, meaning that their hip structure is similar to that of lizards. Dinosaurs are divided into two different groups, based on their bone structure: *saurischian,* which means "lizard-hipped," and *ornithischian,* which means "bird-hipped." So one thing the brachiosaurus and the allosaurus had in common was that they were both "lizard-hipped."

Both were big, compared to other dinosaurs of their time. However, the brachiosaurus was gigantic! Full-grown, the brachiosaurus reached 90 to 100 feet in length. Supported by its long, strong neck, its head sat some 40 feet high in the air. It was more than twice as tall as a giraffe, the world's tallest mammal today. It was also as heavy as 12 elephants, weighing up to 80 tons. You wouldn't want to be underfoot with these huge beasts running around! Even though the allosaurus was no shrimp, at 30 feet in length and weighing two tons, it was still tiny in comparison to the brachiosaurus.

The two dinosaurs were physically different in most ways other than size, too. The brachiosaurus is known as a *sauropod,* one of two subgroups of the saurischian dinosaurs. Like all sauropods, the brachiosaurus was big and had four pillarlike legs and a long neck and tail. Its head was small compared to its massive body. Its name, which means "lizard arm," describes its front legs, which were thinner and longer than its back legs. The allosaurus, on the other hand, belongs to the other dinosaur group, called the *theropods.* The allosaurus had two long legs and two smaller but powerful arms. *Allosaurus* means "different lizard," to show that it was different from another theropod called the *megalosaurus.*

The physical differences of the two types of dinosaur also tell a tale about their eating habits. The brachiosaurus, like its sauropod counterpart, was a plant eater. Its great height enabled it to eat treetops—leaves, branches, and all. Its chisel-like teeth were perfect tools for cutting off branches. The brachiosaurus also had nostrils that were between and above its eyes. Scientists have developed a theory that the purpose of these nostrils was to help the dinosuars sniff out their favorite kinds of plants.

Scientists also developed a theory about the purpose of the teeth of the allosaurus. Like the other theropods, the allosaurus was a meat eater—a skilled and impressive hunter. Its teeth were razor-sharp, shaped like knife blades, and plentiful. Unlike the brachiosaurus, the allosaurus's head was very large compared to the rest of its body, with huge jaws in which to capture its prey. Its three sharp claws at the end of each hand also came in handy during a hunt. Bony ridges in front and above its eyes made the allosaurus look like it had horns. This probably served to frighten enemies or prey. Although it was a ferocious predator, the allosaurus was thought to be nurturing of its own young. Fossils suggest that these dinosaurs brought portions of sauropods to their nests to feed their babies.

Because they lived during the same time, the two different dinosaurs had their share of meetings. The huge brachiosaurus's best defense most likely was its size—because it was so big, the much smaller allosaurus could not bring it down. Scientists think that the allosaurus might have traveled in packs so that they could take on their larger prey. The allosaurus also probably could attack and kill a baby brachiosaurus, but usually not if its mother was around!

Despite their differences, both the brachiosaurus and the allosaurus thrived. Based on fossil remains found, scientists know that the brachiosaurus lived in Europe, East Africa, and the western United States. The remains of the allosaurus have been found on five continents—North and South America, Africa, Asia, and South America.

Perhaps most amazing, though, is that both types flourished, side by side, predator and prey, for a very long time. The brachiosaurus and the allosaurus had their differences, but one final thing that they must have had in common was a stubborn will to survive.

Fun Fact

The word *essay* comes from the Latin word *exigere*, which means "to weigh or examine." Indeed, when you write an expository essay, you weigh and examine the information you collect.

Reading Your Writing

Remember that to write an effective compare/contrast essay, the things that you are comparing must be the *same* in some way. Comparing a car to a computer, for example, will not work because the two things are completely different *types* of things. Also keep in mind that whenever you do research to get ideas for an essay, you should restate the ideas you find in your own words. That way, you avoid plagiarizing, or copying, another person's words.

Examining the Compare/Contrast Essay

In the sample essay, the writer could have chosen a few different ways to organize the compare/contrast essay.

Ways to Organize the Compare/Contrast Expository Essay

▶ Topic by Topic or Part by Part

In each paragraph, introduce a **topic.** Describe each subject and how they relate to the topic and each other. For example, introduce the topic of **size.** First, describe how big the brachiosaurus was, then describe how big the allosaurus was, and then compare the two. Then go on to the next topic, such as other physical features, and describe those of one dinosaur, then the other, and compare.

▶ Whole Subject by Whole Subject

Describe all of the traits of the first subject of comparison. Then describe all of the traits of the second subject of comparison, reminding the reader about how it compares to the first. For example, describe all of the brachiosaurus's traits in the first half of the essay. Then describe all of the allosaurus's traits in the second half of the essay, mentioning the brachiosaurus for points of comparison.

▶ By Similarities and Differences

In the first half of the essay, discuss how each of the two subjects is similar. In the last few paragraphs, tell how they are different. For example, first discuss how the brachiosaurus and the allosaurus are alike: both are big, and they lived at same time. Then discuss how they are different: one is a plant eater, one is a meat eater, and so on.

Often, the two things that you are comparing will give you a good idea of how to organize your essay. For example, in the sample essay, because there are several different topics to discuss, such as size, physical traits, and eating habits, the writer decided to use the topic-by-topic method.

To ensure that the essay flowed smoothly from idea to idea, the writer used *transition*, or *signal*, *words*. These include *both, same, also, in comparison, in contrast, like, similar to, different from, in the same way, unlike, most, compare, on the other hand*, and so on. These transition words also helped the reader understand the points of comparison.

Finally, the writer's voice shows through in the text, making it an enjoyable read. Exclamatory sentences and informal, amusing observations about the dinosaurs help make the topic more lively.

Tips for Writing an Expository Essay Using Comparison/Contrast

Prewriting Choose a Subject

▷ Think of two things you would like to compare. Make sure they are two of the same type of thing.
▷ Use a Venn diagram or other graphic organizer to note the similarities and differences.
▷ Decide on the best way to organize the information based on the notes you took.

Drafting Follow Your Plan

▶ Include in your introduction the two things you are comparing.
▶ Use topic sentences for each paragraph to tell what points you are comparing.
▶ Include details that help illustrate the similarities and differences.
▶ At the end, consider adding one more new point of comparison to give the reader something new to consider.

Revising Check the Content

▶ **Organization** Make sure the organization makes sense. Is it the best choice for the way you compare the subjects?
▶ **Ideas** Add details if you need to support or explain a point of comparison that you are making. Cut any details that don't have to do with the topic.
▶ **Sentence Fluency** Have you used transition words to indicate points of comparison and contrast?
▶ **Voice** If you haven't done so, add some personal observations and comments.

Editing/Proofreading Examine the Details

▶ **Conventions** Double-check the spelling of any technical terms or proper names. Check for grammar errors.

Publishing Add the Finishing Touches

▷ Make a typed or neatly written final copy.
▷ **Presentation** Consider including illustrations or graphics if you're comparing physical characteristics of two things.

Writing a Research Report

Just like it sounds, a **research report** shares information you have gained through research. Usually, your teacher asks you to write a research paper. Once you decide on your purpose and audience, you can look for a good subject.

Selecting a Suitable Subject

In many cases, your teacher will give you a general topic and then ask you to choose a subject within that topic. Be sure you pick a subject that interests you. Otherwise, not only will you be bored doing the research, you might communicate your boredom to your audience as well.

Suppose you are studying the stars and planets in your science class. Your teacher asks you to choose a subject that deals with one aspect of the study of stars and planets. Think about what interests you. You decide you aren't very interested in one particular planet or star, but you *are* interested in how scientists get information about things in space.

So you have a more specific topic, but you still need to narrow it down. Start by doing some exploratory research. Look through books and magazines about space exploration. Search the Internet for ideas. Take notes about subjects that interest you, using a web like the one below as you go along.

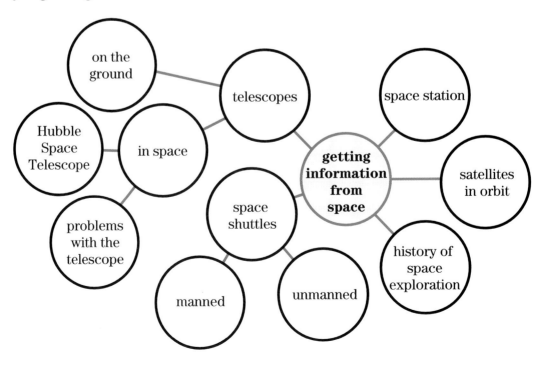

Narrowing Your Subject

As you study the web for possible subjects, keep these guidelines in mind:

▶ Make sure your subject isn't too broad. For example, suppose you are writing a two- to three-page paper. Based on your beginning research, you realize that you probably can't cover the subject "the history of space exploration" in just a few pages. So, you either have to narrow it down or choose a different subject. On the other hand, if there is hardly any information available at all about a subject, then it is probably too narrow to use for a research report.

▶ Avoid subjects that are too technical, such as the chemical reactions that take place during the formation of galaxies.

As you create your web, one subject in particular catches your attention—the Hubble Space Telescope. You decide that this will be the subject of your research paper. Let the research begin!

Gathering Information

Once you have chosen a subject, your next task is to gather information about it from books, magazine and encyclopedia articles, Internet sites, and so on. Use your library's card catalog (computerized or otherwise) to find sources. Take notes to help you organize the information that you are studying. Label your note cards with questions that you have about the subject or with general headings that you come across as you read.

1. Why was the Hubble Space Telescope built?
2. Who built the telescope? When was it built?
3. How does it work?
4. What information does it provide?
5. What problems did it have? Were they fixed?
6. Why is it named "Hubble"?

As you find answers to your questions in your references, add them in the appropriate places in your note cards. Summarize and paraphrase the information you find (refer to pages 96–99 on Writing Summaries to help you). Be sure to include the reference from which you got the information on each card as well.

> *Why Is It Named Hubble?*
>
> *Named after Edwin P. Hubble, American astronomer (1889–1953)*
> *Worked with telescopes*
> *Made many important discoveries*
> *One of first astronomers to show that the universe is expanding*
> *—Sipiera, p. 21*

Narrowing Your Focus

The next step is to use the notes you took to narrow the focus of the subject you chose. What *about* the Hubble Space Telescope do you want to concentrate on in your research paper? Try to figure out how you can present the information you found in a fresh and interesting way. You decide to focus on the long and bumpy path the Hubble traveled to success.

Try It

Decide which topic or topics below are narrow enough for a short research report.

▶ *Charles Dickens: His Life and His Works*

▶ *How World War II Changed Japanese Life and Politics*

▶ *Why the Legal Age for Driving Should Be Changed to 18 Across the Country*

Writing an Outline

If necessary, do some more research to find additional information that deals with your new, narrow main topic, making note cards as you proceed. Then use the note cards to create a loose outline for your paper.

Outline for Research Report on Hubble Telescope

I. The Hubble Took a lot of Resources to Build
   A. Serious plans for planning and building began in 1960s
   B. NASA concentrated on other things until 1970s
   C. Cost more than a billion dollars, with more than ten thousand people helping build it
II. Expectations Were High
   A. Description of Hubble—reasons expectations were high
   B. Compared to other telescopes
III. Encountered Major Problem Right Away
   A. Images were blurry
   B. Had to develop and implement a solution
IV. Accomplishments
   A. Gives scientists better understanding of happenings in space
      1. Found thousands of objects in space
      2. Narrowed age of universe
      3. Found evidence of black holes
      4. Recorded comet hitting Jupiter in 1994

Writing Your Report

Use your outline to write your report. If necessary, make corrections to your outline if you find that a certain train of thought is not working.

Keep your audience in mind as you write. Ask yourself what they need to know to get a better understanding of your main topic. For example, how much do they need to know about how Hubble works? What do they need to know about its history?

Include important details that will help the reader understand your ideas. Also, try to include a direct quote or two from someone about your main topic. This makes the paper more interesting and lively.

Include an introduction that includes your main point and gets the reader's attention. Add a conclusion that not only summarizes your main point but also gives the reader a new piece of information to consider.

Use your own words, and let your audience get a sense of your interest and enthusiasm through your writing.

Then create a bibliography of all of the resources you used to write your report, as explained after the model shown on the next page.

Here is a sample research report about the Hubble Space Telescope.

The Hubble Telescope

Introduction ▶   Picture it: the Hubble Space Telescope, almost as long as a school bus, uses solar panels to produce the electricity it needs to operate and radio antennas to communicate with Earth. It orbits Earth at an amazing 4.5 miles per second, taking sharp pictures of nearby planets, as well as galaxies 10 billion light-years away. It

sends the pictures to eager scientists back home, who use the information to develop new theories about our universe. Indeed, this is the role of the Hubble Space Telescope. Although it has been successful in its role, Hubble's road to success has been a long and bumpy one.

Middle ▶   The planning and making of a large space telescope took a huge amount of time and resources. The first serious study for putting a large telescope into space was conducted as early as 1962, about 28 years before Hubble would orbit Earth. Why did it take so long? Well, NASA had other things on its mind (and draining its pocketbook) in the 1960s and 1970s, such as getting a man on the moon and launching the Skylab space station. Finally, after NASA got funding approval from Congress in 1977, it took about ten thousand people throughout the United States and the world—and cost more than a billion dollars—to build. It was stalled another four years after the shuttle *Challenger* was accidentally destroyed, along with its crew. Finally, on April 24, 1990, amid much excitement, the space shuttle *Discovery* released the Hubble Space Telescope into orbit.

   The scientific community waited in anticipation for the first pictures from Hubble. The main reason for launching a telescope into orbit was so that it didn't have to look through Earth's atmosphere, which can distort and blur images. (The atmosphere is what makes stars appear to "twinkle.") Although other telescopes had been launched into orbit, none compared in size and complexity to Hubble. It weighs 25,000 pounds and is 43 feet long. The mirror, used to collect light from stars, is 8 feet across. Hubble is capable of observing ten times farther than telescopes based on Earth and can see objects that are 50 times fainter than can be seen from Earth. It's so accurate that it could produce an image of a small coin that is 400 miles away!

However, when the first pictures finally arrived a month later, project scientists got a huge shock. The pictures were blurry! Although the pictures were still better than any that could be produced from telescopes on Earth, they should have been much clearer. Under a lot of pressure from Congress and the media, project scientists scrambled to find the problem. They quickly figured out that the shape of the main mirror was a tiny bit off—it was 0.002 millimeters too shallow at the outer edge. This made the mirror unable to properly focus the light that the telescope collected. Retrieving the mirror and fixing it on Earth would cost hundreds of millions of dollars. The scientists decided to send astronauts to correct the fuzzy "vision" of the mirror by adding corrective lens—much in the same way that glasses or contact lenses correct a person's poor vision. Astronauts made the repairs in 1993, during a scheduled maintenance trip to Hubble as it orbited in space. The repairs did the trick!

Despite its problems, Hubble has lived up to its expectations. In its first ten years, it has found more than 13,000 objects and made more than a quarter of a million individual observations. It has achieved its goal of narrowing the estimate of the age of the universe. Hubble has found conclusive evidence of black holes, which are so dense that nothing can escape their gravity—not even light! It has provided images of the comet that hit Jupiter in 1994. In 1995, it took pictures of the birth of a star and gave scientists a glimpse of galaxies 10 billion light-years away. (Note that a light-year equals 5.9 *trillion* miles—the distance that light travels in one year.)

Conclusion ▶ Hubble will be replaced in 2010 by a telescope with a mirror that is several times as big as Hubble's. Hubble was named for Edwin Hubble, an American astronomer who helped explain how the universe works. Scientists hope that for the last ten years of its life, like the *man* Hubble, the *telescope* Hubble will lead them to make many more exciting discoveries about our universe and beyond. Hubble project scientist David Leckrone thinks that Hubble has already done more than anyone ever expected: "Not since Galileo aimed a small … telescope into the night sky in 1609 has humanity's vision of the universe been so revolutionized in such a short time span by a single instrument."

Writing a Bibliography

As you take notes for your research paper, you should keep track of the sources you use. A **bibliography** is a list of books or other materials used by the author in producing a piece of writing. It is usually found at the end of a book or piece of writing.

To create a bibliography, alphabetize the sources you have used by each author's last name, followed by a comma and the first name. If there is no author's name, alphabetize the work by the title. Don't count *A*, *An*, or *The*.

The following bibliographic entries are from the research report about the Hubble Space Telescope.

Book

Author's last name, author's first name. *Title of Book.* City of publication: name of publisher, year of publication.

Vogt, Gregory. *The Hubble Space Telescope.* Brookfield, CT: The Millbrook Press, 1992.

Newspaper Article

Author's last name, author's first name. "Title of Article." *Title of Newspaper.* volume number, issue number, page number.

Cowen, Robert C. "Hubble at 10: A Universe of Discoveries." *Christian Science Monitor,* Vol. 92, Issue 106, p. 4.

Encyclopedia Article

Author's last name, author's first name (followed by "and" and the second author's first and last name, if applicable). *Title of Encyclopedia.* City of publication: name of publisher, year of publication.

Couper, Heather, and Nigel Henbest. *Space Encyclopedia.* New York: DK Publishing Inc., 1999.

Online Source

Name of Web site, date accessed. <URL of Web site>.

HubbleSite, accessed 20 September 2000. <http://hubble.stsci.edu>.

Reading Your Writing

Keep in mind that a research report isn't just a restatement of facts you have found. Instead, it presents a main idea and organizes the information found to support that idea. So, don't just list fact after fact that you found from your research; instead, use the facts to support your ideas.

Tips for Writing a Research Report

Prewriting — Find a Topic

▶ Think of a topic that interests you. Do some research to find out more about it.

▶ If the topic is too broad for your paper, narrow it to a main idea.

▶ Research and take notes on your new main idea.

▶ Use your notes to make an outline.

Drafting — Report the Information You Found

▶ Use your outline to guide you in writing your report.

▶ Include details that support your main topic.

▶ Use topic sentences in your paragraphs. Follow topic sentences with supporting information.

▶ Include a bibliography at the end.

Revising — Be Sure It Is Correct and Makes Sense

▶ **Sentence Fluency** Use transitions to move smoothly from one idea to the next.

▶ **Word Choice** Use your own words by summarizing and paraphrasing.

▶ **Ideas** Are enough facts included to support your ideas? Add more facts if necessary.

▶ **Ideas** Be sure that you don't just list fact after fact after fact. Your report should be guided by your ideas and supported by facts and details.

Editing/Proofreading — Look Closely at the Details

▶ **Conventions** Check the spelling and capitalization of proper names and technical or scientific terms.

▶ **Conventions** Make sure the titles and authors in your bibliography are spelled correctly. Also check the punctuation.

Publishing — Get Ready to Share Your Report

▶ Make a neatly typed or written final copy.

▶ **Presentation** Add a title page and any illustrations that are necessary to the reader's understanding of the ideas presented.

Narrative Writing

Narrative writing tells a story. The story can be true, such as a biography or autobiography. These are about real people and real events. The story can be fictional, or make-believe. Some fiction stories can be realistic, with characters and events that could really happen. Others, such as fantasy and science fiction stories, contain characters and events that could never really happen.

When you do narrative writing, you are telling your readers what happened. Narrative writing has a beginning, a middle, and an end. It also needs a setting, a problem and solution, and characters. It may also need dialogue. Look on the following pages for some of the different kinds of narrative writing.

Personal Narrative

A *personal narrative* is a story about something that happened to you. That's really all it is. When you come home from school and tell about your day, you're telling a personal narrative. When you tell a friend of yours how you felt about something that happened, that's a personal narrative, too. In fact, your whole life is full of personal narratives, yours and other people's.

Getting Ideas for a Personal Narrative

Most written personal narratives concern something that stands out a little bit from the rest of the writer's life. It doesn't have to be something of major importance, though. It can be an event that you thought was kind of funny or a time when you figured out something. It can even be a moment when you realized something about yourself.

Making a Point

You may have noticed that some people are interesting when they tell stories and some aren't. One person can tell about walking to school and everyone pays attention. Another person can tell about visiting the Grand Canyon and everyone is bored.

There's nothing worse than a story that just drones on and dribbles out. Before you begin a personal narrative, think about the point you want to make. Don't start your story with it. Guide your story toward that point and end with it. Suppose you were going to tell about getting your new shirt muddy. You could start with getting the shirt and go on to describe how great you felt wearing it and *then* tell about getting mud on it.

Also, think about the special moment when you saw, heard, or felt something that led you to your point. Maybe it was seeing your dog running toward you with muddy feet and knowing that those feet were about to end up on your shirt. Be sure to describe that moment.

Putting the Reader There

Another way to interest people in what you're talking or writing about is to help them see or feel what you did when it happened. If you saw a beautiful sunset, for example, you might say, "I saw a beautiful sunset last night." On the other hand, you could say "The sunset last night was purple and pink with streaks of gold in it." Now you've come much closer to making your reader see what you saw. A really creative writer might use a comparison. "The sunset was like gold light shining through pink and purple cotton candy."

You can also use the words people spoke, or something very close. "My mom said, 'Go to your room!'" is just a little more interesting than "My mom told me to go to my room."

A graphic organizer like the one below might help you plan a personal narrative.

The Point
I figured out how to get a car unstuck.

→

The Beginning
• describe snowy day
• tell about going to the store

↓

The Special Moment
I saw the wheels spinning on the smooth snow.

←

The Event
• describe the stuck car
• tell about Mom and Dad helping

Try It

Think of a joke you know. Try telling it with the punch line—or the point—at the beginning. Does it work?

I Save the Day

Yesterday it was really cold and snowy. The snow in the air looked like little white feathers. It was making parked cars look like big marshmallows. I was sitting in the kitchen by the stove. I was glad I was inside. Then my mom said, "Let's go stock up."

Sometimes it snows for a long time. Then it's hard to go places. It's better to have lots of food and candles and stuff like that in the house. So, my mom and my dad and I put on our boots and our heavy coats and mittens. We got in the car and went to the store.

The streets were already filled up with snow. It was hard to drive, but we got to the store. We bought lots of soup and a gallon of milk. We also got apples and oranges and some extra boxes of cereal. Mom bought some yeast so she could make bread. I got a box of raisins and some little carrots and oatmeal cookies. We got dog food and cat food and kitty litter.

We loaded all the bags in the car. Then we started back home. My dad was

driving and he skidded once. We didn't hit anything. My mom said, "That was close." It really wasn't. She was kidding my dad. She always says she's a better driver. He says he's a better driver.

We got back to our block and turned into the alley. We have a garage and that's how we get to it. Yesterday, we couldn't get to our garage, though. There was a car stuck in the alley. Its wheels were spinning around and around. We could see the driver through the windshield. He looked really unhappy.

My dad turned off our car and got out. He talked to the man in the other car. Then he started pushing on the front of the car. I guess the guy put it in reverse. It started to go back a little bit, but then it stopped.

Then my mom got out. She started to push the other car, too. The driver started to argue with her. That doesn't usually work. I try to argue with her sometimes. My dad tries, too. She just goes on doing what she's doing. So she just kept pushing the car. It didn't move.

I got out of the car. My dad said, "Back off, Won. It's not safe." I stood there and watched for a minute. The snow under the guy's tires was really smooth. It looked like a kitchen floor. The tires were just spinning on top of it.

"It's too smooth," I said. My dad said he knew it was. They were trying to push the car back where the snow wasn't so smooth.

"We should make it rough," I said. My mom said we didn't have any sand. That's what they use to make icy roads rough.

My mom and dad kept pushing. Sometimes they stopped and talked to the guy. Then they started pushing again. I watched them for a while and then I got back in the car. I started looking through the bags for the oatmeal cookies. I found the kitty litter.

I jumped out of the car. "Hey, Mom. What about kitty litter?"

For a minute, my mom and dad didn't know what I was talking about. Then they figured it out. They got the big bag of kitty litter out of the car. They opened it and put kitty litter all around the guy's tires. He backed up just like that. We put our car in the garage. Then he drove right on out of the alley.

My mom says we're going to keep a bag of kitty litter in the car all winter long.

Analyzing the Model

The Beginning

The student model begins well before Won and his family see the stuck car. Because of this, we get a real feeling for the kind of snowfall they're experiencing. It's serious enough that Won's mother thinks they should stock up. We wouldn't know that if the story began, "We were just turning in our alley on our way home from the store . . ."

Starting that far back also gives us some feeling for who Won and his parents are. The more you know about someone, the more you're likely to care about him or her.

The Special Moment

The special moment begins when Won gets out of the car and starts thinking about the problem. No matter where the writer chose to begin the story, this part would have to be in it. Things begin to move a little faster. The reader can sense that the point is coming.

Description and Dialogue

The model begins with a description of the day and the snow. That description puts us right into the story. It may make us think of a time when we saw cars look like "big marshmallows." Very soon, the writer uses some spoken words—"Let's stock up." They add a sense of reality.

Characterization

By including the conversation between his parents about driving, the reader gets a sense of the type of relationship Won's parents have. By telling that it was his mother who thought of stocking up, who continues pushing even when people argue, and who decides to keep a bag of kitty litter in the car, the reader can tell that Won's mother is determined but is accepting of other people's ideas. Writers can reveal a lot about characters by telling what they say and do.

Describing Feelings

Compare these two bits of narrative.
"The door opened. I walked in."
"When the door opened, I was scared. But I walked in anyway."
Adding your own feelings gives your writing a point of view. It helps put the reader in your place.

Tips for Writing A Personal Narrative

Prewriting — Make a Plan

▷ Decide on an event in your life that you would like to tell about.
▷ Figure out the point you want to make.
▷ Decide where to begin your story in order to make your point more powerful.

Drafting — Get Your Ideas on Paper

▶ Use descriptions to put your reader into the story.
▶ Use short lines of speech to liven up your story.
▶ Move toward your point, giving your reader enough information and not getting sidetracked.

Revising — Be Sure It Makes Sense

▶ **Ideas** Go over the moments leading up to the point of your story to make sure you haven't left out anything important.
▶ **Word Choice** Use colorful words and comparisons to make your descriptions effective.

Fun Fact

Novelist Herman Melville once told some friends a story of a fight he had seen in the South Seas. He vividly told about a Polynesian warrior who waded into the fight with a heavy club. Later, the friends realized that he had left their house without the club he had been using to demonstrate, but they couldn't find it. The next day, Melville assured them there was no club. His narrative had made them imagine it.

Editing/Proofreading — Look Over the Details

▶ **Conventions** Make sure you've used quotation marks to set off speech.
▶ **Conventions** Proofread for spelling errors.

Publishing — Get Ready to Share Your Personal Narrative

▶ **Presentation** Type your narrative or rewrite it neatly.
▶ **Presentation** Think about illustrating your story.

Autobiography

An *autobiography* is the story of one person's life, written by that person. It covers a lot more than a personal narrative. A full-length autobiography starts with the author's birth, or even with his or her parents or grandparents. It tells the story of the author's life. A partial autobiography may cover only one period in a person's life.

Putting Things in Order

Autobiographies are almost always written in chronological order—the order in which things happened. Sometimes, however, a writer will begin an autobiography in the present and then go back to the beginning. That's a way of getting the reader interested. A movie star, for example, might talk about his or her latest movie before telling about being born and growing up.

Choosing Details

Nobody includes every detail in an autobiography. It would take as long to read it as it did to live it. Writers have to decide what to put in. They choose details that are important first. These are the things that might be called landmarks along the way—birth, parents, hometown, school, first job, falling in love, and so forth. Next there are the details that are simply interesting. If your family left you behind at a rest stop and had to drive back to get you, that wouldn't be a landmark, but it would be an interesting story.

Doing Research

At first it doesn't make sense for a person to have to research his or her own life, but think about it. You don't actually remember being born. Someone had to tell you when and where it happened. There are other things about your very early life that you might have to find out about if you were writing an autobiography. You could ask your parents, of course. Your family might have a scrapbook that would have information in it. Your older brothers and sisters could also answer questions and tell you stories.

The graphic organizer below might help you plan an autobiography. Remember, notes on a graphic organizer do not need to be complete sentences.

Opening really an Oklahoman	Details born in Chicago ended up in Chicago		
	Landmark parents	Details mother—Land Rush, Dust Bowl father—Twenties married—World War II	

	Landmark birth	Details in Chicago while father in college	
Details red clay school playground friends Mrs. Cotter		Landmark moved back to Oklahoma	
Details I didn't know many people who were born in Chicago like I was.		Conclusion moved back to Chicago	

Take a Look

This model tells a little about the early life of the writer.

Early Years

It's funny that I was born in Chicago and ended up in Chicago, because I'm really an Oklahoman. You see, my mother's family went to Oklahoma during the Land Rush. They lined up on the border in a wagon and rushed in at the sound of the pistol to claim a piece of that free land. They ended up in western Oklahoma and managed to make it through the Dust Bowl. They had neighbors who lost their farms and went to California to find work, but my mother's family held on. My grandfather worked on the town newspaper as a linotype operator. My mother went off to college right before World War II and met my dad.

My father's family moved to Oklahoma during the Roaring Twenties. They lived in Oklahoma City, where there were streets and tall buildings and indoor plumbing. My grandfather was art director of the Oklahoma City newspaper.

My father met my mother on a blind date and they got married before he went off to war. Their first baby, my big sister, was two years old before my father ever saw her. My mother took about a million pictures of her to send to him, though. My parents always insisted that was why there were twenty pictures of my sister for every one picture of me. I was born after Daddy came home.

Now, the reason I was born in Chicago is that my father was going to the University of Chicago on the G. I. Bill. The government would pay for college for any soldier who fought in the war. My parents and my uncle and his wife all lived together with me, my sister, and my two cousins. Then Uncle Dan and Aunt Jeannie decided they didn't like Chicago and went home. It took my parents a few years longer to come to the same decision. I was five when we went back.

So there I was, growing up in Oklahoma. Before long, I didn't even remember what Chicago looked like. As far as I knew, all dirt was like the red clay under my feet. I didn't know what a mountain looked like, and big trees were something pretty special. The first house I really remember was a one-story ranch house. Grass didn't grow very well in the dry climate, so my mother didn't complain when I dug holes in the backyard.

I can remember standing on the playground during recess watching a dust storm. Sometimes the dust would swirl into what looked like tiny tornadoes. It would blow against my bare legs and sting. We all kept on playing, though. We were used to it.

I also remember some of my friends from the first grade. There was a boy named Larry whose mother was from Cuba. She came to our class and taught us how to count in Spanish. There was another boy, named Ronnie, who was older than the rest of us because he'd been held back. He was handsome and very sweet.

I liked school, even though I was bored sometimes. My fourth-grade teacher, Mrs. Cotter, was very strict, but I thought she was great. She sang country-western music on a television program that came on too late for me to watch.

It would be a long time before I got back to Chicago. When I did, I was one of the few people I knew who was actually born there. It was funny, though, because I was really an Oklahoman.

Try It

Think of a memory you have of your early life that would be interesting to include in an autobiography.

Analyzing the Model

The Beginning

The writer of this model began with a statement about herself. She was born and lives in Chicago, but she's really an Oklahoman. This is a good way to get a reader interested because it immediately raises a question. Why is she really an Oklahoman? That question, although never stated, is in the minds of readers as they go on.

Chronological Order

Having made her introductory statement, the writer goes back to the beginning. She chooses to talk about her mother's family all the way back to the Oklahoma Land Rush, which happened near the end of the nineteenth century. She is explaining her roots in Oklahoma. For many people, this kind of information seems important in telling who they are.

After telling about her parents, the writer tells how she happened to be born in Chicago and why she ended up back in Oklahoma. The introductory question is partly answered now, but why did she stress that she was *really* an Oklahoman?

Details

The details the writer has chosen to share fill in the picture of a person who relates strongly to a place. She talks about the red clay and the lack of tall trees. She tells about the dust storms on the playground. These are not major events in the writer's life, but they are important. They help show us what shaped her way of looking at the world. They are the kinds of details that make an autobiography different from even the best biography.

Reading Your Writing

An autobiography shares what the writer thinks is important about his or her life. Be sure you give more than bare facts when you write.

Tips for Writing an Autobiography

Prewriting Make a Plan

▷ Decide what part of your life you want to write about.
▷ Research details that you don't know about personally.
▷ Look at pictures and scrapbooks to jog your memory.

Drafting Get Your Ideas on Paper

▶ Begin with a statement that will make your reader want to know more about you.
▶ Put the events of your life in chronological order.
▶ Include descriptions and details that will help your reader understand who you are.

Revising Be Sure It Makes Sense

▶ **Ideas** Read over your material to make sure you have included more than the simple facts of your life. Check to make sure your dates are right.
▶ **Word Choice** Look for general words like *nice* and *good* and try to replace them with more specific words.
▶ **Organization** Make sure your events are in chronological order so your reader can easily follow your narrative.

Editing/Proofreading Look Over the Details

▶ **Conventions** Check to see that you have used complete sentences.
▶ **Conventions** Look up the names of places to be sure they are spelled correctly.

Publishing Get Ready to Share Your Autobiography

▶ **Presentation** Type your story or rewrite it neatly.
▶ **Presentation** Think about illustrating your story with family photographs.

Fun Fact

English writer Samuel Johnson said that autobiographers have one advantage over biographers. At least they know what the true story is, whether they decide to tell it or not.

▶ Biography

A *biography* is the story of one person's life written by another person. Often, the subjects of biographies are people who are famous for their accomplishments. However, a biography goes beyond the fame to tell the story of a life. Many writers use the form of a biography to convey a message of courage, values, or perseverance.

Choosing a Subject

The best biographies are written by people who are interested in their subjects. If you're interested in sports, you might choose a sports figure to write about. If you have serious problems in your life, you might choose to write about someone who has succeeded in spite of obstacles. To get ideas, you can make a list of the things that interest you and then look in a reference book or on the Internet to find names of people connected with those things.

The *tone* of a biography is the writer's attitude towards the subject. If you like the person you are writing about, the tone of your biography will show that. The opposite is also true.

Doing Your Research

Writers of biographies have to do a great deal of research. Often, they interview friends and relatives of the subject. They may use letters or journals written by the subject. They search in public records and read any other biographies written about their subjects.

If you choose a famous person to write about, you will probably use mostly published material—encyclopedia entries, magazine articles, Internet articles. It helps to start with a short entry from an encyclopedia or biographical dictionary. It will give you the important events in the subject's life, as well as significant dates and names.

If you choose someone you know, you will probably begin with an interview, making notes of the things that strike you as important. You can then ask other people about those things.

Try It
Choose one of your parents or some other adult you know well. Think about what the important events of that person's life would be.

Organizing the Material

The material in a biography is usually presented in chronological order. However, it helps to begin the biography with the reason you're writing it—why the person is important. Your readers will then be able to understand everything else you tell them in terms of that information. A graphic organizer like the one below might help you plan a short biography. Find a short entry in a reference book or online to help you decide what you need to research.

Encyclopedia Entry

O'Reilly, John Boyle (1844–1890)

<u>Writer, editor, poet</u>; born near Drogheda, <u>Ireland</u>. Apprenticed as a printer, he worked in Ireland and England before being <u>arrested and tried in 1866 as an Irish freedom fighter</u> and traitor to England. He was convicted and <u>deported to a prison colony in Australia in 1868</u>. He <u>escaped in 1869</u> with the help of a priest and came to the United States. Living in Boston, he <u>became a newspaper editor, lecturer, and poet</u>.

Name	John Boyle O'Reilly
Accomplishment	editor, lecturer, poet
Born	1844, Ireland, parents? find out more
Early life	find out more
Events	worked as printer, reporter arrested for political reasons (1866) deported to Australia (1868) escaped (1869), how? find out more came to United States became an editor, etc., what did he write?
Died	1890, how?

Take a Look

This student model tells the life of the fascinating Irish American poet John Boyle O'Reilly.

Rebel Poet

John Boyle O'Reilly was a famous editor and poet in America in the nineteenth century. He was born in Ireland in 1844. His father, William David O'Reilly, was a schoolmaster. There were eight children in the family. His mother, Eliza Boyle O'Reilly, taught him to love poetry. She also taught him that Ireland should be free from England, which had ruled Ireland for generations.

John began working for a printer when he was nine, as an apprentice. He worked for a newspaper called the <u>Argus</u> until he was fifteen. Then he went to England and got another job as a printer's apprentice. He ended up as a reporter.

When he was nineteen years old, John returned to Ireland. He joined a group called the Fenian Order. The Fenians were fighting for Irish independence from England. At the same time, he enlisted in the English Army. O'Reilly secretly recruited other soldiers in his regiment to work with the Fenians. In fact, he recruited 80 of the 100 Irish soldiers in the regiment.

O'Reilly was caught in 1866 and court martialed. At first, he was sentenced to death. That sentence was changed because he was so young. He went to prison instead. First, he was in solitary confinement. Then he was on a work gang, but he managed to escape in a thick fog. Then he was sent to Australia. Many English convicts were deported to Australia at that time.

Some of the other convicts thought John O'Reilly should be free to work for Irish freedom. There was a priest near the Western Australian Settlement who thought so, too. The priest helped O'Reilly escape from the prison and get to a whaling ship. The captain of the ship was the priest's friend. He helped the young rebel get to America.

The Irish community in Boston knew about O'Reilly's work. He was a hero to them. He got a job on an Irish American newspaper called the <u>Pilot</u>. His writing made him famous. He got married in 1872 to Mary Murphy. She was a journalist, too. They had four children. Later he became the editor of the <u>Pilot</u>.

John Boyle O'Reilly also wrote a novel and many books of poetry. He was the most famous Irish American writer of that time. Irish Americans were discriminated against in those days, and O'Reilly fought for their rights. He didn't just write about Irish people, though. He defended the rights of Jews, African Americans, and Native Americans, too. Some of his opinions were unpopular. Some people criticized him. He always stood up for what he believed.

John O'Reilly had many friends. They were all sad when he died in 1890. He was only forty-six years old.

Analyzing the Model

Setting up the Background

This student model begins by telling the reader why John Boyle O'Reilly was famous. This helps interest the reader and put everything that follows into a context. The writer then begins a chronological account of O'Reilly's life.

Chronological Order

After the opening statement about O'Reilly's achievements, the student model follows the poet's life as it unfolds. The reader can place an event in O'Reilly's life not only by dates and other written time cues but by the order it appears in the biography. This makes the biography clear and easy to follow.

Time and Place

Because O'Reilly lived a long time ago, the writer had to explain some things, such as the situation in Ireland and the fact that English convicts were often sent to Australia. Later, the writer has to explain about the discrimination against Irish people in the United States. These are all necessary to make sense of O'Reilly's life.

Tone

The tone of this biography is admiring. The writer clearly feels sympathy for O'Reilly's point of view and actions. This tone makes the reader more likely to admire O'Reilly as well.

Reading Your Writing

Choosing a subject who interests you is crucial in writing a biography. Everything in the biography then becomes a way to explain your interest.

Tips for Writing a Biography

Prewriting · Make a Plan

▶ Choose a subject who interests you.

▶ Begin with a short entry from a reference book, or a personal interview, to determine the important events in your subject's life.

▶ Use a graphic organizer to put the events in chronological order.

▶ Determine what the message of the biography will be.

Drafting · Get Your Ideas on Paper

▶ Begin with a statement of your subject's accomplishments or importance to you.

▶ Try to put yourself in your subject's place as you write.

Revising · Be Sure It Makes Sense

▶ **Ideas** Go over your biography to see that you have explained things from a different time or place that might be confusing to your reader.

▶ **Word Choice** Word choices affect the tone of your biography. Make sure that you have made the right choices.

Fun Fact

Carl Sandburg once described his biography of Abraham Lincoln as "a book about a man whose father could not sign his name, written by a man whose father could not sign his."

Editing/Proofreading · Look Over the Details

▶ **Conventions** Proofread your story for spelling errors.

▶ **Conventions** Check to see that names of people and places are capitalized.

Publishing · Get Ready to Share Your Biography

▶ **Presentation** Type your story or rewrite it neatly.
▶ **Presentation** Think about illustrating your story.

Realistic Story

A *realistic story* has characters and settings that seem real. It's that simple. The characters behave the way people do in real life. The events don't have to be true, but the things that happen in the story *could* happen in real life. The setting might be your own neighborhood, or it might be a city you've never visited. It would not be an alien galaxy. There are no giants or dragons in a realistic story. People can't fly and animals can't talk.

Getting Ideas for a Realistic Story

Writers get ideas for realistic stories from things that happen to them. They also get ideas from newspaper stories or people they see on the street. You can get an idea for a realistic story almost anyplace. The events in a realistic story can be ordinary or they can be unusual and important. You could write a realistic story about your family eating breakfast. You could write one about a president being elected. You could write about getting sick or going to the beach or finding a dollar on the street. What's important is that the events in a realistic story must be ones that could really happen.

The Point

A realistic story should have a point or a message or a theme. It may be about courage, perseverance, or standing up for your beliefs. The events of the story can help the reader understand the message. The writer makes the decision that a realistic story, instead of a biography, fantasy, or science fiction story, is the best way for the writer to convey the message.

Try It

Imagine yourself in a situation where you have to make a choice. Suppose you saw a kitten with a collar and tags wandering lost through your neighborhood. What would you do? What could that say about your personality?

Making Something Happen

To make your story interesting, something has to happen to your characters. At least one of your characters should make a discovery, solve a problem, or make a decision. When you're thinking about the plot of your story, consider what would make your characters learn or change.

If you want to show how brave one of your characters is, for example, you could put someone close to him or her in a difficult position. To show that a young girl is brave, you could have her parents accuse her brother of something the girl herself did. If she admits that she is guilty when she doesn't have to, the reader will see that she is brave and honest. If she lets him take the blame, the reader will see the opposite. That's just an example, of course. You will think of your own plot events. A graphic organizer might help you plan a character-based realistic story.

MAIN CHARACTER		
AGE	PERSONALITY	MALE/FEMALE
13	kind, loving	girl

SETTING
city neighborhood, mostly Hispanic

EVENT THAT REVEALS PERSONALITY
new neighbor shows more interest in her than in her more popular sister

Take a Look

This student model was written about some ordinary sisters who are very different.

The Quiet One

Laura and Carolina were sisters. Laura was thirteen years old. Carolina was eleven. They were born in Mexico, but their family moved to Chicago when they were little. They lived in a neighborhood with lots of people from Mexico and Puerto Rico. The grocery store sold the kind of food they were used to, like plantains and black beans. Even the red and white hot dog stand sold tamales.

Carolina was only five when the family moved into the yellow house on Dickens Street. She learned English very quickly. Now she could speak it as well as kids who were born in the United States. She was very friendly and laughed a lot. She was also curious about everything.

Laura was seven when the family got to the United States. She learned English more slowly than Carolina. Sometimes she still couldn't remember how to make her sentences work. That made school hard for her. She was quiet and a little bit shy. Lots of times, she tagged along after Carolina, even though she was older.

One day, a new neighbor moved in. She was kind of old. She had curly gray hair and blue eyes. She laughed and talked with the movers who were carrying her furniture into her house. Carolina was very curious about her, of course.

"Why do you think she moved here?" she asked her sister. She leaned way out from their porch so that she could see better.

Laura looked down the street. "It's a nice house," she said.

"But she's not Mexican," Carolina said. "Just about everybody here is Mexican or Puerto Rican."

"I don't know," said Laura. Then she went back to petting her puppy. Laura and Carolina's parents had just bought them both puppies.

The next day was bright and sunny. Laura and Carolina were playing with their new puppies. Carolina was tearing up and down the sidewalk. One of the puppies ran after her. Laura was sitting on their front step petting the other puppy. The new neighbor came down the street.

"Those are wonderful puppies!" the neighbor said. She smiled so big she was almost laughing. Carolina started chattering to the neighbor. She asked all kinds of questions. She told the neighbor all about the people who lived on the block. She talked about the puppies and herself and her sister. Then the new neighbor asked a question.

"How do you say 'puppy' in Spanish?"

Carolina just looked at her. She couldn't remember. Then Laura answered quietly. "Perrito," she said.

"Perrito," said the blue-eyed neighbor. "Thank you. Gracias."

"My sister still speaks a lot of Spanish," said Carolina. The way she said it sounded a little like an apology. Laura blushed. But the neighbor looked interested.

"Really?" she asked. "Do you think you could teach me some? I really need to learn some Spanish for my work."

Laura smiled. "Yes, I can teach you." Then she looked at her sister. Carolina's smile was gone. "And my sister Carolina can help me."

Making Your Story Realistic

Writers of realistic stories work to make their readers feel that the story is real. They include things from real life that will make their readers think, "Oh, yes, I've seen that," or "I know how that feels." Descriptions of the setting in a realistic story usually have details that the reader will recognize. The description of the neighborhood in the student model has enough details, like the kind of food in the stores, to make it seem real. The writer tells us both the color of the girls' house and the name of the street they live on. These details make the story seem more realistic.

Organization

The way you organize your story gives the reader a clue about what is going to be important. "The Quiet One" begins with the present and then goes back to tell us something about the early life of the two girls. Then, before it goes on with the plot, it describes the two characters. The writer takes us to the fourth paragraph of the story before he or she says, "One day . . ." This is where the plot actually begins. This way of organizing a story indicates that characters are going to be very important.

Using Your Own Experience

When you're writing, put yourself in the character's place to make your story more realistic. You can use your imagination. You might be a boy who lives on a farm, but you could ask yourself, "How would I feel if I were a shy girl living in a big city?" "Is there anything in my own life that would help me understand a girl whose sister always outshines her?"

Characters

You can show the reader about your characters as well as tell them. This writer told us that Carolina was friendly, talkative, and curious. Laura, on the other hand, was quiet and shy. Later, we see Carolina running up and down the sidewalk while Laura quietly pets her puppy. Then, Carolina chatters to the new neighbor while Laura listens.

Reading Your Writing

Realistic stories should seem as though they could really happen. When you write a realistic story, put yourself in each character's place to make his or her actions true to life and use descriptive details.

Tips for Writing a Realistic Story

Prewriting Make a Plan

▶ Think of characters who interest you. They can be inspired by real people, but they should be made up.

▶ Put your characters in a setting that you like.

▶ Think of an event that will bring out the personalities of your characters.

Drafting Get Your Ideas on Paper

▶ Help your readers imagine your characters. Describe what they look like or the way they think and feel.

▶ Try to put yourself in the characters' place. Imagine what they would do, say, and feel.

▶ If your characters talk to each other in your story, try to make them sound real.

Revising Be Sure It Makes Sense

▶ **Ideas** Do your characters behave in a realistic way? Is your reader going to believe in their actions?

▶ **Word Choice** Even simple words can work for you if you choose them carefully. Be sure your verbs say exactly what you want.

Editing/Proofreading Look Over the Details

▶ **Conventions** Proofread your story for spelling errors.

▶ **Conventions** Check to see that names are capitalized.

Publishing Get Ready to Share Your Realistic Story

▶ **Presentation** Type your story or rewrite it neatly.

▶ **Presentation** Think about illustrating your story.

Fun Fact

Katharine Anne Porter said she never began a story at the beginning. "I always write my last line, my last paragraphs, my last page first."

Historical Fiction

Historical fiction is just what its name says—part history and part fiction. The writer sets the action of the story at some time in the past. That time may be a thousand years ago or it may be fifty years ago. Either way, the details of the story have to fit the moment in history the writer chooses. There must not be cars in 1820 or televisions in 1890 or personal computers in 1950.

Even more important, the problems that the characters in the story face must be problems of that time and place. In *Catherine, Called Birdy*, by Karen Cushman, young Catherine's biggest problem is that her father, a twelfth-century English knight, is trying to marry her off at the age of fourteen. She won't have any choice in the matter, and her father isn't choosy. Now, that is not the kind of problem a young teenager faces in twentieth-century America. Historical fiction writers choose this form to convey their message of courage, perseverance, or values.

Characters

Most of the characters in the usual work of historical fiction are imaginary. However, they must act the way a person of the past would act. They should be true to the period the writer has chosen in the same way that the details and the problems faced are. That doesn't mean that these characters have completely different feelings from you and your friends. In fact, one of the interesting things about writing and reading historical fiction is that you get to see how a person who is a lot like you might react in a world that is not much like yours. In Cushman's book, Catherine hardly ever bathes, has to pick off fleas, and lives in a castle. She also has a sense of humor, is sometimes gross, and has the usual assortment of teenaged insecurities.

Try It

Choose a period in history. Now, think of three things you wouldn't know about the life of a twelve year old in that time. What could you do to find out about those things?

Researching the Background

Writers like Mildred Taylor, author of *Roll of Thunder, Hear My Cry*, don't just happen to know a lot about the time periods they choose; they do research. Taylor used details from her own family, but she also researched the period of the Great Depression to make her story of the Logan family accurate. Historical writers have to know what their characters would eat, wear, and do for fun. They need to know methods of transportation and kinds of houses. If there is dialogue in the story, they have to know how people talked.

A great many of these facts can be found in books of history or in magazine articles. You can also find a lot of information on the Internet. There are even clubs that host Web sites about particular periods in history.

Anachronisms

The word *anachronism* comes from the root *chron*, the same root that is in *chronological*. The root means "time," and *anachronism* means "out of its time." When something in a work of historical fiction is wrong for the time period, it is an anachronism. One of the most famous anachronisms happened in the filming of the movie *Ben-Hur*. Somehow, one of the actors forgot to check his costume after lunch. So there, in a close-up, in the middle of a huge chariot race in ancient Rome, is a wrist with a watch.

This kind of thing happens on television and in movies a great deal. You will have to be careful to see that it doesn't happen in any historical fiction you write. An anachronism jerks the reader out of the story, no matter how well it is written otherwise.

Take a Look

This model shows how one writer took basic facts of American history and imagined a young heroine to fit into them.

The Mission

Richmond was still dark as Susie slipped quietly along. The stone streets were wet with dew. Only a hint of the sun brightened the eastern horizon. Soon, the city would be waking up. Sellers of fruit and vegetables would push their carts out onto the street, and customers would straggle in from all over the city.

Susie felt the morning chill in spite of her long skirt and wool petticoat, but she couldn't think about being cold. She could think only about her mission. She slowed down a little to protect the eggs in her market basket. They were wrapped carefully in a clean cotton cloth. Even wrapped eggs break sometimes and these mustn't.

As she passed through the market area, a Confederate soldier looked her way. She smiled and bobbed her head, but her heart almost stopped. He probably thought she was a slave, running an errand for her master. That would be good. It would be better if he did not wonder about her for even a moment.

The soldier looked at her grimly but turned back to his work. After all, she was just a little girl carrying a basket. She was fifteen but was small and looked no more than twelve. She was not a slave. Her former mistress had freed Susie in her will, and Susie had the papers with her to prove it. She had been working as Miss Van Lew's housemaid for a year, ever since she was freed, but now she had a more important job.

The checkpoint grew nearer. There, she would have to talk to the soldiers. She would tell them quietly and firmly that she was taking eggs from "Crazy Bet" Van Lew to an ailing friend outside town. All the Confederates thought that the wealthy Miss Van Lew was really crazy. The people who worked for her knew her craziness was an act. She actually headed a group of Union spies.

Just last night, one of Miss Van Lew's workers, Mary Elizabeth Bowser, had served dinner in Jefferson Davis's house. The Confederate president hired her because he thought she was too dim-witted to understand the plans he was discussing with his generals. Mary Elizabeth's slowness, however, was as much an act as Miss Van Lew's craziness. She memorized everything she could. When she got home to Miss Van Lew's, she wrote it down.

There was the checkpoint. Two large soldiers turned to Susie.

"What's in the basket?" one of them growled.

"Eggs for Mrs. O'Hara," said Susie.

"I'll take a look," he said.

Susie held her breath. He poked around in the basket and looked under the cloth. Then he looked at her again. "All right, go on. Be sure you're back before sundown."

Susie murmured thanks and walked on. Her mission would succeed. Mrs. O'Hara would get her eggs. The Union army would get Elizabeth Bowser's information. It was written in the tiniest handwriting on the thinnest tissue . . . and hidden inside one hollowed-out egg.

Analyzing the Model

Setting

As a work of historical fiction, this story takes place in the past. Susie is walking down the streets of Richmond, Virginia, during the Civil War. The writer does not have to tell us this straight out. We can pick up clues. The most important clue, of course, is that Susie refers to Confederate soldiers and the Union army.

Plot

The plot of the model story involves smuggling information through Confederate lines to the Union army. Susie's mission is one that could take place only at this point in history. It is also the kind of mission that a young girl would be doing *only* during a time of crisis.

Characters

Susie behaves in the story the way a young African-American woman of the time would behave. She is cautious about the first soldier and very polite to the checkpoint soldiers who hold the fate of her mission in their hands. She also bravely participates in what she saw as a war for freedom, as did thousands of African-American women during the Civil War.

Details

In this story, the first historical detail is probably the stone streets. From there on, we read about the carts in the market, Susie's long skirt and wool petticoat, and eggs in a cotton cloth and a basket instead of an egg carton. These details match the time period.

Real People and Real Events

Mary Elizabeth Bowser and Elizabeth Van Lew were real people, and they did exactly what the story says they did.

Tips for Writing Historical Fiction

Prewriting — Make a Plan

▶ Decide on a historical setting. It should be a time you know about or can research.

▶ Do some reading about your time period. Make notes of details you might need for your story.

▶ Create a character to put into the setting.

▶ Choose a problem for your character that fits the time.

▶ Think about the point you want to make to your reader by telling this narrative.

Drafting — Get Your Ideas on Paper

▶ Try to see the setting in your mind and then choose historical details that will help your reader see it.

▶ Make your characters behave like real people.

▶ If your characters talk to each other in your story, try to make them sound like people of the time period you choose.

Fun Fact

Historical novelist Edna Ferber always did her writing looking at a blank wall when she could. Anything else distracted her.

Revising — Be Sure It Makes Sense

▶ **Ideas** Check your story for anachronisms. If you're unsure about a detail, research it.

▶ **Word Choice** Look carefully at words and phrases, such as slang, that do not fit your time period.

Editing/Proofreading — Look Over the Details

▶ **Conventions** Proofread your story for spelling errors.

▶ **Conventions** Check to see that names are capitalized.

Publishing — Get Ready to Share Your Historical Fiction

▶ **Presentation** Type your story or rewrite it neatly.

▶ **Presentation** Think about illustrating your story.

Science Fiction and Fantasy

Science fiction looks at the way science and technology might affect our lives. It tries to answer the question "What if . . . ?" What if people could travel anywhere they wanted in an instant? What if human beings met aliens from another planet who could read our minds? What if somebody invented a machine that could make food out of the atoms in the air?

Fantasy is very much like science fiction because it also tries to answer "What if . . . ?" However, instead of telling about what could really happen because of science, it tells about wizards and sorcerers and other imaginary characters. Many people who like science fiction also like fantasy.

Setting

The setting for most science fiction is the future. That's because we already know how science affects us today. The story may take place on a future Earth or it may take place on planets and space vehicles that the writer imagines. The *Star Trek* television show took place mostly on a starship called the *Enterprise*.

Plot

In every episode of *Star Trek*, the crew of the starship dealt with a problem. Sometimes it was aliens on the attack. Sometimes it was aliens in trouble. Sometimes it was the crew members in conflict. Either the problem or the solution always involved the possibilities of science. That is true of most science fiction. In Madeleine L'Engle's *A Wrinkle in Time*, Meg Murry must rescue her long-missing father from evil forces who are trying to dominate the universe. To do this, she and her brothers and friends must travel by means of "tesseracts," which L'Engle has imagined as wrinkles in time. In this case, both the problem and the solution have to do with imagined elements. Science fiction writers use this form to tell a story about courage, fear, or perseverance.

Characters

The main characters in science fiction are usually realistic, with ordinary human feelings. Writers use the imagined parts of their stories to explore the real reactions of their characters. *This is very important.* You can make your setting as outrageous as you want, but you then must try to make your characters' behavior true to life. You will have to put yourself in that outrageous setting and use your imagination to find out how you would react. Good science fiction is a combination of imagination and realism. A graphic organizer like this one might help you work out that combination.

IMAGINARY ELEMENTS	REALISTIC ELEMENTS
in the future	human boy
some aliens living on Earth	family
people make everything with machines	friends
	birthday

COMBINATION THAT MIGHT PRODUCE PROBLEM
best friend is an alien

Try It

Think of some scientific discovery that would change life on this planet.

Take a Look

Look at this student model that explores what might happen if a boy's best friend were an alien.

The Problem of Xyvo

One day, Jacob woke up early. He looked through the wall of his bedroom. He could see the city clock up in the sky. The numbers said it was six o'clock. He sat up and pushed a button on the table next to his bed. A glass of cold orange juice appeared on the table. He drank the orange juice and thought about his problem.

Jacob's best friend was an alien. That wasn't the problem, though. Xyvo was a great best friend. The problem was getting Xyvo a birthday present.

Jacob got out of bed. He stepped on a button in the floor. His closet opened. He picked a blue skinsuit and a thick black vest.

Xyvo had powers. That was very good, sometimes. Xyvo could see tribullons in the creek better than anybody. He could take Jacob anywhere without a Zenon transporter. He could make Saturn slushes without a materializer. That was the problem. He could make anything he wanted.

Jacob went downstairs. His mother was surprised to see him so early. "Good morning, Jacob. You're up so early. Is anything wrong?"

"Kind of," Jacob said. Then he explained about Xyvo and the birthday present.

"Don't worry," Jacob's mother said. "He'll like whatever you give him."

Jacob didn't feel a lot better. He put his transporter on his belt. He started to push the code for his school. Then he remembered it was too early. He pushed the code for the creek instead. A second later he was standing next to it.

Jacob sat and watched the tribullons swimming. Their hundreds of legs were purple and green and gold. There were milicons, too. You could see right through them. There were lots of animals on Earth from other planets. Xyvo knew almost all their names.

Jacob reached into his vest pocket. He took out a wooden puzzle. His grandfather had made it for him. He liked to play with it when he was thinking. He slipped the wooden pieces in and out.

Xyvo was like the tribullons. He came from another planet, too. His father was an ambassador to Earth from Bjsdfs. Bjsdfsians could see better than humans. They could hear better, too. They could also materialize things. Jacob had to use a materializer. He or his parents had to pay for anything he made. Xyvo could just do it himself.

Xyvo could make Saturn slushes, but he couldn't make milicons. He couldn't make anything that was alive. Maybe Jacob could give him a whole can of milicons. No, that wasn't any good. Xyvo could catch milicons for himself.

Except for live things, Xyvo could make anything he could think of. Jacob looked down at his puzzle. Xyvo could make the puzzle if he saw it just once. Of course, it wouldn't be the same.

Suddenly, Jacob stood up. It wouldn't be the same. Jacob loved the puzzle because his grandfather made it. Xyvo would love something Jacob made. It was a whole week until Xyvo's birthday. Jacob could make something really good in a week. He wouldn't use the materializer, either. Maybe he would make a puzzle. Maybe he would make a toy. He would think of something. Then he would make it with his own hands.

Jacob put the puzzle back in his pocket. He pushed the code on his transporter. "Hi, Xyvo," he said as he walked into school.

Analyzing the Model

Setting

As a work of science fiction, this story takes place in the future. Jacob wakes up in his bedroom and immediately looks *through* his walls. The reader doesn't know what the walls are made of, but this is a clue that something unusual is going on. Other clues come quickly. Jacob's orange juice appears at the touch of a button. He wears something called a "skinsuit." Again, we don't know exactly what it is, but we know it's not jeans and a T-shirt.

Characters

Jacob is the main character of the story, and he is obviously a normal boy. He has a best friend, whom we do not meet. His friend, Xyvo, is an alien, but he also sounds as though he has the usual feelings and thoughts of a normal boy.

Plot

The plot of the model story involves Jacob's worries about getting a birthday gift for Xyvo. Xyvo not only *has* everything, he can *make* everything in an instant. That doesn't leave much for Jacob. He has to look at what he values in the world to discover what he can give Xyvo.

Reading Your Writing

Science fiction should explore human life today by imagining scientific changes. When you write a science fiction story, try to keep your characters as real as your setting is imagined.

Tips for Writing Science Fiction

Prewriting — Make a Plan

▷ Decide on your future setting. Make notes about some things that might be different from now.

▷ Create a character to put into the setting. He or she can be realistic or imaginary, but feelings and thoughts should be true to life.

▷ Choose a problem for your character that either is caused by scientific change or can be solved by it.

▷ Decide what message you want to convey about your characters and setting through a science fiction story.

Drafting — Get Your Ideas on Paper

▶ Have fun with the details of your setting. Let your imagination go!

▶ If your characters talk to each other in your story, make their conversations sound real.

Revising — Be Sure It Makes Sense

▶ **Ideas** Check your imagined details to make sure they stay the same throughout the story.

▶ **Word Choice** If you have made-up names for animals, machines, and so on, be sure they remain the same.

Editing/Proofreading — Look Over the Details

▶ **Conventions** Proofread for punctuation problems.

▶ **Conventions** Check to see that names are capitalized.

Publishing — Get Ready to Share Your Science Fiction

▶ **Presentation** Type your story or rewrite it neatly.

▶ **Presentation** Think about illustrating your story.

Fun Fact

English novelist Robert Louis Stevenson said, "The difficulty of literature is not to write, but to write what you mean." Think about it and you'll figure out what he meant.

Myth

A *myth* is a lot more than just a story. It's a culture's way of explaining how things came to be as they are. Why do plants grow only in summer? Why does water fall from the sky? Long ago, people created myths to answer these questions.

Myths don't have authors in the usual sense. We can only guess at who began each story, but we know that myths were added to and changed by generation after generation. The ancient Greeks believed that there was a group of gods and goddesses who directed the lives of human beings. Their mythology is important to much European literature.

Sometimes, writers create their own "myths." These are not actually myths, because they do not come out of a culture's attempts to explain the world. However, they can be interesting because they are one individual's way of making us look at the world another way. Writers use the form of a myth to teach a lesson or send a message to their readers.

Elements of a Myth

The most important thing in a myth is the plot. It is the plot that explains nature for us. The characters are often very simple. Sometimes they don't even have names. They don't usually have complicated personalities. Because myths come to us from ancient times, the setting is a time long ago. However, some writers have set myths in modern times.

Retelling a Myth

A single myth can be the basis for many different works of literature. A myth can be retold in a poem, a play, a short story, even a novel. Take the example of Demeter and Persephone.

Demeter was goddess of agriculture. Her daughter, Persephone, was kidnapped by Hades, god of the underworld. While Demeter mourned for her, the earth became cold and nothing grew. Finally, Zeus, the leader of Greek gods, negotiated with Hades for Persephone to spend six months of each year with her mother and six months in the underworld. He could not get her freed completely because she had eaten six pomegranate seeds while she was with Hades. Now, the months Demeter misses Persephone are the cold months between one year's harvest and the next year's planting.

That is the bare bones of the myth, the basic plot. The story can be told in various ways. The difference is in the details.

Try It

A myth explains something in nature or human behavior. Think of something in the world you know that could be explained by a myth.

Using Details

Details are everything when you retell a myth. The plot is already there for you. The basic characters are there, although you can play with their personalities and motives. The basic setting is there, although you can use descriptions to make it come alive.

A writer who was retelling the story of Persephone might make her a devoted daughter who falls in love with Hades against her will and then is torn in her feelings. On the other hand, she might become a restless teenager who wants adventure and goes with Hades without a struggle, only to find that the underworld is dark and dangerous. A third writer might make her battle Hades every step of the way and eat the pomegranate seeds only to keep up her strength.

Here is a graphic organizer to help you plan a myth retelling.

Plot of Original Myth	Notes about Your Own Details
There is no sun.	sky is gray, colors are dull
Man finds a trunk and opens it.	describe trunk / man wonders where trunk came from
Man puts on brightly colored clothes.	describe clothes, talk about colors
Man dances into sky and becomes sun.	man can't resist dance / use good verbs like "twirl"

Take a Look

This student model retells a myth from the Maya of Guatemala about the origin of the sun.

The Sun Dancer

Once, there wasn't a sun in the sky. Everything else was the same. Flowers grew. Trees lost their leaves. Animals hunted each other. People got mad at one another for no reason. The sky was gray, like a rock. Then all that changed. This is how it happened.

One dull gray day, one of the people was walking in the forest. He saw a big box. It was a trunk. It was taller than a jaguar and had gold hinges. It was probably the most beautiful trunk he had ever seen. He looked around to see if it belonged to anyone. Maybe some traveler had stopped here. Maybe someone was lost or hurt. He saw no one. There was no camp and there were no burros.

The man walked up to the trunk and looked at it carefully. It was carved all over with plants and animals. He didn't see a lock, so he opened it. What he saw was amazing! The trunk was filled with clothes, and the clothes were colors no one had ever seen before. There was blue the color of turquoise and yellow the color of cactus blossoms.

Now, remember that no one had ever seen the bright colors of the turquoise and the cactus flower. The turquoise was not as gray as the sky, but it was like a pool where the mud has been stirred up. The cactus flower was like a tortilla made with white corn.

The clothes in the trunk, however, shone brightly in the forest. Some clothes were red like a ripe tomato and purple like grape juice. The colors were so brilliant the man could only look at them for a moment. Then he reached out for a poncho of rich green. He pulled it over his head. He took a scarf of gold and draped it around his neck. He slipped his feet into a pair of blue moccasins. One after another, he took up the clothes and put them on.

Suddenly, the trunk was empty. The man stood there in his brilliant clothes. Then he felt his arms begin to move. They were turning him. They were twirling him! He felt his right foot lift and pound onto the ground. Again and again it pounded. He was dancing and he couldn't stop.

The man in the bright clothes danced through the forest. His scarves touched all the trees. His blue moccasins stirred the pine needles. Still, he couldn't stop. He twirled and twirled until he came to the edge of a cliff. He screamed, afraid he would fall over the cliff. His next twirl, however, took him into the air and up. He went higher and higher. Finally, he was just a glowing ball in the sky, and the earth was filled with light and color.

Analyzing the Model

This student model has all the elements of a myth. It explains something in nature, in this case the origin of the sun. It has a simple character and a setting long ago. The setting is Guatemala, but it is also simply "the world."

Details

Poet Marianne Moore once wrote about "imaginary gardens with real toads." The details in a myth retelling are the real toads, the touches of reality in a story that isn't about a realistic event. In the model, the writer describes the world before there was a sun. "Flowers grew. Trees lost their leaves. Animals hunted each other. People got mad at one another for no reason." These details describe a world that really was like the one we know. The description works much better than "There were flowers, trees, animals, and people."

Details show up again when the man wonders about the trunk. Could a traveler have left it behind? Is there a traveler still there, hurt or lost? There's no camp and no burros. These details give us a sense of a real human being confronted by a mystery. Later, the writer describes the colors in the clothing by using comparisons. This is another way of introducing details.

Word Choice

Because so many of the elements of a myth are simple, a lot of the interest lies in the words. The myth can be beautiful, moving, or funny, depending on the words you choose. This writer used good, strong verbs to make the man's dance come alive for us.

Reading Your Writing

Retelling a myth involves using details. When you write a myth retelling, try to "see" your setting and use specific details in describing it.

Tips for Writing A Myth

Prewriting   Make a Plan

▶ Read some myths from various cultures.

▶ Choose a myth that explains something that interests you or that you think could be beautiful or funny.

▶ Use the graphic organizer to make notes of details you might use.

Drafting   Get Your Ideas on Paper

▶ Make your descriptions detailed and specific by trying to "see" what you're describing.

▶ Try to put yourself in the characters' place. Imagine what they would do, say, and feel.

▶ Within the limits of the myth, show your reader something about your view of the world.

Revising   Be Sure It Makes Sense

▶ **Ideas** Are there real toads in your garden? Be sure your story has detail and imagery.

▶ **Word Choice** Increase the interest of your myth retelling by choosing words that are strong and specific.

Editing/Proofreading   Look Over the Details

▶ **Conventions** Proofread your story for punctuation.

▶ **Conventions** Be sure you spell names correctly.

Publishing   Get Ready to Share Your Myth

▶ **Presentation** Think about reading your story aloud to a group.

▶ **Presentation** Practice your reading.

Fun Fact

Author Truman Capote wrote all of his work while he was lying down.

Play

A *play* is a narrative plan for a theatrical performance. It's true that you can read a play in a book, but that's not the best way to experience it. Plays are written for actors to perform, for set designers to design, for costume designers to costume, and for lighting designers to light. The playwright is part of a theatrical team, and that's true even if the play was written four centuries ago. More important, of course, is that plays are written for audiences to watch. It's not half as much fun to hear a description of J. M. Barrie's *Peter Pan* as it is to see Peter fly across the stage and hear Captain Hook snarl and watch Tinkerbell's light dim and then grow brighter. Playwrights choose the form of play to convey their messages of courage, perseverance, or taking a stand.

Dialogue

The most interesting thing about writing a play is that it is made entirely of dialogue and movement. *Dialogue* consists of the words characters say to each other and it is the heart of the play. Most of the time, you don't need to tell the actors where to move and what to do. It comes naturally out of the dialogue. You can write descriptions of the characters and what they're feeling, but no one will ever hear your descriptions. You can write descriptions of the setting, but no one will ever see them, except the rest of your theatrical team. Basically, writing a play is writing dialogue.

Before they write a single line of dialogue, playwrights listen to the way people talk. Do they talk in complete sentences? Do they repeat themselves? Do they interrupt each other? Some playwrights sit for hours in diners and bus stations just listening. That's how important dialogue is.

Character, Setting, and Plot

Plays are usually very much like stories in terms of characters, settings, and plot, except for one thing. The audience members are not going to read about any of those things. In a realistic production of a play, they are going to be looking at a stage set that duplicates a real house or forest or classroom. In other productions, they imagine the setting, based on what they hear in the dialogue. The dialogue also tells them about the characters and the plot. For example, what would you learn from this line of dialogue?

Freda: There's Bette. She looks better today than she usually does.

That line could tell us either that Bette is usually not very snappy or that Freda is not being very nice. The next line clears it up.

Luis: Oh, you're just jealous, Freda.

Staging and Theatricality

You can have a lot of fun with a stage. You can have music or thunder. Lights can go out or burst on. People can overhear each other. They can slip on banana peels, chase each other, start yawning during a conversation, or dance like Fred Astaire and Ginger Rogers.

Staging is all the movement that takes place on the stage. *Theatricality* includes all the dramatic, showy, funny, wonderful things that only theater can offer. You may write a short story in which you describe a storm, and that can be very interesting. In the theater, you can have thunder and lightning and, in some cases, even rain. In a story, you can tell about a dog howling in the night. In the theater, you can make an audience's blood run cold when the silence is broken by a loud but distant cry.

Try It

Think about one of your friends or someone you know from school. What line of dialogue would tell people something about that person?

Take a Look

Look at this student model to see how dialogue—and a little theatricality—can tell a story.

Welcome to My World

Cast of Characters

Rita, a girl of twelve   Truman, a dragon

It is a sunny afternoon in the park. There is the sound of a baseball hitting a bat, then cheering, and Rita runs on backwards.

RITA: I've got it! I've got! (Falls down) Oh, darn!

TRUMAN: (Appearing from behind a bush) What's going on?

RITA: Oh, my gosh, a dragon! (Dives under a bush)

TRUMAN: Oh, my gosh, a girl! (Ducks back behind his bush)

RITA: (Coming out from behind the bush slowly) Hold on. That wasn't a dragon, you dope. There's no such thing as a dragon. It must have been the way the sunlight was shining on that bush or something. (Starts to run back to the ballfield)

TRUMAN: (Coming out from behind his bush) What kind of idiot are you, Truman? Girls only exist in fairy stories. You fell asleep and dreamed her. (Sees Rita) And apparently you're still dreaming!

RITA: (Stopping in her tracks) It wasn't the sunlight. It's some kind of animal, some kind of beast.

TRUMAN: Hold it right there, girlie. Dragons are not beasts.

RITA: It can talk.

TRUMAN: That's right. And "it" can breathe fire, too. So you'd better watch what you say.

RITA: I must have hit my head when I fell. Jason's father is a doctor. He's watching the game. He can—

TRUMAN: What am I doing? I'm talking to a girl. A girl! There's no such thing as a girl! They're imaginary creatures.

RITA: Excuse me? You're trying to say that I'm fiction?

TRUMAN: Only if you're a girl. If you're a dream, then you're just that pickle I had after dinner. My mom told me not to. She said it would upset my stomach and I'd have nightmares.

RITA: Oh, now I'm a nightmare.

TRUMAN: Welllll . . .You don't exactly look like the maidens in the legends.

RITA: You mean the ones that have to be rescued by knights? From dragons?

TRUMAN: Oh, come on. Everybody knows dragons rescue maidens from knights.

RITA: Oh, right. What fantasy world do you live in? Wait a minute, wait a minute. That's a good question, isn't it? You obviously come from some other world.

TRUMAN: I am in the world I've always been in, Toots.

RITA: Rita.

TRUMAN: Okay. I'm in my regular old world, Rita. The only thing different is you. A girl.

RITA: I can't believe I'm having this conversation. I'd better find Jason's father right away. (She leaves.)

TRUMAN: Thank goodness! No more midafternoon naps for me. No more pickles, either. Well, maybe every once in a while. I really do—

RITA: (Rushing back on) Gone! It's gone!

TRUMAN: She's back.

RITA: The ballfield is gone . . . everybody . . . my family . . . my team.

TRUMAN: Your world, you mean? Your world is gone? And that would mean you're in my world?

RITA: Oh. Oh, no! Now, I'm really in a pickle!

TRUMAN: Actually, you are a pickle. And if I'm not mistaken, that means I can get you back to your world.

RITA: How? Oh, please, whatever you are, if you can—

TRUMAN: Truman. I'm a dragon and my name is Truman.

RITA: Fine, fine. You're Truman. Can you really get me back home?

TRUMAN: I think I can. I think all I have to do is wake up.

RITA: Great! Wake up.

TRUMAN: Have you ever tried to wake yourself up from a dream? It's not so easy.

RITA: Try, Truman, try!

TRUMAN: Okay. (Closing his eyes and frowning) Wake up, wake up, wake up, wake up, wake up . . .

As he chants, RITA falls in slow motion to the ground. Her hand goes behind a bush and comes out with a ball. She jumps up and runs off, holding up the ball and shouting, "Got it!"

TRUMAN: (Opening his eyes) Now, that was really weird. (Lumbers off in the other direction) Mom!

Working with Dialogue

When you write a play, each line of dialogue follows the name of the character who speaks it, as in the model. Usually, the character's name is in capital letters, followed by a colon. Do not put quotation marks around the lines of dialogue. You'll notice in the model that most of the lines are not long. Some are no more than a word or two. That's the way people talk in real life. The characters repeat themselves or each other. One character cuts off the other character. This all makes the dialogue more realistic.

Plotting

In the model, two characters stand around talking to each other for most of the play. Even if they're fun to listen to, this would eventually get boring, except for one thing. There's a kind of mystery—what's a dragon doing in the park?—and the audience enjoys trying to figure it out.

Playing with Theater

There is a lot of theatricality in the model. There are sound effects at the beginning. One of the characters would be costumed in an imaginative, creative way. Finally, there is the final staging, when we see Rita return to her own world. When you're writing a play, you can put directions for actions and effects in the *stage directions*. Those are the words in parentheses and italics.

Reading Your Writing

Dialogue is the heart of a play. If you're used to writing stories, you may put too much in the stage directions. Look at the model to see just how little is written in those parentheses.

Tips for Writing A Play

Prewriting Make a Plan

▷ Look around you for play ideas. You can find them in paintings, photographs, real life, and so on.

▷ Decide on the message you want to convey with your narrative in play form.

▷ Choose a setting or a character that would be fun, interesting, or dramatic on a stage.

Drafting Get Your Ideas on Paper

▶ Focus on dialogue. Don't try to put your story into the stage directions.

▶ Say your dialogue out loud as you write, or try to hear it in your mind.

▶ As you write, look for opportunities for staging effects that can make your play more fun to watch.

Revising Be Sure It Makes Sense

▶ **Ideas** Do your characters behave in a realistic way? Even an imaginary character can seem true to life.

▶ **Word Choice** Choose words that your characters would actually use.

Editing/Proofreading Look Over the Details

▶ **Conventions** Be sure stage directions are italicized or underlined.

▶ **Conventions** Check to see that characters' names are in all capital letters.

Publishing Get Ready to Share Your Realistic Story

▶ **Presentation** Practice reading the different parts with a partner.

▶ **Presentation** Make neat final copies for cast members.

▶ **Presentation** Present your play to an audience.

Fun Fact

The great French playwright Moliére insisted, "I always do the first line well, but I have trouble doing the others."

Descriptive Writing

Descriptive writing provides the reader with a clear, vivid picture of something or someone. Think about the best place you ever visited. What do you remember about the way it looked, sounded, and smelled? When you use those kinds of details in your writing, you help your readers see what you see, hear what you hear, and feel what you feel. The following lessons will give you tips on writing good descriptions.

Writing a Description

Descriptive writing is writing that *describes* something, such as a memorable event, or someone, such as a character in a story. The key to writing a good description is to use words that have to do with the senses—*seeing, hearing, smelling, touching,* and *tasting.* This means choosing vivid adjectives and adverbs and precise verbs that put pictures in the reader's mind and help the reader imagine being in a particular place. This descriptive sentence uses the senses of sight and touch to tell what it was like being at a rainy soccer game:

▶ We ran onto the soaking wet field, feeling the cold, thick mud splatter onto our legs as our cleats sank into the ground.

Notice how the following descriptive sentence also appeals to the reader's sense of hearing:

▶ Six tiny, black puppies wiggled in the smooth cardboard box and squeaked softly.

Sometimes a description is a piece of writing that stands on its own. Otherwise, it is used to make the supporting points in another piece of writing precise, vivid, and memorable.

Take a Look

Which of the two pieces of writing tells you more? Why?

▶ *The warm ocean water gently lapped against my feet, the sand soft and squishy between my toes. As I peered out at the vast blue horizon, the crashing, rhythmic sound of the ocean's ebb and flow filled my ears.*

▶ *The water hit my feet, which were in the sand. I looked at the horizon. I heard the ocean's sound.*

Try It

Think of a place you know well. What adjectives, adverbs, and verbs would you use to describe it so that your reader could picture that place?

Mood

Another element of descriptive writing is **mood,** or the overall feeling a reader gets when reading a description. The mood in the first "Take a Look" example is one of peace and calm, created by words like *gently lapped*, *rhythmic sound*, and *soft and squishy*. The second example, on the other hand, creates a mood of distraction or unrest—the reader cannot vividly picture the scene, and the short, choppy sentences don't flow the same way that the longer sentences do in the first example. By carefully choosing your words and sentences, you can create any mood that you wish in your descriptive writing.

Organization

In any description, it's important for readers to understand where things are in relation to one another. To help you do that, here are a few different ways to organize the details of your descriptions.

▶ Left to right (or right to left): description begins at the left and continues to the right; suited to horizontal things, such as a train or an alligator.

▶ Top to bottom (or bottom to top): description begins at the top and continues to the bottom; useful for things that are vertical, such as a person standing or a waterfall.

▶ Near to far (or far to near): description begins with what is near and continues to what is in the background; good for such scenes as landscapes or rooms in a house or restaurant.

It's also important to begin your description with a sentence or sentences that tell the reader what to expect or that summarize the main point of the description. Take a look at the first few sentences in each of the models on the following pages.

Left-to-right Description Notice how the writer not only describes a familiar monument but also the description as a way to comment on the monument.

First sentence summarizes main point of description ▶

Exact modifiers (underlined)

Carved in Mount Rushmore's <u>gray</u> granite in the Black Hills of South Dakota, the faces of four <u>celebrated</u> presidents sit silent. Interestingly, their positions make a statement about their places in history. From their mountain 5,675 feet high, George Washington, Thomas Jefferson, Theodore Roosevelt, and Abraham Lincoln look out to different points on the horizon. <u>Serious</u> and <u>thoughtful</u>, and a much <u>lighter gray</u> than the surrounding mountaintop, each stone face ranges in height from 50 to 70 feet, twice the size of the <u>ponderosa</u> pines that grow below.

The head of "the father of his country," George Washington, stands higher and juts out farther than any of the others. Seeming to grow out of the mountain, his is the first face on the left—the first in line, facing straight ahead. Behind and to the right of Washington is Thomas Jefferson, our third president, who helped draft the Declaration of Independence. His head is lower, with his chin resting on Washington's left shoulder. The shadow of Washington's head covers a portion of Jefferson's right cheek.

To the right of Jefferson is Teddy Roosevelt, the Rough Rider, the youngest man to become president, positioned the lowest of all four. His head is turned to the right so that part of the left side of his face is hidden. <u>Thick</u> eyebrows cover <u>deep-set</u> eyes that also stare in the distance. And finally, on the far right, is the face of Abe Lincoln, the Great Emancipator. A space about half the width of a face separates a <u>serious</u> Lincoln from the others. He alone faces to the left, pondering a view all his own.

Top-to-Bottom Description Here is a description of the setting in a story. Notice how the writer sets the mood right away by choosing certain words.

Precise action verbs (underlined)

The July sun <u>blazes</u> overhead as the ocean's foam <u>sprays</u> in the humid air. Seagulls <u>glide</u> above our heads. At the surface of the water, beachgoers ride the gray, foamy waves on inflatable rafts. They <u>wince</u> as they taste the salty flavor of a million dead sea animals. On the shore, hermit crabs <u>burrow</u> in the sand, dotting the beach with little air holes that look like tiny dome-shaped houses. Nearby, a group of crows <u>pick</u> at a dead fish, and the curious seagulls <u>step</u> gingerly toward them to assess the situation. The contents of the Atlantic Ocean are well hidden, except for the tiny, clear fish that <u>dart</u> back and forth in the shallow water that meets the sand.

Near-to-Far Description In this example, the writer describes a familiar place with action verbs, vivid modifiers, and transition words.

Words and phrases that show location (underlined)

The rookie surveyed the infield. Ninety feet away at first base, his teammate Jones the Jet crouched, taking a big lead. <u>Beyond</u> the pitcher at second base, Hernandez the Hammer slouched a few feet from the bag. Out of the corner of his eye, the rookie made out Charlie "the Chicken" Club hopping around at third base. The other team's infielders stood <u>around the infield</u>, staring at the rookie, knees bent, waiting to make a play.

<u>Beyond</u> the dirt of the infield, the outfielders paced, small, blurry figures in the tall grass. The stands that <u>surrounded</u> the field held a sea of faces, small dots that ran together. The scoreboard high <u>above</u> the orange fence at straight-away center field, four hundred twenty feet from home plate, told the tale: Bottom of the ninth inning, two outs, and the home team was down by three runs. The rookie held up a sweaty hand to the blue-suited umpire <u>behind</u> the catcher and croaked, "Time."

Analyzing Descriptive Writing

Each sample description is organized according to what is being described. For example, the first description is organized from left to right, because what it describes—the Mount Rushmore carving—is horizontal. Because the second one describes a beach scene—from the sky to the fish just beneath the water—it is organized from top to bottom. Finally, the third begins with what is nearest the batter—the infield—and goes farther away.

Although the three descriptions are organized differently, they are similar because they all use vivid language that appeals to the senses. The second description, for example, describes the waves as "gray" and "foamy," allowing the reader to picture the ocean. Most of the verbs chosen in each description are active—"slammed," "juts," and "crouched." They show rather than tell the reader what is happening. The vivid language also helps set the mood of the descriptions. For example, the words and phrases used to describe the baseball field make the scene suspenseful.

The descriptions also use location words that tell the reader where things are in relation to one another. The Mount Rushmore description, for example, uses words such as "left," "right," "next to," and "lower," and exact measurements, such as "from 50 to 70 feet." Notice also how the writer begins the description with a topic sentence that sets the mood and gives the reader an overview of the scene.

Try It

How would you organize writing that describes the photograph on this page?

Reading Your Writing

Remember that if *you* are familiar with what you are describing, your audience may not be. Use location words such as "behind" and "next to" to make your descriptions clearer, and use vivid words that appeal to the senses.

Tips for Writing a Description

Prewriting Explore the Subject

▷ Think of a person, place, thing, or event that you know well, or study a photo or illustration.

▷ List some descriptive details about the subject you chose. Try to list details that appeal to at least four of the five senses.

Drafting Bring the Sights and Sounds to Life

▶ If appropriate, include a topic sentence that previews what is to come.

▶ Include details that support and make clear the subject you are describing.

▶ Use comparisons to bring your descriptions to life ("the hail was the size of golf balls," for example).

Revising Bring It into Focus

▶ **Ideas** Do you need to add any details to clarify what you are describing?

▶ **Organization** Do you use location words and transitions to help the reader picture the scene and move easily from one description to the next?

▶ **Word choice** Do your words stimulate the reader's senses and bring the description to life?

Editing/Proofreading Look Closely at the Details

▶ **Conventions** Double-check the capitalization and spelling of proper names and other proper nouns.

▶ **Conventions** Make sure you've used commas to separate nouns or adjectives in a series.

Publishing Get Ready to Share Your Description

▷ **Presentation** Consider attaching a picture or drawing of your subject to your final draft.

▷ You may wish to practice giving a dramatic reading of your description and then share it with your class.

Writing an Observation Report

If you've ever watched a fish swim back and forth in its tank or taken note of the sights, sounds, and smells at a local festival, you have made observations. An **observation report** is a report based on what you can observe with your five senses.

We're constantly observing our surroundings, whether we're aware of it or not. Maybe you've observed people around you on a bus. What sounds did you hear? What did you see? What did the seat feel like? If you've taken care of a baby brother or sister, what did your senses pick up? What did the baby look like? How did his or her skin feel? What sounds did the baby make? Any of  these situations, and countless more, can be used as the focus of an observation report. Just record on paper what your senses are recording about the scene around you.

Try It

Here are some sample topics for an observation report. For each one, tell what you might observe through each of your five senses.

▶ *a restaurant*   ▶ *your room*

▶ *a high school football game*   ▶ *a bowling alley*

▶ *science class*   ▶ *a holiday gathering*

Science Observation Report

A special kind of observation report is the *science* observation report, in which you make observations about an experiment or a science project. The nature of your report depends on the subject that you choose.

To gather information for an observation report, use a graphic organizer. Geraldo decided to do an experiment to see what makes iron rust. He had noticed that cars tend to rust in a wet environment, but he wondered if exposure to water is the only reason that iron rusts. To find out the answer, he put iron nails in jars of water as follows and recorded the results every few hours. The chart on the next page shows how Geraldo recorded the results of his experiment.

Jar Description	3 hours	6 hours	24 hours
Jar 1: 1 nail lying at bottom in 1 oz of water, uncovered	no change	bit of rust spot at sharp end of nail	rust over more than half of nail, most concentrated near point and under head; scattered rust bits floating in water—water still fairly clear
Jar 2: 4 nails lying in 1 oz of water, placed side by side, touching, uncovered	tiny specks of orange rust visible on top surface of two middle nails where they touch	rust covers almost half of all nails; is concentrated on surface where they touch and at top under nail head and bottom at point; water is a light orange; bits of rust lie at bottom and also float in water	most of nails are covered with brown-orange rust; water is dark orange color; rust bits cover the bottom of the jar, float thickly in water
Jar 3: 1 nail lying in 1 oz of water that was boiled (to get air out), filled to brim, sealed tight	no change	no change	a small speck of rust covers point of nail
Jar 4: 4 nails lying in 1 oz of water (placed side by side, touching) that was boiled (to get air out), filled to brim, sealed tight	no change	no change	rust covers a little over a quarter of midsection of middle two nails, on surface where they touch; a few specks of rust on ends of two outermost nails
Jar 5: 1 nail coated with clear nail polish, lying in 1 oz of water, uncovered	no change	no change	no change

Student Model—Science Observation Report

Here is the report that Geraldo wrote about his rust experiment, based on his observations.

Problem: Does water alone make iron rust?

Hypothesis: Water makes iron rust, but iron also needs air to rust.

Procedure: I used five glass jars of the same size and iron nails about 2 1/2 cm long and 1/2 cm in diameter, with the head about 1 cm in diameter. In Jar 1, I placed one nail in one ounce of water, uncovered, and in Jar 2, I placed 4 nails, touching, side by side, in one ounce of water, uncovered. In Jar 3, I placed 1 nail, filled it to the brim with water that I had boiled for ten minutes (to get the air out), and sealed it tight with its lid. I did the same for Jar 4, except I used 4 nails, placed side by side touching each other. In Jar 5, I placed a dry nail that I had painted with nail polish into one ounce of water, uncovered. I then observed the jars after 3 hours, 6 hours, and 24 hours.

Observations: Jar 2 showed the most signs of rust the most quickly. After 24 hours, the 4 nails were almost completely covered with rust, and the water was orange with rust specks. I did notice, however, that most of the rust was on the surface and the ends of the nails; there was hardly any rust in between the nails. The nail in Jar 1, which also was uncovered, was the next most rusted—from the point to halfway to the head and under the head. The nails in the jars that had the boiled water and were sealed—Jar 3 and Jar 4—showed only a little bit of rust. Jar 3, which had only 1 nail, showed only a speck of rust on the point, whereas rust covered about a quarter of two of the nails in Jar 4. The nail in Jar 5, covered in three coats of clear nail polish, showed no signs of rust.

Conclusions: My hypothesis that it takes both water and air for iron to rust was correct. The reason that the nails in the sealed jars did rust a little, I think, is that a little bit of air remained in the water and between the water and the lid. Because there was less air, they rusted more slowly. One observation I made, though, leads me to another experiment: I want to find out why when there were four nails, the rust took over much more quickly than when there was only one nail. Also, why did the four nails rust only at the tops and sides but not in between where they touched?

Another kind of observation report is one in which you use sensory details to describe a scene or event that you have observed.

The doors to the bus open with a hiss and a squeak. Inhaling exhaust fumes, I step up the three tall stairs and let the warm air bathe my frozen face. I take off my mitten to drop the coins with a clink into the collector. I mumble a hello to the driver, who mumbles back. Like most bus drivers, she is dressed in navy blue from head to toe.

As usual, the "Whisperer"—a tiny woman dressed in a sweat outfit behind the driver—rocks back and forth and whispers softly to herself. I scan the seats. The bus is packed with passengers bundled in thick coats and hats, staring straight ahead, eyes slightly dazed and tired. A few boys near the back doors talk and laugh loudly, earning them a pursed-lip look from a blue-haired woman across the aisle.

Aha! Two seats from the driver, across from the whispering woman, I spy the only open seat! A scowling gray-haired man in a dark wool coat sits in the seat next to it. I scramble to the seat. I smile smugly to myself as I watch the searching eyes of the passengers who followed me on the bus. They grab onto a steel pole and brace themselves.

But wait! The last passenger to get on is an old woman with a back so crooked she is almost bent over double. She can barely raise her head to search for a seat. I pull myself up and say, "Here, take my seat." Her twinkling blue eyes meet mine as she says, "Now, here's a girl who was brought up right." She sits down with a sigh.

Analyzing Observation Reports

Take another look at the sample observation reports. What do they have in common? They both are based on observations made by the writers. Geraldo's experiment relies mostly on data he collected using his sense of sight. Can you think of other science experiments that would rely on other senses, such as smell or touch? Justine, on the other hand, recorded observations using most of her senses.

Try It

Look over Justine's report, and give an example of an observation based on each of the following: sight, sound, smell, and touch.

Both reports use words that appeal to the senses of the reader. For example, instead of saying, "The doors opened," Justine tells *how* they opened—"with a hiss and a squeak." She uses strong verbs and colorful adjectives and nouns. Geraldo appeals to the reader's sense of sight by using exact words—"rust covered about a quarter of two of the nails in Jar 4." Without sensory details, an observation report cannot give an accurate picture of what the writer observed.

Notice how the two reports are organized differently. Most science observation reports have similar organization:

 I. Present the problem
 II. Make a hypothesis
 III. Explain the procedure
 IV. Describe what was observed
 V. Draw conclusions based on the observations

Justine organizes her report by telling the observations she makes in the order she makes them. For example, her first observation is of the doors opening, the next is of her climbing the stairs, and so on. This kind of organization works well because it is easy to follow as she moves naturally from one observation to the next.

Reading Your Writing

When you're writing your observations, it's easy to get caught up in writing only about what you see and hear. Don't forget about your sense of touch to observe the textures or temperature of something. Try to include tastes and smells in your report, too.

Tips for Writing an Observation Report

Prewriting Choose a Subject

▶ For an observation of a scene, list some places you think would be good places to observe. Choose a place, go there and observe, and jot down notes in a notebook. Write your observations on a chart that lists the five senses.

▶ For a science observation report, decide on a topic or experiment, and use a chart or other organizer to record your observations. Think about what conclusions you can draw based on your observations.

Drafting Write It Out

▶ For an observation of a scene, decide on the best way to organize your observation report.

▶ For a science observation report, use the standard organization of Problem, Hypothesis, Procedure, Observations, and Conclusions.

Revising Make Necessary Changes

▶ **Ideas** Have you recorded observations based on as many senses as possible?

▶ **Word Choice** Do your words give the reader a good idea of the scene you are describing? For a science observation report, make sure you use words that exactly describe your subject.

▶ **Organization** Do your observations flow from one to the next? Add transition words if necessary.

Editing/Proofreading Look Closely at the Details

▶ **Conventions** Check the capitalization of proper names of the places and people in your observation report.

▶ **Conventions** For a science observation report, check the spelling of scientific terms.

Publishing Get Ready to Share Your Observations

▶ **Presentation** For an observation of a scene, add any photos or illustrations that give your report eye-appeal.

▶ **Presentation** For a science observation report, add any necessary diagrams or charts.

Persuasive Writing

Persuasive writing encourages readers to think or feel a certain way or to see the writer's point of view. It can also motivate readers to take action. Sometimes persuasive writing can do all of these things at the same time. To do this, you, the writer, must attract and keep the attention of your readers. The following lessons will show you how.

Persuasive Writing

You think your school cafeteria should serve frozen yogurt, so you write a persuasive article about how good yogurt is for kids and submit it to your school newspaper. An article or essay that persuades is just one type of **persuasive writing.** In persuasive writing, you influence others to think, feel, or act in a certain way.

The goal of writing to persuade is to change the reader's mind. You choose an issue you care about and try to convince your readers to accept your point of view. Your opinion and the facts, details, and examples to support it are most important.

Try It

Think of how you could support or oppose each argument:
▶ *The rating system for movies is too strict.*
▶ *Students should be able to eat and drink in the classroom.*
▶ *Talking on cell phones should not be allowed in cars.*

Another type of persuasive writing is used by advertisers. They use words that appeal to the reader's emotions or interests, as in the following example.

Take a Look

Do you find yourself drifting off in class? Do you fight to stay awake? Get that burst of energy you need from power-packed Energy Bar! It's chock-full of crunchy peanuts, chocolate, crisp rice, and vitamins. Start every day with Energy Bar, and you'll start your day out right!

Persuasive writing comes in many forms: radio and TV ads, letters to the editor, and editorial cartoons, to name a few. Before you begin your persuasive writing, as with all forms of writing, you need to determine your purpose and audience.

Purpose and Audience

Imagine that your purpose for writing is to convince the principal that the strict dress code does not benefit students and should be changed. Your purpose should be stated as your central idea, or claim, at the beginning of your piece of writing:

Our school would benefit from relaxing the dress code.

Next, consider your audience and select facts and other evidence that will convince that person or group to support your claim. For example, the results of a survey of students and parents about the dress code might persuade the school principal to see your point of view. Once you know the main points you want to make, organize your information in the most effective way. Sometimes, saving the strongest piece of evidence for last is the most persuasive strategy. Other times, it makes more sense to present it first.

One way to make your writing more persuasive is to figure out what those opposed to your opinion might say and then present evidence that disproves their viewpoints.

Those who disagree say that a dress code allows students to concentrate more on their studies and to get better grades. However, based on the research I have found on our local schools, grades in schools without a dress code have been about the same as grades in schools with a dress code for the past five years.

At the end, restate your claim, summarize your main points, and suggest a plan of action. For example, you might suggest that the principal present your argument at a parent-teacher meeting.

Reading Your Writing

Stating your opinion is a key part of writing to persuade. Make sure that you include facts or examples to support your opinions. The audience is more likely to be persuaded if they are presented with concrete information that cannot be argued against.

Persuasion in Advertising

Advertisements are everywhere—on television, the radio, billboards, and the Internet; in magazines and newspapers; at sporting events and on buses and taxis. This type of persuasive writing appeals to people's emotions, senses, or interests to sell a product or make a point.

Take a Look

The following ads appeal to the audience's emotions, senses, interests, or a combination of the three:

Just-So Jeans are just the most popular brand of jeans today. Just look at what your friends—and their friends, and their friends—are wearing. You just have to have Just-So Jeans.

Are you bored with your old board games? Then try Puzzlemaker, the exciting new mind-bending game by Board Games Unlimited. It's guaranteed to cure your board-game blahs.

Dark circles under your eyes? Gone in one swipe. Wrinkles? Hidden in seconds. The advanced, state-of-the art makeup system of Yung-Again lets you put your best—and youngest—face forward.

When writing an ad, keep in mind your purpose and your intended audience. For example, the Yung-Again ad is clearly intended to sell beauty products to middle-aged or older women. Also, decide where the ad will appear: in print in a magazine, on television, on the radio, and so on. This will affect how you write the ad, including how long you will make it.

Choose your words carefully. Use short, direct sentences. You may even use sentence fragments, made of a few words, that are catchy and attract the reader's attention. Repetition of words or phrases is also an effective way to attract the reader's attention.

Public Service Ad

Have you seen billboards urging kids not to smoke or TV ads that tell kids to say "no" to drugs? These advertisements are known as public service ads. Public service ads try to persuade the audience to take certain actions that some believe are in its best interest and the best interest of the public. Not smoking, for example, makes for a healthier person and a healthier society.

Stay on the bus to somewhere
Stay in charge of your future
Stay in the game
STAY IN SCHOOL

Take a Look

Here are some public service advertisements that combine words and pictures:

For what issue would you like to create a public service ad? Think of an issue that is important to you. If nothing comes to mind, flip through a magazine or newspaper to get an idea. The issue might have to do with the environment, such as recycling, or maybe you would like to help get drunk drivers off the road. Determine what your purpose is—what you want to accomplish with the ad—and who your audience is. What kinds of words and images would work best?

PLANT YOUR FUTURE

PLANT A TREE

Reading Your Writing

Ads are a type of persuasive writing that urges the audience to either buy a product or take action on an issue that affects people's lives. Make sure that the ads you write are accurate and not misleading. Although you might be tempted to "bend the truth" to get people to take a certain action, false advertising is dishonest and unfair to your audience.

In advertising writing, it is especially important that your final version is free of errors in punctuation and spelling. Ads with errors will make your audience lose confidence in the ad and the issue or product you are "selling."

Fun Fact

What do you think about advertising? One newspaperman, E.W. Scripps, didn't think much of it at all, saying: "As you know, I recognize the advertiser as the enemy of the newspaper."— 1907

Writing a Letter to the Editor

One way you can share your opinion with others is in the form of a letter to the editor. A letter to the editor usually enjoys a wide audience because it appears in a newspaper or magazine. This type of letter not only expresses an opinion but, like other kinds of persuasive writing, also tries to influence readers to think or feel a certain way or to take a certain action. This purpose makes a letter to the editor different from other types of letters. A personal letter, for example, is usually meant for a much smaller audience—usually someone you know well. More often than not, its purpose is just to let the reader know about what is going on in your life. Similarly, a business letter usually has a small audience, such as a store manager or government official. In many cases, its purpose is to request information or to complain about a service or policy.

You begin a letter to the editor by stating your viewpoint. You then support your viewpoint by

▶ including concrete facts and logical reasons,
▶ using specific examples, or
▶ providing a possible solution to a problem.

You might also use a combination of all three to support your opinion.

Take a Look

On the next page, read a letter to the editor that Vivian wrote to her school newspaper. Look at how she organizes her letter. She begins by stating her viewpoint and then uses examples from her own experience to support her viewpoint. At the end she adds a bit of new information, and then she sums up what she has said previously.

Vivian Schmidt
2181 Trelawn Ave.
Avon, MI 12345

Editor
The King Star
Martin Luther King, Junior, Middle School
Avon, MI 12345

November 22, 2003

Dear Editor:

   I think that our school should do away with "Take Your Child to Work Day." I went to my father's work in fourth grade and then my mother's work in fifth grade. At both places, although it was fun to get out of school, I didn't really learn anything valuable at all.

   For one thing, I already knew what my parents did at work because they talk about their work at home. Also, because I didn't really have any of the knowledge or skills needed for the jobs they do, all I could do was some clerical stuff to help them out a little. In fact, I think that I might have gotten in the way more than I helped because they were trying to find things for me to do. The best part of the day for me was going to lunch.

   In addition, the whole time I was away from school, I felt a little nervous about what I was missing at school. Each time, not even half of our class went to "work," so our teachers had to plan a lesson for those who stayed. At the same time, the kids who stayed didn't like the fact that we got to get out of school and they didn't.

   The purpose of Take Your Child to Work Day is to give kids a chance to see what the work world is like and to help guide them in choosing their careers. I think this purpose can be accomplished much more efficiently in other ways.

Sincerely,
Vivian Schmidt
Grade 6

   In the letter on the next page, Jason not only presents his viewpoint about school lunches, but he also provides a solution to a problem. Notice how he first explains the problem, proposes a solution, and then explains how his solution can be carried out. He uses questions to keep his writing interesting. He also presents the opposing argument and then responds to it. At the end, he tells why this solution is beneficial to all involved.

Jason Cho
129 Elk Ave.
Sunny, NE 00001

Editor
The Freedom Press
Abraham Lincoln Middle School
Sunny, NE 00002

April 7, 2003

Dear Editor:

In last week's paper, several students wrote letters to the editor complaining about the quality and freshness of the cafeteria food. I think that students should be allowed to buy their lunches from one of the two fast-food places across the street.

"Fast-food places?" you may ask. "Aren't they even worse in nutritional value than the cafeteria food?" Not so! At Burgers 'N Stuff, you can get a salad with five different vegetables and low-fat dressing. And Cluck's menu includes broiled chicken breasts, side salads, corn on the cob, and other nutritious, low-fat dishes.

It's simple. The principal should contact the two restaurants to make sure they agree to handle so much more business. If they agree, students could place their weekly orders with the manager of the restaurant each Monday and pay for their meals then. The orders could then be delivered at lunchtime.

With this plan, students have more of a choice in what they eat, and the school cafeteria will probably improve so that they don't lose a lot of business.

Sincerely,

Jason Cho
Grade 6

Try It

Study the student models. For each one, think about how you might plan a letter that takes the opposite view. What evidence would you use? How would you organize your letter?

Reading Your Writing

Letters to the editor are a great way to express your opinion and reach a wide audience.

Tips for Writing a Letter to the Editor

Prewriting   Choose a Topic

▷ List some current school issues about which you have an opinion. Choose the one that interests you most.

▷ Decide which newspaper or magazine will publish your letter, and write to that audience.

▷ Figure out exactly what your opinion is about the issue and do some research to find supporting facts and examples.

Drafting   Get Your Thoughts on Paper

▶ Let the reader know right away the issue you are discussing and your viewpoint on it.

▶ Include reasons, facts, or examples—or a combination of the three—to support your opinion. You may also present a solution to a problem.

▶ Write a conclusion that restates your viewpoint.

Revising   Take Another Look

▶ **Ideas** Do you include *accurate* information that supports your opinion? If you propose a solution to a problem, is the solution really doable? Also, make sure your opinion and the issue you are writing about are clear from the beginning.

▶ **Organization** Do the ideas in the middle paragraphs logically follow each other?

Editing/Proofreading   Look Closely at the Details

▶ **Conventions** Double-check the names of people or places you include in your letter. Make sure the greeting is followed by a colon.

Publishing   Prepare to Send Your Letter to the Editor

▶ **Presentation** Use the proper format for a business letter.

▶ Make sure you have the correct address for the newspaper or magazine. Address your envelope to "Letters to the Editor." Use a business-sized envelope.

Editorials and Editorial Cartoons

An **editorial** states an opinion about a current topic of interest. It is called an *editor*ial because it is usually written by an editor of a newspaper or magazine. Editorials appear near the front of a magazine and in the first section in a newspaper. Often, an editorial calls for specific action.

Take a Look

Here are some topics for an editorial that you might find in a school newspaper:

▶ *The new grading system is unfair and should be discontinued.*

▶ *Students should be allowed to have cell phones or pagers in school.*

▶ *Physical education should be optional, not required.*

A good editorial is short (about 100 to 200 words in length), interesting, and to the point. It presents an opinion with authority and backs it up with sound reasoning, facts, and examples.

Sometimes, an illustration can express an opinion as or more effectively than can words alone. An **editorial cartoon** is just what it sounds like—an editorial in the form of a cartoon. It uses images and a few words to share an opinion with readers. In newspapers, editorial cartoons appear with the other editorials and letters to the editor.

Editorial cartoonists often use exaggeration to make a point. For example, to show that a certain football star has a big ego, a cartoonist may give him a huge head in the shape of a football. Cartoonists may also draw **caricatures,** or illustrations of people whose features are exaggerated. For example, if a specific person has a bushy mustache, the cartoonist may make the mustache huge. Although some editorial cartoons have no words at all, most use a few words or sentences to explain what is happening.

Here is an editorial and an editorial cartoon written by Yoko about a school issue.

I think the school's decision to change our dress code to uniforms will hurt students more than help them.

School officials and parents argue that uniforms will help make us focus more on our studies and less on what we and other kids are wearing. However, in a survey I did of 100 students from all three grades, only six thought that wearing a uniform would help them make better grades. On top of that, our school already receives above-average ranking on statewide tests.

In our school, individual accomplishment, not conformity, is encouraged. Both our Spelling Bee champ and our star basketball player were congratulated at a recent school assembly. In addition, part of our school curriculum is celebrating diversity. We even have a "Diversity Day." How can the school encourage us to be individuals and celebrate diversity, on the one hand, but at the same time tell us what to wear every single school day?

Finally, the uniforms are just plain uncomfortable and not very practical. The girls, who have to wear skirts, will be unnecessarily cold in winter. The boys, who have to wear ties, will waste 20 minutes every morning just trying to tie them right! Uniforms cost a lot of money, too.

The students of Thomas Jefferson Middle School should be able to have a say in what they wear every day, just like they have for twenty years. Tell your teacher, talk to your parents, write a letter to the principal, sign a petition. Let's work together to get out of the uniforms and into our own clothes!

Analyzing the Editorial

Although the editorial is made of words, and the editorial cartoon is made mostly of illustrations, they both present the same basic opinion— that school uniforms will only hurt student achievement.

The editorial and the editorial cartoon also have some differences. For example, Yoko ends the editorial with a call to action, telling students what they need to do to stop the dress code from becoming school policy. However, the cartoon doesn't include this message. It would be hard to create an editorial cartoon that includes two main ideas—the opinion that uniforms are unfair *and* the call to action, or what we should do about it. There would be too many things going on in the cartoon, and the message would most likely be confusing to the reader.

Because the editorial is all words, it can give more detailed information than the cartoon. Yoko includes statistics from a survey she conducted to support her opinion. She also uses writing techniques to keep the reader interested in her editorial, such as asking questions and varying the length of her sentences.

Try It

Think of a school issue about which you feel strongly. How might you turn it into an editorial cartoon? What would be the main images and how would they express your opinion?

Reading Your Writing

One way to make your editorial persuasive is to think about what someone who takes the opposite view might say in response to your ideas. Then, include the opponent's opinion and write your own response to that point of view. This way, the audience sees that you understand both sides of the issue.

Tips for Writing an Editorial

Prewriting   Choose a Topic

▷ List some current school issues or topics in the news. Make sure that the issue you choose is current—an editorial about something that has long since passed is usually not very interesting.

▷ Think about who will read your editorial, and gear your writing towards that audience.

▷ Decide what your opinion is about your topic by researching the different sides of the issue.

Drafting   Get Your Thoughts on Paper

▶ Introduce the issue and state your opinion on it right away.

▶ Include reasons and facts to support your opinion.

Revising   Make Necessary Changes

▶ **Ideas** Do you have enough research to support your opinion? Are your facts and examples convincing?

▶ **Ideas** Are the issue and your opinion on it clear from the beginning?

▶ **Organization** Does the opening catch the reader's attention? Does the ending sum up your point and ask the readers to take action?

▶ **Word Choice** Do you use comparisons and vivid words that appeal to the reader's senses?

Editing/Proofreading   Look Closely at the Details

▶ **Conventions** Proofread your editorial to check for spelling mistakes. Double-check the names of people or places you include.

Publishing   Prepare to Share Your Editorial

▶ **Presentation** Make a neatly typed or written final copy. Take a look at the editorial section in your school or local newspaper and try to match the format.

Writing a Persuasive Report

A **persuasive report** tries to convince readers to think, feel, or act in a certain way. For this reason, a persuasive report is different from an informational report, which mainly passes along knowledge to the reader.

Look at the topics for an informational report, compared to similar topics for a persuasive report. How are they different?

Informational	Persuasive
History of the cell phone	Using cell phones in cars should be outlawed.
How speed bumps affect traffic	Our street needs speed bumps.

There are many ways to influence a reader regarding a certain issue. One way is to state a viewpoint and then provide facts and reasons to support that viewpoint. Another way is to present a problem, and then propose a solution to that problem.

Before you start your report, though, you need to know your audience and your purpose. Exactly what group of people are you trying to persuade? The audience you choose will affect how you write your report. What is the purpose of your report? Do you simply want to persuade your readers to agree with your opinion, or do you want to influence them to take an action?

Take a Look

Here is an example of a topic for a persuasive report with a problem-solution organization:

Topic: *We need to have speed bumps put on our street.*
(Problem: *Cars speed through our neighborhood, putting people in danger.)*
Audience: *All of the people on our street*
Purpose: *To convince the people who live on our street to sign a petition, the first step in getting speed bumps*
(Solution: *Get neighbors to sign a petition.)*

Try It

Think of a problem in your school, community, or even your personal life that you might use as the basis for a persuasive report. How would you present the problem? Who would your audience be? Your purpose? What solution or solutions would you propose?

Once you have chosen a topic, use a web to help you generate ideas for your persuasive report. You might need to do some research first.

Take a Look

Bonnie used this web to help her write her persuasive report.

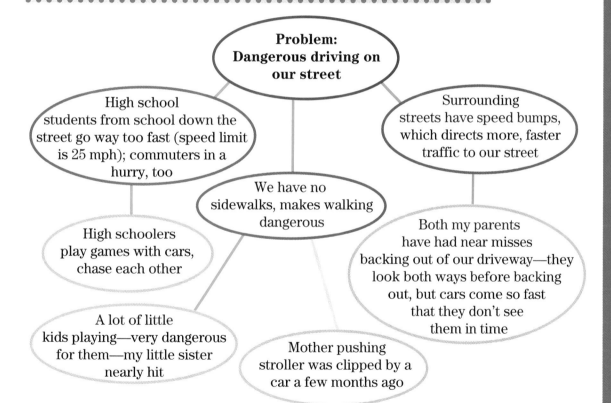

Take a Look

Here is the persuasive report that Bonnie wrote, using her web.

A Bumpy Road to Safety

Cars whiz by, even though street signs tell them the speed limit is 25 mph. Tires screech. Horns honk. Loud music makes the doors and windows shake. This is what happens every day at 3:30 in the afternoon on our street, when the high school lets out. At rush hour, it's the same scene, but usually without the loud music. Because we have the only street in the area without speed bumps, drivers who want to go fast go on our street. We need peace on our street. We need speed bumps.

You may ask, can a little fast driving for a few minutes a day make a difference? How does it hurt anything? For one thing, it's dangerous. We don't have sidewalks on our street. So this means that people have to walk on the street to get anywhere. Also, there are a lot of little kids on our street who sometimes don't watch out for their own safety. A few weeks ago, I was walking my little sister home from school, and I had to pull her out of the way of a car speeding right at her. The driver didn't even see us; he was trying to catch up with his friends in the car ahead of him.

There's more! My parents have had several near misses backing out of our driveway. Even though they look both ways when backing out, sometimes the cars come so fast that they don't see them until it's almost too late. Other drivers haven't been as lucky. There have been five accidents on our little street in the last five months. That's one accident a month on a street that's only three blocks long! I talked to an officer at our local police station, and he agrees that this is way too many accidents for such a small side street. Police officers patrol the area as much as they can, but they can't be there all the time. We need something to force people to drive slowly on our street—and that something is speed bumps.

Speed bumps are a proven way to keep people from driving fast—that's the whole point of them. It's why all of the streets near ours have gotten speed bumps. Most people who live on these streets completely support having the speed bumps. Sure, they're frustrating when you're in a hurry, but most agree that they feel a lot safer and their street is a lot calmer. Parents aren't afraid to push their babies in strollers.

No, speed bumps won't solve all of our problems. We'll probably still have a lot of traffic from the school. However, if drivers know that our street has speed bumps, they probably won't always choose to drive down our street.

You can help us get speed bumps on our street. All you have to do is sign the petition I got from our city's department of transportation. I'll be going door to door for the next few weeks. Sixty-five percent of the households on our street need to sign it in order for a committee to review it. If we get the okay from the committee, it can take up to a year before the speed bumps are actually put on our street. So we need to act now!

It takes only a few days to put in bumps. Yes, it'll be noisy and inconvenient for a little while, but it'll be worth it to make our street peaceful and safe again. Let's take back our street. Let's show some community spirit. Let's let drivers know that this is a street where people live—not a race track. Don't wait for someone to die before we do something. Sign the petition.

Analyzing the Problem-Solution Persuasive Report

The first paragraph of your persuasive report should not only grab the reader's attention; it should also tell the reader what the problem is, as well as your proposed solution. Bonnie does all of this in her report on speed bumps. She begins by "setting the scene," using interesting and vivid details to give the audience a clear picture of the problem. She then proposes a solution to the problem.

In the middle paragraphs of your persuasive report, you should provide evidence to support the ideas you introduced in the first paragraph. Bonnie has done this in several different ways. First, she presents some of the opposition's arguments: it's only a little fast driving for a few minutes a day; speed bumps are a hassle when you're in a hurry, speed bumps won't solve all of the traffic problems; putting in speed bumps will be noisy and dirty. She gives her own response to each of these arguments.

Bonnie also uses facts to support her proposed solution. She gives survey results, accident statistics, and the opinion from the local police station. Because facts are hard to dispute, they provide powerful support for her viewpoint. She also clearly explains exactly what action her audience needs to take to help get her solution underway—sign the petition she already has in her possession.

The conclusion of a persuasive report should end on a strong note. It may summarize the points already made, introduce a new idea, ask for the reader's support, or a combination of these. In her final paragraph, Bonnie appeals to the emotions of her readers by urging them to "take back our street." She tells them not to "wait for someone to die." She also asks for their support by encouraging them to sign the petition.

To write an effective persuasive report, you must be clear about your purpose and write to your intended audience. Throughout her paper, Bonnie always has her audience—her neighbors—and purpose—to get speed bumps installed—in mind.

Fun Fact

Mark Twain once said, "Our opinions do not really blossom into fruition [fullness] until we have expressed them to someone else."

Reading Your Writing

It may be tempting to include only *your* side of an argument when writing a persuasive report. However, sometimes it is more persuasive to present an opposing viewpoint and then explain why your viewpoint is more reasonable. This way, the audience sees that you understand and appreciate the opposing side and that you are a sensible person.

Tips for Writing a Problem-Solution Persuasive Report

Prewriting   Make a Plan

▷ List some current issues that deal with your school or community or even your personal life.

▷ Choose a subject that you feel strongly about and decide exactly what your viewpoint is on it. Use this as the main idea for your report.

▷ Decide what your purpose is and who your audience is.

▷ Use a graphic organizer or outline to help you decide how to organize your arguments or supporting points.

Drafting   Put Your Thoughts Together

▶ Grab the reader's attention in your introduction. State your subject and your opinion on it up front.

▶ Use facts and reasons to support your main idea.

▶ End on a strong note. Summarize your ideas, and give the reader something to consider.

Revising   Make Your Report Stronger

▶ **Ideas** Are your message and purpose for writing clear?

▶ **Ideas** Are the facts accurate and your argument logical?

▶ **Organization** Is your report organized logically? In most persuasive reports, the strongest points are presented either first or last.

▶ **Organization** Is your conclusion effective? It should summarize your ideas, restate your opinion, end with a call to action, or do a combination of these.

▶ **Voice** Does it sound like you care about your subject?

Editing/Proofreading   Check the Details

▶ **Conventions** Double-check the spelling of any proper nouns you use; make sure your capitalization is correct.

Publishing   Get Ready to Share Your Report

▶ **Presentation** Consider preparing handouts or transparencies that outline the main points of your report.

Poetry

Poetry is very different from other forms of writing. For one thing, it looks different. Think of some poems you have read. They look very different from stories or articles. The capitalization and punctuation are different. The familiar patterns of sentences and paragraphs are not present in poetry.

There is something else about poetry. It can describe things in a way that you may never have considered. Poetry often contains thoughts and feelings of the writer. It also contains images, or word pictures, that can make a deep impression on readers. The following lessons will give you a chance to explore some different kinds of poetry.

Rhyming Poetry

To define the word *poetry*, the poet Samuel Taylor Coleridge compared it to *prose*, which is the kind of writing you find in newspapers and novels:

"Prose—words in their best order; poetry—the best words in their best order."

Poetry is a certain kind of writing that expresses deep thoughts and feelings using the sound and meaning of words. Indeed, creating a poem is all about choosing the "best" words and putting them in the "best" order.

Poetry is different from other kinds of writing. It is written in **stanzas,** or lines of poetry that are grouped together. In poetry, lines may be shorter than those in prose. A line in a poem may end in the middle of a sentence or thought.

Sound and Pattern in Poetry

The sounds of words in poetry are more important than in other writing. Both the sounds and the pattern, or arrangement, of words can affect a reader's reaction to a poem. **Rhyme** is a pattern in which words end with the same sounds, such as *see* and *tree.* In a lot of poetry, words are arranged into a pattern of accented and unaccented syllables—this pattern is a poem's **rhythm,** or *meter.* Here are two lines of Joyce Kilmer's poem "Trees." The accents show the stressed syllables.

I `think that `I shall `never `see,
A `poem `lovely `as a `tree.

Another kind of pattern is **alliteration,** which occurs when the same sound is repeated at the beginning of words:

The <u>s</u>nake <u>s</u>lithered <u>s</u>ilently across the <u>s</u>and.

Alliteration contributes to the mood, or feeling, of a poem. It also helps a line of poetry flow, making it easier to read.

Imagery in Poetry

Imagery is a tool used by most poets. It is the use of figurative language to create pictures or images in the mind of the reader. One way to create images is to use similes or metaphors, which are kinds of comparisons. A **simile** is a comparison that uses the word *like* or *as.*

My love is like a red, red rose....
                    –Robert Burns

Here, "my love" is compared to a "red, red rose." The comparison creates the image of a deep red rose in the reader's mind and suggests that the person who is the object of the poet's affection is as beautiful and delicate as a rose.

A **metaphor** is also a comparison, but it doesn't use *like* or *as.* It says one thing *is* another thing. Shakespeare provides a good example of a metaphor in his play *As You Like It.*

All the world's a stage
And all the men and women merely players....

Here, a character in Shakespeare's play says that the world *is* a stage, but he is really comparing the world *to* a stage and the lives of men and women to actors and actresses in a play. He uses a metaphor to make an observation about the world and people's behavior. The world sometimes seems like a stage because people often "act" differently than who they really are when they are around others.

Another kind of poetic technique is **personification,** which is giving human qualities to things that are not human, such as objects or ideas.

> The car's engine gasped and then was still.
> Freedom died.

Traditional Forms of Poetry

Poems come in all kinds of forms and styles. Here are some traditional forms of poetry.

A **couplet** is made of two lines of poetry that rhyme and that form a complete thought. The lines of a couplet usually are about the same length and have the same rhythm.

> Water crashes on the sand,
> Then it mingles with the land.

A poem may be made completely of couplets, or couplets may be used throughout a poem that has a different pattern. A poem that is made of just one couplet is called a **closed couplet.**

A **triplet** is like a couplet, except instead of two lines of verse, there are three. The following poem by Alfred, Lord Tennyson, is made of two triplets.

The Eagle
He clasps the crag with crooked hands;
Close to the sun in lonely lands,
Ringed with the azure world, he stands.

The wrinkled sea beneath him crawls;
He watches from his mountain walls,
And like a thunderbolt he falls.

A **quatrain** is a stanza or poem made of four lines, usually with every other line rhyming. Here's a quatrain from Lewis Carroll's poem "The Crocodile."

… How cheerfully he seems
    to grin!
How neatly spread his
    claws,
And welcomes little fishes in
    With gently smiling jaws!

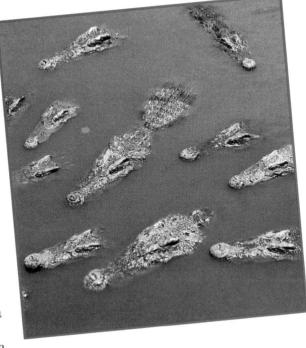

Quatrains may have other kinds of rhyming patterns as well. For example, the first two lines may rhyme, and the last two lines may rhyme. Or the first and last lines may rhyme, with the middle lines rhyming as well.

A **ballad** is a poem that tells a dramatic or exciting story. It usually is written in the form of a quatrain and has a simple rhythm and rhyming pattern. Ballads are often set to music. Here's the first stanza from "The Streets of Laredo."

As I walked out in the streets of Laredo,
As I walked out in Laredo one day,
I spied a poor cowboy wrapped up in white
    linen,
Wrapped up in white linen as cold as the
    clay.
                    –Anonymous

A **lyric** is a poem that expresses strong personal emotion. Many times a lyric sounds musical when read aloud because of its rhythmic sound patterns.

I love to see the starry flag
That floats above my head.
I love to see its waving folds
With stripes of white and red.
"Be brave," say the red stripes,
"Be pure," say the white.
"Be true," say the bright stars,
"And stand for the right."
                    –Anonymous

An **internal rhyme** is a rhyme that appears within one line of a poem.

I found no **joy** in the **toy**,…

Try It

Read some poems and find a few that you like. Do they follow any of the rhyming patterns described? If so, which one(s)?

Fun Fact

Lyric **poetry gets its name from the lyre, a small, harplike instrument originating in ancient Greece. It was used to accompany recited or sung words.**

Reading Your Writing

The reason for writing poetry is to communicate deep thoughts and feelings to your reader. However, don't forget that poetry also appeals to the ear. You may want to "test" your poem by reading it out loud or tape-recording it and playing it back. Listen carefully, and fix any parts that sound awkward—maybe your rhythm is off or a certain phrase or line just doesn't work.

Tips for Writing a Rhyming Poem

Prewriting Choose a Subject

▷ List some things you feel strongly about, that interest you, and that you know well (a person, a pet, a special place, something in nature).

▷ Write down ideas and sensory details about your subject.

Drafting Put the Poem Together

▶ Write a poem that has a beginning, a middle, and an end.

▶ Use some poetic techniques, such as rhyming, alliteration, and comparisons.

▶ Use words that are concrete, appeal to the senses, and get across the feelings you want to express.

Revising Polish Your Poem

▶ **Word Choice** Do your words create colorful and vivid images? Do they relate a certain feeling to the reader?

▶ **Word Choice** Do you use creative comparisons that help you get your ideas across? Include a simile, a metaphor, or a personification, if possible.

▶ **Organization** Does your poem move logically from one idea to the next? Does it have an interesting beginning? Does the ending complete the poem well? Try adding a thought-provoking surprise at the end.

Editing/Proofreading Put on the Finishing Touches

▶ **Conventions** In most traditional poetry, each line begins with a capital letter, even if it doesn't begin a sentence. Make sure your capitalization is correct.

▶ **Conventions** Are your end punctuation marks correct? Do they make sense?

Publishing Get Ready to Share Your Poem

▷ Decide on the best way to read your poem out loud. Which parts will you read slowly? Quickly? Loudly? Softly?

▷ Be sure to add a title to your poem. It should make the reader want to read the poem but not give away the whole poem.

Nonrhyming Poetry

A poem doesn't have to rhyme to be a poem. In fact, a lot of poems don't rhyme. Here are a few kinds of nonrhyming poetry.

Cinquain

A **cinquain** is a poem made of five lines. It follows this pattern:

Line 1:   2 syllables   subject (title of the poem)
Line 2:   4 syllables   description of the subject
Line 3:   6 syllables   action involving the subject
Line 4:   8 syllables   a feeling about the subject
Line 5:   2 syllables   another name or synonym for the subject

> My mom,
> With cool, soft hands,
> Touches my hot forehead
> Murmurs soothing words when I'm sick.
> Mama.

Diamanté

Diamanté (DEE uh MAHN tay) comes from the French word for "diamond," because this kind of poem is diamond-shaped. There are different versions of diamanté poems; some are five lines and some are seven lines. A diamanté follows a pattern of a certain number of words in each line, which is how it gets its diamond shape.

Justin followed this pattern to write a diamanté about himself.

Line 1:   1 noun—the subject
Line 2:   2 adjectives—describe subject
Line 3:   3 verbs—show action
Line 4:   4 adjectives—show feelings
Line 5:   1 noun—name of subject

> Justin
> smart, strong
> competes, thinks, laughs
> happy, intense, healthy, proud
> Justin

Haiku

A Japanese form of poetry, **haiku** is an unrhymed, three-line poem with seventeen syllables: five in line 1, seven in line 2, and five in line 3. A true haiku is about nature. It often refers to a certain time of year, either by naming or describing a season. Usually written in the present tense, a haiku captures a moment in time.

Here is a haiku that Tanisha wrote about the changing seasons.

Cold, hard rain beats down,
tearing colored leaves off trees.
Winter is coming.

Free Verse

Free-verse poetry does not follow specific rules, and it usually doesn't rhyme. In free verse, the poet decides when the lines will break. Free-verse poems often use blank space instead of a comma or period to show a pause. Here is a short free-verse poem by Kobayashi Issa.

Mosquito at my ear—
does it think
I'm deaf?

Try It

Think of a subject for a poem. What kind of pattern would best suit this subject? Haiku? Free verse? A cinquain? Why?

Here is a longer free-verse poem written by American poet Walt Whitman. Notice how the poem follows a unique format, and the lines do not rhyme.

I Hear America Singing

I hear America singing, the varied carols I hear,
Those of mechanics, each one singing his as it should be blithe
    and strong,
The carpenter singing his as he measures his plank or beam,
The mason singing his as he makes ready for work, or leaves off
    work,
The boatman singing what belongs to him in his boat, the
    deckhand singing on the steamboat deck,
The shoemaker singing as he sits on his bench, the hatter singing
    as he stands,
The wood-cutter's song, the ploughboy's on his way in the
    morning, or at noon intermission or at sundown,
The delicious singing of the mother, or of the young wife at
    work, or of the girl sewing or washing,
Each singing what belongs to him or her and to none else,
The day what belongs to the day—at night the party of young
    fellows, robust, friendly,
Singing with open mouths their strong melodious songs.

Fun Fact

The term "free verse" was made popular by French poets in the late 1800s. Inspired by American poet Walt Whitman, they wanted to break free of the formal patterns used in French poetry and instead use the "free" rhythms of natural speech.

Reading Your Writing

An important part of writing poetry is being willing to experiment with words and arrange them in the order that best suits the meaning of your poem. Whether the pattern you choose is rhyming or nonrhyming, be sure to select one that adds to the reader's understanding and enjoyment of your poem.

Tips for Writing a Free-Verse Poem

Prewriting   Choose a Subject

▷ List some things you feel strongly about that are a part of your everyday life, such as a person, a pet, a special place, or something in nature.

▷ Choose a subject and freewrite about it for a few minutes. Write words that tell how the subject looks, feels, smells, and so on.

Drafting   Put the Poem Together

▶ Decide where you want to break the lines. You might break them where there is a natural pause or break them in a not-so-natural place to create a certain effect.

▶ Use vivid modifiers and precise verbs.

▶ Include comparisons and other poetic techniques.

Revising   Polish Your Poem

▶ **Word Choice** Are your words colorful and vivid? Do they express emotion?

▶ **Word Choice** Do you use similes, metaphors, or personification to help get across your ideas?

▶ **Organization** Are the ideas in your poem logically connected?

▶ **Organization** Do your line breaks make sense? Do they make the poem stronger?

Editing/Proofreading   Put on the Finishing Touches

▶ **Conventions** Check your punctuation. In free verse, it's sometimes easy to forget about a period or comma. Make sure your capitalization is consistent.

Publishing   Get Ready to Share Your Poem

▶ **Presentation** Add any artwork to your final copy that reflects your poem's message.

Structures of Writing

Words, sentences, and paragraphs are the building blocks of writing. Think about what you do when you write. You use words to build sentences. You use sentences to build paragraphs. You use paragraphs to build reports, stories, and other kinds of writing.

In this unit, you will find out how sentences and paragraphs are constructed. You will also learn how to combine short, choppy sentences into one flowing sentence. You can use what you learn in these lessons in many different kinds of writing.

Writing Sentences

Good writing begins with good sentences. It's difficult to define a sentence. One definition is that a **sentence** is a group of words that has a subject and a predicate and expresses a complete thought. The **subject** is who or what the sentence is about. The **predicate** is what the subject is, does, or has. There are many different ways to write a sentence, but all sentences have some things in common. Every sentence starts with a capital letter and ends with one of the following punctuation marks: a period, a question mark, or an exclamation point.

Take a Look

In the following sentences, the subject is green, and the predicate is red.

Dakota is running for class president.
Dakota and her friends made campaign signs.

Kinds of Sentences

Different kinds of sentences are used to express different ideas. The four kinds of sentences are declarative, interrogative, imperative, and exclamatory.

A **declarative sentence** makes a statement. Declarative sentences end with a period.

Jerome got a pet turtle for his birthday.
Alisha got an A on her science test.

An **interrogative** sentence asks a question. Interrogative sentences end with a question mark.

> Who gave him the turtle?
> What does a turtle eat?
> Did you study with her?

An **imperative** sentence gives a command or makes a request. If an imperative sentence expresses a strong emotion, it ends with an exclamation point. All other imperative sentences end with a period. The subject of an imperative sentence is not stated. Instead, it is understood to be the pronoun *you*.

> Take good care of your pets.
> Hand me the book, please.
> Do your homework now!

An **exclamatory** sentence expresses strong emotion, such as fear, surprise, or excitement. Exclamatory sentences end with an exclamation point.

> That turtle is really cool!
> Don't drop it!
> She finished the test just in time!

Try It

Rewrite the following sentence to change it from an imperative sentence to an interrogative sentence.

▶ *Let me use the microscope.*

Combining Sentences

Good writers look for ways to combine sentences or parts of sentences to avoid repeating words unnecessarily. Combining sentences can also add variety and interest to your writing.

Combining Subjects, Objects, Verbs, and Modifiers

You can combine parts of two short sentences to make one sentence that reads more smoothly. Use the conjunctions *and, but, or, both . . . and, neither . . . nor,* or *either . . . or* to create compound subjects, objects, and verbs.

Pluto is an outer planet. Neptune is an outer planet.
Pluto and Neptune are outer planets. (compound subject)

Satellites send signals. Satellites send pictures.
Satellites send **signals or pictures.** (compound object)

The shuttle blasts into space. The shuttle glides back to the ground.
The shuttle **blasts into space but glides back to the ground.** (compound verb)

I have never visited the Kennedy Space Center. My friends haven't visited it either.
Neither I nor my friends have visited the Kennedy Space Center. (compound subject)

You can see launches there. You can also see landings.
You can see **both launches and landings** there. (compound object)

You can also combine modifiers from different sentences. Use commas or conjunctions to combine these sentence parts.

Pluto is a dark planet. Pluto is an icy planet.
Pluto is a **dark, icy** planet.

Earth orbits the sun slowly. Earth orbits the sun steadily.
Earth orbits the sun **slowly but steadily.**

Combining Phrases

Phrases from separate sentences can sometimes be combined to improve the flow of your writing. You might even be able to combine several sentences to avoid repeating words.

> The astronauts climbed up the steps. The astronauts climbed to the shuttle.
> The astronauts climbed **up the steps to the shuttle.**
>
> Latasha looked through a telescope. Latasha saw the moon.
> Latasha **looked through a telescope and saw the moon.**
>
> Comets are balls of ice and rock. Comets move in huge orbits. Comets move around the sun.
> Comets **are balls of ice and rock** that **move in huge orbits around the sun.**
>
> A meteoroid is also known as a shooting star. A meteoroid vaporizes when it enters Earth's atmosphere.
> A meteoroid, **also known as a shooting star, vaporizes when it enters Earth's atmosphere.**

When you combine words or phrases from different sentences, be sure to organize the new sentence in a way that makes sense. Otherwise, you could confuse your readers.

> Latasha used a telescope to look at the planets. Latasha used a telescope in her bedroom.
>
> Latasha used a telescope to look at the planets in her bedroom. (This sentence is confusing. The planets aren't in Latasha's bedroom.)
>
> Latasha used a telescope in her bedroom to look at the planets. (This sentence correctly combines the two original sentences.)

Creating Compound Sentences

Two simple sentences that are related can be combined to form a compound sentence. Both parts of the compound sentence still express a complete thought. Use a conjunction, such as *and*, *but*, or *or*, between the two simple sentences, and place a comma before the conjunction.

John Glenn was an astronaut. He was also a senator.
John Glenn was an astronaut, **and** he was also a senator.

Some people think the sun is a planet. It is really a star.
Some people think the sun is a planet, **but** it is really a star.

Does the moon make light? Does is reflect light from the sun?
Does the moon make light, **or** does it reflect light from the sun?

Creating Complex Sentences

Another way to combine sentences is by creating complex sentences. A complex sentence is made of an independent clause and one or more dependent clauses. An independent clause can stand alone as a sentence, but a dependent clause cannot. A dependent clause begins with a word such as *after*, *although*, *because*, *that*, *when*, and *which*. To combine two sentences into a complex sentence, make the idea from one sentence into a dependent clause. Note that a comma is not always used between the independent and dependent clauses.

Voyager 2 is a space probe. It was sent into space in 1977.
Voyager 2 is a space probe **that was sent into space in 1977.**

Triton is Neptune's biggest moon. It is very cold.
Triton, **which is Neptune's biggest moon,** is very cold.

Sentence Starters

Another way to add interest to your writing is to begin sentences in a variety of ways. This will not only keep your reader's attention but will make sentences more fun to write.

The natural order of a sentence is for the subject to come first, followed by the predicate.

Marcia fixed a salad for lunch.

However, there are many other ways to organize your thoughts. Experiment with some of the following sentence starters.

Begin with an adverb: **Suddenly,** Marcia realized she needed carrots.

Begin with one or more prepositional phrases: **At the store on the corner,** they sell fresh vegetables.

Begin with a clause: **When Marcia got there,** she saw Nathan buying the last bunch of carrots.

Begin with an infinitive phrase: **To solve her problem,** Marcia invited Nathan to lunch.

Begin with a participial phrase: **Knowing that Marcia is a good cook,** Nathan accepted her offer.

Reading Your Writing

A sentence can be a statement, a question, a command, or an exclamation. You can combine sentences to avoid repetition and make your writing easier to read. There are many different ways to begin a sentence, and using a variety will help keep readers interested.

Sentence Problems

Good writers know how to recognize and correct mistakes in their writing. Sentence fragments, run-on sentences, and rambling sentences are some common problems to watch for as you proofread your work.

Fragments

A **fragment** is a group of words that is punctuated as a sentence but is not a sentence. It may be missing a subject, a predicate, or both.

> Talked to the doctor yesterday. (missing a subject)
>
> Surgery and a cast. (missing a predicate)
>
> Nothing to worry about. (missing a subject and a predicate)
>
> All of the doctors and nurses in the hospital. (missing a predicate)
>
> Helped her recover quickly. (missing a subject)
>
> On Saturday afternoon. (missing a subject and a predicate)

Fragments are confusing because they provide incomplete information. Adding the missing parts to these sentences makes their meaning clear to readers.

> **Alex** talked to the doctor yesterday.
>
> Surgery and a cast **are needed.**
>
> **She said there is** nothing to worry about.
>
> All of the doctors and nurses in the hospital **were friendly.**
>
> **They** helped her recover quickly.
>
> **Her parents will pick her up** on Saturday afternoon.

Try It

How would you correct this sentence fragment?

▶ *The patient with crutches.*

Run-on Sentences

A **run-on sentence** contains more than one independent clause without the proper connections. To correct a run-on sentence, add a comma and a conjunction, use a semicolon, or rewrite it as two separate sentences.

Run-on: Danielle came home from the hospital yesterday we thought she looked tired.

Correct: Danielle came home from the hospital yesterday, and we thought she looked tired.

Or Danielle came home from the hospital yesterday. We thought she looked tired.

Or Danielle came home from the hospital yesterday; we thought she looked tired.

Rambling Sentences

A **rambling sentence** is one in which too many thoughts are connected with conjunctions. You can correct this problem by writing a separate sentence for each thought. Note that some parts of a rambling sentence might actually belong together. In this case, add a comma before the conjunction.

Rambling: I came upon a large field and stopped to explore it and my bike fell and there was a loud crash and I knew I would have a hard time riding my bike home.

Correct: I came upon a large field and stopped to explore it. My bike fell, and there was a loud crash. I knew that I would have a hard time riding my bike home.

Reading Your Writing

The most common sentence problems are fragments, run-on sentences, and rambling sentences. Knowing how to identify and correct these mistakes will help you communicate more clearly with your readers.

Paragraphs

A **paragraph** is made of two or more sentences about a single topic. The three basic parts of most paragraphs are a topic sentence, supporting sentences, and a closing sentence.

Topic Sentence

A **topic sentence** clearly states the paragraph's main idea. Often, it is placed at the beginning or the end of a paragraph. A strong topic sentence names a particular subject and states a direction or focus relating to that subject. The subject and direction should be small enough to deal with in one paragraph. Your story or report may have a larger focus, but the topic sentence of each paragraph should make that paragraph able to "stand alone." Although every paragraph you write should be focused, not all paragraphs have topic sentences. Some narrative paragraphs, for example, do not need topic sentences. In those cases the purpose of the paragraph is to move the story along by narrating events as they occur in time order.

Supporting Sentences

Supporting sentences provide information about the main idea. The main portion of a paragraph is made of one or more supporting sentences. Sentences that do not support the main idea of a paragraph do not belong. Supporting sentences should be arranged in a logical order. For example, you might present information chronologically (order of time), by order of location, or by order of importance. You can compare the supporting sentences in a paragraph to the strong support structure of a bridge. A bridge needs many steel beams to keep it standing, just as a paragraph needs a variety of strong supporting sentences to help it stand on its own.

Closing Sentence

A **closing sentence** is the last sentence of a paragraph. Sometimes the closing sentence is also the topic sentence. Other times, it provides a final thought about the main idea, a summary of the paragraph, or a smooth transition to the next paragraph.

Topic Sentence ▶ Reading is the best hobby a person could have.

Supporting Sentences ▶ It is a hobby that you can do almost anywhere. People read on airplanes, in doctors' waiting rooms, in bed, and at the beach. Another great thing about reading is that it doesn't require any special equipment. In fact, books are easy to get. If you can't buy them at a bookstore, you can borrow them from a library.

Closing Sentence ▶ The best thing about reading is that no matter what you like to do or where you like to go, you can experience it in a book.

Supporting the Main Idea

Writers use different kinds of information to support their ideas. Examples, facts, and evidence can make your writing more realistic and believable.

Take a Look

The student who wrote this paragraph supported the main idea with facts and examples. He crossed out one sentence because he realized it did not support the main idea of the paragraph.

> Although the cost of postage stamps has risen, they're still a great bargain. For only 34 cents, you can communicate with someone who lives thousands of miles away. It would be impossible for a person to travel that far for such a small amount of money. Most telephone calls cost more than 34 cents, even if you talk for just a few minutes. ~~Some long distance calls cost less after 7:00 p.m.~~ Many people think e-mail is free, but not if you consider the cost of a computer. I will not complain about the increased price of stamps. To me, the excitement of finding a letter in the mailbox with my name on it is worth every penny.

Staying on topic is another important part of supporting the main idea of a paragraph. If you include a sentence that doesn't belong, like the one crossed out in the sample paragraph, you might confuse your readers. However, if you find a sentence that doesn't belong in one paragraph, don't automatically throw it out. It might be a good main idea or supporting sentence for another paragraph. Look for ways to include all of your interesting information in an organized way.

Some Things to Remember

▶ Indent the first line of each paragraph.
▶ Watch the length of your paragraphs. They should be neither too long nor too short.
▶ When you start a new idea, it's time to start a new paragraph.
▶ Write transition sentences that help your writing flow smoothly from one paragraph to the next.

The following paragraphs are from a speech that Suki wrote. Each paragraph focuses on a different main idea, but Suki has used smooth transitions to tie them all together.

The street in front of our school is unsafe for students. Because trees and shrubs have grown up in front of the School Zone signs, many drivers do not realize that they need to slow down. The nearest stop sign is one mile away, so cars are able to work up to a very fast speed by the time they reach our building.

Another problem with this area is the sidewalks. The sidewalks are only wide enough for one person. When two students pass each other, one of them has to step off the sidewalk. That means a student is dangerously close to the road. The concrete sidewalks are also crumbling. Students who ride their bikes to school have skidded and fallen because of the gravelly path. Something must be done about this.

Improvements must be made to make the area in front of our school safer. Branches that block the School Zone signs should be trimmed. We also need to add a stop sign and a clearly marked crosswalk. Finally, the sidewalks have to be repaired and widened. Making these changes will help students travel much more safely to and from school.

Try It

Reread the paragraphs above. Which sentences make the transition between paragraphs smooth?

Reading Your Writing

A paragraph is made of two or more sentences, including a topic sentence in most cases, supporting sentences, and a closing sentence. You can support the main idea of a paragraph with different kinds of information, but be sure that all of the information relates to the topic.

Types of Paragraphs

Writers have different methods for communicating their ideas. Their paragraphs might be narrative, descriptive, expository, or persuasive. Use different types of paragraphs for different purposes.

Narrative

Narrative writing is used for telling stories, either fiction or nonfiction. Narrative writing is usually written to entertain, so it is especially important for the writer to consider his or her audience. Elements of narrative writing include building suspense to keep readers wondering what happens next and using description and dialogue to bring a scene to life.

Take a Look

The narrative paragraphs below are from *The Wright Brothers: How They Invented the Airplane,* by Russell Freedman.

Orville took the pilot's position, his hips in the wing-warping cradle, the toes of his shoes hooked over a small supporting rack behind him. Like his brother, he was wearing a dark suit, a stiff collar, a necktie, and a cap. Wilbur turned to the lifesaving men and told them "not to look so sad, but to . . . laugh and holler and clap . . . and try to cheer Orville   up when he started."

"After running the motor a few minutes to heat it up," Orville recalled, "I released the wire that held the machine to the track, and the machine started forward into the wind. Wilbur ran at the side of the machine, holding the wing to balance it on the track. Unlike the start on the 14th, made in a calm, the machine, facing a 27-mile-per-hour wind, started very slowly. Wilbur was able to stay with it till it lifted from the track after a forty-foot run. [John] snapped the camera for us, taking a picture just as the machine had reached the end of the track and had risen to a height of about two feet."

Wilbur had just let go of the wing when John Daniels tripped the shutter. The lifesavers broke into a ragged cheer. The Flyer was flying!

Descriptive

A descriptive paragraph uses vivid words to create an image or experience for the reader. Word choice is particularly important in this kind of writing. Writers should use words that appeal to the readers' five senses—sight, taste, hearing, smell, and touch.

Take a Look

This descriptive paragraph is from **"Windows on Wildlife,"** by Ginny Johnson and Judy Cutchins. Notice the vivid words that help readers feel as if they are seeing the exhibit themselves.

This rain forest is completely indoors, so the temperature and amount of moisture in the air can be carefully controlled. Above one of the exhibit's four waterfalls, fog machines spray mist into the air. The moisture forms clouds that drift over the jungle. It is always warm and steamy here, just as it is in a tropical forest. Heating coils hidden beneath the realistic riverbanks at JungleWorld simulate sun-warmed basking areas for monitor lizards and crocodilelike gharials.

Try It

Think of a descriptive sentence you could add to the sample paragraph on this page. Remember to appeal to the readers' senses.

Expository

Expository writing is used for giving information or explaining. You will find expository writing in newspapers, textbooks, and essays. When you write to explain something, remember to think about who your audience is. Ask yourself what they already know and what they might want or need to know.

Take a Look

The expository paragraph below is from **The Most Beautiful Roof in the World,** by Kathryn Lasky.

Other ants visit the canopy but live underground in great fungus factories. The leafcutter ants do their farming in reverse, trudging up to the canopy day and night to cut dime-size disks. They then hoist the pieces overhead and carry them back down to underground chambered caverns. In the dark damp maze of tunnels and caves, the leaves begin to grow mold and fungi, which in turn feed the ants. The long, silent lines of tiny, quivering green disks move across the rain forest floor. If you peer closely, you notice that on each disk rides an even smaller ant. This one protects the carrier ant from attacks by deadly micro wasps. For lateral protection alongside the column march lines of larger soldier ants. Each leaf disk, no bigger than a dime and only a fraction of a gram in weight, must get to the fungus factory. Once there, other ants will check the leaves to see if they are right for the kind of fungus the ants are producing. If they are not, the disks are discarded and the ants must turn around and climb one hundred or more feet (thirty meters) into the canopy again in search of the right kind of leaf.

Try It

The paragraph above contains descriptive words to make the explanation more interesting for the reader. What are some of those words?

Persuasive

A persuasive paragraph is used to convince readers to think, feel, or act a certain way. There are several good strategies writers can use in persuasive writing. For example, you might present your opinion as a problem, then suggest a solution. Providing evidence, or facts and reasons, to support your idea can also be an effective way to persuade. Another strategy is to present the points of your argument in order of their importance. This leaves readers with your most convincing point fresh in their minds. Choose the strategy you think will work best for a particular audience.

Take a Look

Aracelli, a student living in Chicago, wrote the following paragraph about ice skating at Navy Pier. She used evidence to support her view.

The best place to go ice skating in Chicago is at Navy Pier. Many people think that it is too cold to skate there because it is right on the lake, but I disagree. In fact, I work up a sweat while skating at Navy Pier because the rink is so large that everyone has plenty of room to move freely, even during busy times. The rink also has a great view of Lake Michigan. When you do need a break from skating, you can go to one of the nearby restaurants for a good lunch and hot chocolate. With a large rink, a beautiful view, and good food, Navy Pier is the best skating spot in town.

Reading Your Writing

Use different kinds of writing for different purposes—to tell a story, describe, explain, or persuade.

Graphic Organizers

A graphic organizer is a tool for collecting and organizing information in a logical manner. Writers use many different graphic organizers for different purposes. The following pages contain some examples of graphic organizers you might use to plan your writing projects.

Time Line

A time line organizes information in chronological, or time, order. In addition to showing the order in which events occurred, a time line can show relationships among events. Time lines can be drawn either horizontally or vertically, as long as the dates proceed chronologically in one direction. This time line was prepared by a writer planning a report on United States national parks.

U.S. National Parks Established before 1920

1872	Yellowstone (Idaho, Montana, and Wyoming)
1890	Yosemite (California)
1890	Sequoia (California)
1899	Mount Rainier (Washington)
1902	Crater Lake (Oregon)
1903	Wind Cave (South Dakota)
1906	Mesa Verde (Colorado)
1910	Glacier (Montana)
1915	Rocky Mountain (Colorado)
1916	Lassen Volcanic (California)
1919	Grand Canyon (in Arizona)
1919	Zion (Utah)

Collecting Grid

A collecting grid, or chart, is used to record information gathered from several different sources. Collecting grids are especially useful for preparing research papers or factual reports.

The collecting grid below shows details the writer is gathering on the subject of world population. The first column on the left lists the questions researched. The first row across the top lists the various sources used; you may write out the full title of the source or abbreviate it, as shown. It is a good idea to check facts in more than one source to make sure they are accurate.

	World Book Encyclopedia	GOED	DPG	UCB
world population?	5.9 billion		5.9 billion	
smallest country?		Vatican City, 840		
largest country?		China, 1.2 billion		
largest city?				Tokyo, Japan, 26.9 million

Venn Diagrams

A Venn diagram is used for comparing and contrasting two items. Recording information in a Venn diagram might show you that two things had more, or less, in common than you thought.

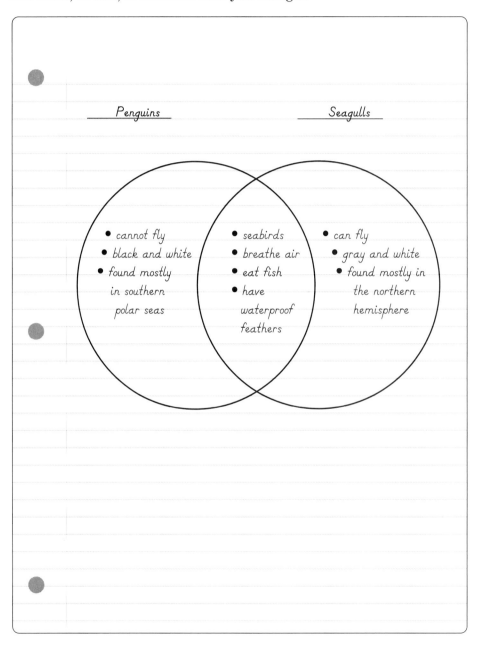

Penguins
Seagulls

- cannot fly
- black and white
- found mostly in southern polar seas

- seabirds
- breathe air
- eat fish
- have waterproof feathers

- can fly
- gray and white
- found mostly in the northern hemisphere

5 W's Chart

A 5 W's chart is used to organize information that answers the questions *who? what? when? where?* and *why?* These charts are especially helpful in collecting details for newspaper articles or narrative stories.

Karen used the 5 W's chart below to help her organize information for an article she is writing for the school newspaper.

Who?	What?	When?	Where?	Why?
Carly Harper, 6th grader	• Won school spelling bee • Is going to compete in county spelling bee	• School spelling bee was held January 8 • County spelling bee will be held March 23	• School auditorium • Main branch of the county library	Carly's mother won the county spelling bee when she was in 6th grade; Carly wants to carry on the tradition

Web

A web is a graphic organizer that shows how information relates to a main idea or topic. It is also useful for sorting information into categories.

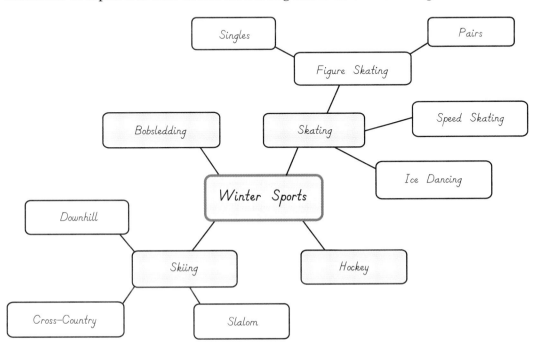

Cause and Effect Diagram

A cause-and-effect diagram shows connections among events. This type of graphic organizer can be helpful for preparing stories, papers about historical events, and science reports.

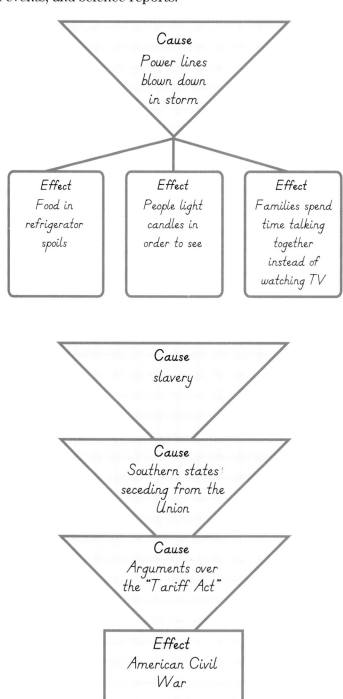

Expository Diagram

An expository diagram helps you sort information into topics and subtopics. An outline is one way to organize this kind of information. Another way is to create a line diagram like the one shown below. Using an expository diagram is especially helpful for organizing any type of informative report, such as a research report.

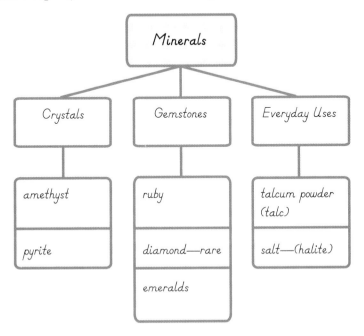

. . . .

Reading Your Writing

There are many kinds of graphic organizers that writers can use to collect their thoughts and information. Different organizers are used for different kinds of writing. Using a graphic organizer to plan what you write will help you and your readers stay focused.

. . . .

Writer's Craft

Like anything else that's worth doing, writing requires some skill and a lot of practice. The lessons in this unit will help you learn some of the skills that make good writing better. Just like athletes or musicians, writers learn the skills they need to improve, and then they practice, practice, practice. Look for new ways to improve your writing as you read these lessons.

Purpose and Audience

The goal of writing is to communicate with others. Achieving this goal requires some thought about your reason for writing and who will read your finished work. Keep these things in mind as you write in order to communicate successfully with readers.

The **purpose** of what you write is your reason for writing, or your goal. To identify your purpose for writing, ask yourself what you hope to achieve with a particular piece of writing. Are you writing to entertain, to describe, to explain, or to persuade?

Take a Look

The purpose of the first paragraph below is to entertain, or tell a story. The second paragraph was written to persuade.

We were all on the edge of our seats in the movie theater. I knew something scary was about to happen, and I didn't want my friends to see that I was afraid. I kept looking down into my bag of popcorn instead of at the screen, hoping I would miss the big moment. Then it happened. A loud, ringing sound broke the silence. Popcorn and licorice flew through the air as my friends and I threw up our hands to cover our eyes. Our hearts were pounding so hard, it took us a minute to realize that the sound hadn't even come from the movie. Someone in the row behind us had gotten a call on her cell phone.

Cell phones should not be allowed in public places where people are trying to watch a performance. It is getting harder and harder to enjoy a concert or a movie without being disturbed by someone talking on the telephone. Even if the person doesn't talk for long, the sound of a ringing phone is disruptive. It might distract a performer or spoil a suspenseful scene. Many of us go to plays and other shows to relax and take a break from our daily routines. When phones ring and people have personal conversations during a performance, it ruins the experience for other members of the audience.

In addition to having a clear purpose when you write, it is important to think about your audience. An **audience** is the person or people who will read what you write. Identifying your audience will help you decide the best way to communicate your message. For example, a letter to a friend or relative would be more casual than a letter you write to a business or newspaper. Also, you would use different words for an audience of five-year-olds than you would if your audience were an adult.

Take a Look

Suki wrote the following thank-you notes. She used a casual tone in the note to her grandparents and a formal tone in the one to her dentist.

Dear Grandma and Grandpa,

Thanks so much for the money you sent for my birthday. Mom and Dad said I had to put some of it in the bank, but I spent the rest on art supplies. I bought some new pastels and drawing paper. I'm sending you one of my new works of art. I hope you like it!

I can't wait to see you next summer.

Love,
Suki

Dear Dr. Lawrence,

Thank you very much for allowing me to interview you last week. I appreciate the time you spent talking with me and showing me around your office. After learning more about your profession, I'm even more interested in becoming a dentist someday.

I look forward to seeing you at my next check-up.

Sincerely,
Suki Mak

Formal Versus Informal Writing

Once you decide on your purpose and audience, you can choose the kind of writing style you want to use. **Formal writing** is used for serious kinds of writing, such as research reports, essays, articles, and business letters. **Informal writing** is a more casual way of writing that is used for friendly letters, stories, and note taking.

Formal writing
▶ sounds serious
▶ includes carefully worded, complete sentences
▶ does not have contractions, shortened words, or slang
▶ often includes long, technical words

Informal writing
▶ often sounds friendly and personal
▶ may include incomplete sentences, similar to everyday conversation
▶ has contractions, shortened words, and sometimes slang
▶ includes simple, ordinary words

Take a Look

The formal writing in this paragraph from the nonfiction book *Natural Fire: Its Ecology in Forests* by Laurence Pringle includes complete sentences and technical vocabulary.

> The study of fire ecology is complex and fascinating because there are many kinds of forests and many kinds of fires. To understand the natural role of fire, scientists observe current fires and also investigate fires that occurred centuries ago.

Many stories have an informal style. Notice the incomplete sentence and dialogue that make this paragraph from Gary Paulsen's fiction book *Hatchet* sound more casual.

> What makes fire? He thought back to school. To all those science classes. Had he ever learned what made a fire? Did a teacher ever stand up there and say, "This is what makes a fire . . ."

Sometimes you might want to communicate the same message to different groups of people. To achieve the same purpose with different audiences, adjust your word choices and the tone of your writing.

Milo wrote the following descriptive paragraphs about his dog. His purpose is the same in both paragraphs, but he is writing for two different audiences.

My best friend is my golden retriever, Ginger. When Ginger sees me come in the door, she gets very excited. She opens her mouth in a way that looks as if she is smiling. Even her brown eyes look happy. Ginger jumps up and puts her paws on my shoulder, then licks my cheek with her rough, wet tongue. Coming home to Ginger after a hard day at school always makes me feel better.

> This paragraph was written for an audience of first-grade students whom Milo tutors. He chose words that these students would understand and used basic sentence structure.

My golden retriever, Ginger, is the best friend a boy could have. As I come through the door, Ginger is always waiting to greet me with great enthusiasm. It seems that she actually smiles at me, not just with her mouth, but with her warm, brown eyes. To make sure that I feel appreciated, Ginger leaps up to embrace me with her paws and give me a slobbery smooch on the cheek. There's no better way to end the day than coming home to a dog who loves you.

> This paragraph is from a paper Milo wrote for an essay contest about kids' pets. Local veterinarians are the contest judges, so Milo used more complicated words and sentences for this audience.

Try It

What words did Milo use in the second paragraph that make it more appropriate for an older audience?

Reading Your Writing

A writer's purpose is his or her goal, or reason for writing, and an audience is the person or people who will read the writer's work. Writers make choices about the words and style they will use based on their purpose and audience.

Orders of Writing

The way you organize your thoughts can be as important as what you write. To communicate clearly, you must present your ideas in a logical order. Choose from a variety of ways to arrange your thoughts, depending on your purpose for writing.

Time

Writers often organize their writing chronologically, or in time order. This kind of order is almost always used in biographies, autobiographies, and history reports. Words that tell when events occur are called **indicators of time.** For example, words such as *yesterday, today, this evening, last week,* and *next year* let readers know when things happen.

> The opening ceremonies for the Winter Olympics were ***last week.*** ***Yesterday*** I watched figure skating and downhill skiing. ***Today*** I saw the bobsled and speed skating events. ***Tomorrow*** I'm going to watch cross-country skiing.

Order

Arranging your ideas by order of events is another way to present information chronologically. Words that show the order in which things happen are called **indicators of order.** You can lead readers through a series of events with words such as *before, then, now, later, first, next,* and *soon.*

> ***At first*** I could barely run a mile. ***Then*** as I got into shape, I started running farther and farther. ***Now*** I can run five miles without any trouble. I hope to run a marathon ***someday.***

Try It

Add indicators of time or order to the following sentences to show when things happened.

▶ *Monica's choir group won the competition. They will have a party at the music teacher's house.*

Order of Importance

When writing to inform or to persuade, organizing your ideas by order of importance can be effective. You might begin with the most important detail and end with the least important, or vice versa. Beginning with your most important idea can help you grab the readers' attention; finishing with your most important idea can leave readers with a strong image. The details in a newspaper article are often organized by order of importance. In the following paragraph, the writer saved her most important detail for last.

> Hundreds of people turned out yesterday to protest the destruction of Hanley Park to make space for a new shopping center. Hanley Park has been a favorite spot for neighborhood picnics and family outings since it was established 75 years ago. In addition to their sentimental attachment to the park, protestors are concerned about how the planned changes will affect the environment. Many trees in the park are more than one hundred years old. Bulldozing the trees will mean destroying the homes of birds, squirrels, and other wildlife in the area.

Order of Location

When writing a description, giving directions, or telling where events in a story take place, writers use **indicators of location.** These include words such as *beside, down, in front of, near,* and *underneath,* which help the reader visualize what is happening.

There are different ways to organize details by order of location, but you should use only one method in a particular paragraph. Choose the method that makes the most sense for your subject and will be the easiest for readers to follow.

Top to Bottom

Describing a scene or item from **top to bottom** is one way to order information by location.

It was the most interesting snowman I have ever seen. A tall, white chef's hat balanced on top of the snowman's head. His mismatched eyes, one walnut and one cherry tomato, stared straight ahead. Centered beneath his eyes, a banana hooked out and down to form the snowman's nose. Below that, six green olives curved up in a crooked smile. His left arm was a wooden spoon, and his right arm was a soup ladle. Tied around the snowman's middle was an apron that read "Kiss the Cook." For the finishing touch, a large skillet made of aluminum foil was built around the snowman's base.

Left to Right

When describing a large object, a room, or an outdoor scene, it might make sense to order your details from **left to right.** Most people are comfortable with this organization because it is familiar—we think from left to right when reading and writing.

We entered the gym through large double doors. To our left was the long row of bleachers where our friends, relatives, and other fans would be sitting that night. Painted on the wall above the top row of seats we saw the name and mascot of our competitors: the Panthers. Mounted high on the wall in front of us was a large, new scoreboard with bright lights. We all imagined looking up at it to see our winning score in the "Visitors" box. Next to the scoreboard was a balcony for the home team's pep band. Their music stands and folding chairs were still scattered there from last week's game. A backboard hung from the ceiling in front of the balcony. The right side of the gym was a mirror image of the left side, except for the table that had been fastened to the third row of bleachers. This is where the announcer and scorekeeper would sit.

Reference to a Focal Point

A third method of ordering information by location is in reference to a **focal point.** A focal point is the main object in a scene. When you order details according to a focal point, you describe where everything else is in relation to the focal point. The focal point should be obvious, such as the purple house in the following paragraph.

When anyone comes down our street, the first thing they notice is Ms. Rivera's house. Her house isn't the biggest, but it is the purplest! She didn't use purple for just parts of the house, like the shutters or the door. The whole two-story house is a celebration of her favorite color. The red brick house to the left of Ms. Rivera's is very charming, and there is a lovely old stone house two doors down on the right. The yard across the street from Ms. Rivera's purple house has a beautiful rose garden and a goldfish pond. As nice as these things are, they all seem plain in comparison to Ms. Rivera's house.

Try It

Find a focal point in the room where you are sitting. Make up three sentences that describe the location of other things in relation to the focal point.

Reading Your Writing

Writing should be organized in a logical way that is easy for readers to follow. Information might be arranged by time, order, importance, or location, depending on what makes the most sense for a particular subject. Using indicators of time and location in your writing will make it easier for readers to follow along and to imagine what is happening.

Transition Words

When you have a lot of different ideas to express in your writing, it's important to help the reader follow along. You can do this by using **transition words,** which connect ideas in a piece of writing. Transition words help make your writing clearer and more accurate, and they help the reader move smoothly from one idea to the next.

Different kinds of transition words are used for different purposes. For example, transition words can signal a time or place, a comparison or contrast, a cause and effect, or a summary.

Showing Time

These are some transition words that can be used to indicate time:

after	immediately	suddenly
as soon as	in the meantime	then
at first	later	third
before	meanwhile	today
during	next	tomorrow
earlier	next month	until
eventually	now	when
finally	second	while
first	soon	yesterday

Yesterday in Social Studies class we got our assignments for research projects. *At first* I didn't want to write about the Anasazi. *Then* I found out more about these ancient Native Americans and the fascinating remains of their civilization. I went to the library *last night* and got some great books. *Now* I'm looking forward to working on this assignment.

Showing Location

The following transition words are indicators of location:

above	by	off
across	down	on
along	far away	outside
around	in front of	right
behind	inside	south
below	left	through
beside	near	toward
between	north	under

They began digging *inside* the red, broken walls of a circular room. Richard found round rooms *in* most of the cliff dwellings. Many were dug *underground,* with firepits and stone benches *around* the walls. He knew that native people farther *south* used circular *underground* rooms for meetings of the tribes' religious clans. The Hopis called the rooms *kivas.*
—from *Searches in the American Desert* by Sheila Cowing

Signaling Facts and Details

Use transition words such as these to point out facts and details:

actually	for instance	specifically
as a matter of fact	in fact	such as
for example	like	to be exact

Many artifacts were left behind in the Anasazi dwellings. *For example,* clay bowls and pots, axes, spears, and woven baskets and sandals were discovered. *In fact,* even the remains of the ancient people who made those items were found.

Making a Comparison

These transition words show comparison:

as	comparable	resembling
alike	equally	same
also	like	similar

Like the ancient Egyptians, the Anasazi *also* preserved the bodies of their dead. The two civilizations must have had *similar* ideas about an afterlife. Mummies from both cultures were buried with items, such as jewelry and tools, for use in their new lives.

Showing Differences

Use these transition words to contrast things:

although	in contrast	on the other hand
but	instead	otherwise
despite	less than	unlike
however	more than	yet
whereas		

Unlike the former residents of Mesa Verde, the people at Grand Gulch had not used pots. *Instead,* they used woven baskets.

Adding Information

The following transition words signal to readers that you are giving them more information:

additionally	another	in addition
also	as well	next
and	besides	other

In addition to being skilled builders, the Anasazi were *also* talented artists. They created beautiful pottery, jewelry, and carvings.

Showing Cause and Effect

Use these transition words to indicate a cause-and-effect relationship:

as a result	due to	then
because	for this reason	therefore
consequently	so	

Because of the dry air in the desert, the remains of the Anasazi were well preserved. **For this reason,** archaeologists have plenty of clues about the ancient people's way of life.

Summarizing

To summarize a point, use transition words such as these:

all in all	finally	lastly
as I have said	in conclusion	to summarize

All in all, I enjoyed this research project more than any other. Although I am finished with my report, I want to keep learning about the fascinating Anasazi people. Someday I hope to visit the Mesa Verde National Park in Colorado to see their cliff dwellings.

Try It

Identify the other transition words used in the sample paragraph above.

Reading Your Writing

Transition words are used to connect ideas in a written work. Different kinds of transition words are used for different reasons. Including transition words can clarify your writing and help guide readers from one idea to the next.

Effective Beginnings and Endings

A good beginning to your story or article gets readers interested and makes them want to keep reading. A good ending helps your readers remember what you wrote. Writers use a variety of methods to create strong beginnings and endings.

A Good Start

There are many ways to grab your readers' attention with a good beginning. Most of these methods can be used for a story or an informational article; however, some work better for one purpose or the other. For example, beginning with an interesting fact or a problem that needs to be solved might work better in an informational piece. Think about story beginnings that you liked. Then, try some of the following techniques for getting your readers hooked.

▶ **Explain a problem.**

> Carrie loved dancing more than chocolate. She practiced her dance moves every day, and she woke up on Saturday mornings ready for class. After next week, however, there would be no more dance class. Her mother was sorry. "We just don't have the money to pay for the lessons now. I know you love it. Maybe next year." Carrie was not ready to give up, though. She would find a way to continue.

▶ **Use details that appeal to the senses.**

> I spread my bright green blanket out on a level section of damp sand. Soon the sun would be blazing down on the beach, burning off all the moisture. I opened my sunscreen and, squeezing the plastic tube, drew long, white lines on my arms and legs. I smelled the tropical scent of coconut as I smoothed the cool cream into my skin.

Fun Fact

The English Department at San Jose State University hosts an annual fiction contest in which all participants must begin their stories with the phrase "It was a dark and stormy night . . ."

▶ **Ask questions.**

What could have happened to my lucky silver dollar? Is it possible that Matthew took it? My grandpa gave me that silver dollar five years ago, and it always brought me luck when I needed it most. I showed it to Matthew after lunch, and he knew the silver dollar was in my backpack.

▶ **Use quotations or dialogue.**

"I'll clean my room tomorrow, Mom," I said as I raced toward the door.

"Tomorrow. Tomorrow. I've heard enough tomorrows," Mom stated emphatically. "Well, tomorrow has come."

▶ **Tell an interesting fact.**

More than 27 percent of the beverages Americans consume are soft drinks. That works out to an average of about 56 gallons of soda per year for every single person in this country! Many of the soft drinks that are popular today are the same as the first ones made in the 1800s.

▶ **Invite the reader into the scene.**

Just inside the tall, blue gate, dreams became reality. Festive music from the merry-go-round filled the air as brightly painted horses cranked up and down in endless circles. Carts suspended from cables carried excited visitors off to exotic lands with roller coasters and water rides. Fuzzy stuffed animals hung in the frames of arcade booths, where cheery young workers called out "Step right up!" It was going to be a great day at the amusement park.

► **Tell something that happened to you or someone else.**

> My most embarrassing moment happened during the school play last spring. Sara, Maria, and I played the part of a Chinese dragon. We wore an elaborate twelve-foot dragon costume. All was going well, until I sneezed.

► **Tell about a problem that needs solving.**

> Landfills are huge garbage piles. What can be done with these sites? Believe it or not, some have been turned into golf courses and ski slopes. Still, there are many more mountains of trash out there that need to be dealt with.

Try It

Which kind of beginning would you use for an informational article about helicopters? Which kind would work well for an autobiographical story?

A Strong Finish

Good writing does not come to a sudden stop. Instead, it leaves readers with a lasting impression or something to think about. An effective ending might also summarize, answer a question, or restate the main idea—these are good techniques for writing a closing sentence for a paragraph.

Take a Look

In the following paragraph, the closing sentence provides a summary.

> Sacajawea was very helpful to Lewis and Clark's team of explorers. She saved the group many weeks of traveling time, guiding them across the land and mountains that she knew well. Sacajawea also acted as a translator between the explorers and the Native American tribes they encountered. When the food supply ran low, Sacajawea gathered and fixed roots, nuts, and berries for the crew. As guide, interpreter, and cook, Sacajawea provided valuable contributions to the success of the expedition.

A concluding paragraph can provide a strong ending for a story or an article. In a report of events, the final paragraph often brings the action to an end. In other kinds of writing, the concluding paragraph can reveal a story's meaning. This is where the writer might make a general statement about life or might turn the reader's focus from the story to himself or herself.

Take a Look

In the concluding paragraph of this piece the writer makes a generalization about life.

As dusk set in, my little sister came charging out of the house and let the screen door slam shut behind her. It was such a beautiful summer night that Mom didn't even bother to remind Allison to close the door gently. Instead, she called out the window, "Josh, could you please help your sister?"

Allison was carrying a freshly washed mayonnaise jar, and she wanted me to poke holes in the lid for her. She was planning to catch fireflies to make her very own night-light. We went to the garage together to find a screwdriver and hammer, and minutes later Allison was on the hunt.

It took so little to make my sister happy—just some shiny bugs in a jar. She brought the jar over and proudly displayed her catch. As we looked at the fireflies together, I saw the smile leave her face. "What's wrong?" I asked.

"They don't look as pretty in the jar. They can't fly," she responded. Allison unscrewed the lid and encouraged all of the little prisoners to escape.

I was proud of my little sister then. She had felt the joy of darting around our yard, free and glowing, just like a firefly. She knew that taking something so good away from another creature could not make her happy.

Reading Your Writing

There are many ways to write good beginnings and endings for stories and articles. A good beginning draws readers in and makes them want to find out more. A good ending leaves readers with something to think about. Use strong beginnings and endings in your writing to connect with your audience from start to finish.

Variety in Writing

Having variety in your writing makes it more interesting and less repetitive. Variety also adds a sense of style to your writing that makes it read more smoothly. Using synonyms and including sentences of different lengths are good ways to add variety to what you write.

Using Synonyms

Synonyms are words that have the same or similar meanings. Using synonyms in your writing helps you avoid repetition that makes your paragraphs weak and dull.

Take a Look

The paragraph below is weak because the word *great* is overused.

I went to a <u>great</u> costume party last week. All of the guests were supposed to come dressed in a uniform. What a <u>great</u> idea for a party! I wore a <u>great</u> pilot's uniform that I borrowed from my aunt. I saw a lot of other <u>great</u> costumes at the party, too.

Using synonyms makes the following paragraph much stronger than the original.

I went to a great costume party last week. All of the guests were supposed to come dressed in a uniform. What a wonderful idea for a party! I wore a fabulous pilot's uniform that I borrowed from my aunt. I saw a lot of other interesting costumes at the party, too.

In addition to using synonyms, you might replace combinations of words with more precise words. For example:

Mika quickly ran into the huge house.
Use a more precise noun: Mika quickly ran into the <u>mansion</u>.
Use a vivid verb: Mika <u>raced</u> into the huge house.

Writing Parallel Sentences

Sentences that are written clearly are made of parallel parts. **Parallelism** is using words and phrases in the same way within a sentence. In addition to clarifying your writing, parallelism makes your writing read more smoothly.

Watch for parallelism in sentences that contain word pairs such as *either/or, neither/nor,* and *not only/but also.* These word pairs are called correlative conjunctions, and they should be followed by words and phrases in parallel form.

Look closely at the words that follow each correlative conjunction to see the difference between parallel and nonparallel sentences. For example, the first sentence below is not parallel because the verb constructions are not parallel (*paying* versus *fix*).

Nonparallel: You are **either paying** for the broken window **or fix** it yourself.

Parallel: You are **either paying** for the broken window **or fixing** it yourself.

Nonparallel: Jake is **not only working** at the gym **but also the** library.

Parallel: Jake is working **not only at** the gym **but also at** the library.

Careful writers also use parallel parts of speech. That means verbs are used with other verbs, nouns are used with nouns, and so on. Watch for parallelism especially when writing words or phrases in a series.

Nonparallel: The mustangs are wild, beautiful, and a thrill.

Change the noun *a thrill* to an adjective to make the sentence parallel.

Parallel: The mustangs are wild, beautiful, and thrilling.

Here are some other examples of how to make sentences parallel.

Nonparallel: I packed my swimsuit, sandals, and am taking shorts.
Remove the verb *am taking* to make a parallel series of nouns.
Parallel: I packed my swimsuit, sandals, and shorts.

Nonparallel: We hung the decorations quickly, quietly, and with care.
Make all of the items in the series adverbs.
Parallel: We hung the decorations quickly, quietly, and carefully.

Nonparallel: I looked for my lost watch on the dresser, under the bed, and checked the bathroom.
Make the sentence parallel by changing the third phrase to a prepositional phrase.
Parallel: I looked for my lost watch on the dresser, under the bed, and in the bathroom.

Writers often have problems with parallelism in sentences that contain infinitives. Watch for sentences in which you should use an infinitive instead of a participle.

Nonparallel: Sheri does yoga to stay fit and clearing her mind.
To be consistent, change the participle to an infinitive.
Parallel: Sheri does yoga to stay fit and to clear her mind.

Also be careful to include the word *to* where it is needed to make a series of infinitives parallel.

Nonparallel: On vacation we plan to tour the castle, visit the museum, and to do some hiking.
Parallel: On vacation we plan to tour the castle, to visit the museum, and to do some hiking.

Try It

Change the following sentence to make it parallel.
▶ *Running out of gas, getting lost, and a flat tire didn't ruin our trip.*

Combining Sentences

Using sentences of different lengths will also help make your writing stronger and more interesting. A paragraph made of many sentences of the same length is often predictable and repetitive. One way to avoid repetitive, choppy writing is to combine sentences or parts of sentences.

Take a Look

There are many ways to combine words and phrases from different sentences to make one sentence that reads more smoothly.

Separate sentences: Twinkling stars filled the sky. The stars were bright.
Combine adjectives: <u>Bright, twinkling</u> stars filled the sky.

Separate sentences: Speak softly into the microphone. You should also speak clearly.
Combine adverbs: Speak <u>softly</u> and <u>clearly</u> into the microphone.

Separate sentences: I can't go to the movie until I make my bed. I also have to fold the laundry and take out the trash before I leave.
Combine adverb clauses: I can't go to the <u>movie until I make my bed, fold the laundry,</u> and <u>take out the trash.</u>

Separate sentences: Quinn's cat sleeps behind the sofa. Sometimes it sleeps in the closet.
Combine prepositional phrases: Quinn's cat sleeps <u>behind the sofa or in the closet.</u>

Separate sentences: The dog howling at the moon is mine. He is running in circles.
Use participial phrases: The dog <u>howling at the moon and running in circles</u> is mine.

Separate sentences: Mrs. Warner lives next door. She is the school principal.
Combine with an appositive: Mrs. Warner, <u>the school principal</u>, lives next door.

Expanding Sentences

Another way to avoid short, choppy writing is to add details to your sentences. One way to do this is by using adjectives and adverbs to create a clearer image for readers. You might also expand your sentences with phrases and clauses. All of these techniques will help add interest and variety to your writing.

Add Details

Make your sentences more interesting and expressive by adding details. Look at your sentences as a reader, and ask yourself what additional information would make the sentence clearer or more vivid. The details you add might answer the following questions: When? Where? How? How often? How much? What kind? Which one? How many?

> *Basic sentence:* I like bagels.
>
> *Tell when:* I like to eat bagels for breakfast.
>
> *Tell where:* I like bagels from the deli on Winthrop Street.
>
> *Tell how often:* I eat a bagel sandwich every day.
>
> *Tell what kind:* I like sesame bagels with cream cheese.

Add Phrases and Clauses

In some of the sample sentences above, prepositional phrases have been added to expand the sentence. You can also use other kinds of phrases and clauses to add interest and variety to sentences.

> *Basic sentence:* The bus stopped suddenly.
>
> *Add a participial phrase:* The bus taking us downtown stopped suddenly.
>
> *Add a prepositional phrase:* The bus stopped suddenly on a steep hill.
>
> *Add an adverbial clause:* The bus stopped suddenly because a duck was crossing the road.
>
> *Add an adjective clause:* The bus that we were following stopped suddenly.

Try It

Expand the following sentence in three different ways: add an adjective, a prepositional phrase, and an adverbial clause.

▶ *The door slammed shut.*

Varying Sentence Beginnings

Starting your sentences in different ways is another good technique for adding variety to your writing. Change the natural order of a sentence (subject then predicate) by beginning with an introductory word, phrase, or clause.

Take a Look

In the first paragraph, all of the sentences have the same structure. A variety of sentence beginnings makes the second paragraph much more interesting and easier to read.

Yesterday was my birthday. Mom and Dad knew I was excited, so they let me open my presents before breakfast. I opened the large box first. The Rollerblades I had wanted were inside! I tried them on right away. I put on knee and elbow pads also, but I didn't think I would need them. I felt fearless as I took off down the driveway. I realized when I got to the intersection that I didn't know how to stop.

Yesterday was my birthday. Knowing I was excited, Mom and Dad let me open my presents before breakfast. First, I opened the large box. Inside were the Rollerblades I wanted! I tried them on right away. Although I didn't think I would need them, I put on knee and elbow pads also. Fearlessly, I took off down the driveway. When I got to the intersection, I realized that I didn't know how to stop.

Reading Your Writing

Use synonyms and sentences of different lengths to add variety to your writing. You can vary sentence length by combining sentences, expanding sentences, and starting sentences in different ways. Remember that sentences should have parallel parts to make them clearer and easier to read. Variety will give your writing a more polished style and keep readers interested.

Figurative Language

A **figure of speech** is an expression in which words do not have their real meanings but are used to create pictures in the reader's mind. Figurative language can be used to create vivid images that are more dramatic for the reader.

In order for readers to understand figurative language, they must know the regular meanings of the words. Therefore, you should think about your audience and whether the figurative language you use will make sense to them. If you use figures of speech that aren't appropriate to the age and experience of your readers, the meaning will be lost.

Following are some figures of speech that can make your writing more vivid and interesting.

Simile

A **simile** compares two things that are not alike by using the word *like* or *as*.

The sailboat bounced like a toy in the rough sea.

Some similes have become clichés, which are worn-out expressions. Clichés have lost their impact through overuse and should be avoided in your writing. It is better to make up original phrases to capture the reader's imagination. Some clichés you might have heard are *light as a feather, run like the wind, quiet as a mouse, cute as a button,* and *work like a dog.*

Metaphor

A metaphor compares two things that are not alike without using the word *like* or *as*. Metaphors are commonly used in poetry to create vivid mental images.

The sailboat was a bouncing toy in the rough sea.

Try It

Make this simile into a metaphor:
▶ *The loaf of bread was hard as a cement block.*

Make this metaphor into a simile:
▶ *The dog's fur was a jungle filled with fleas.*

Personification

Personification is a figure of speech in which an idea or object is given human qualities.

The sports car hugged the curb.
My clothes dryer has stolen another sock.
The flowers smiled up at us with bright faces.

Exaggeration

Exaggeration is overstating the truth. Writers use this figure of speech to emphasize a point.

If I could pass that science test, I could do anything.
Marc had driven that route so often he could do it with his eyes closed.
We think Mr. Richards is the best teacher in the world.

Idiom

An **idiom** is an expression whose meaning cannot be understood by knowing the words that form it.

At first I believed Sue's story, then I realized she was *pulling my leg*.
People *come out of the woodwork* for the community garage sale.
Give me a ring when you get home.

Hyperbole

A **hyperbole** is an extreme exaggeration that writers use for effect.

I went to a million stores looking for the perfect pair of shoes.
From the top of the mountain you can see forever.
Jessie would rather walk on hot coals than give a speech.

Reading Your Writing

A figure of speech is a phrase in which words are used in a creative way to make a picture in the reader's mind. Include figurative language to make your writing more interesting and dramatic.

The Sound of Language

Writers sometimes use the sounds of words to produce a certain effect. Poetry is a type of writing in which the sound and meaning of words are combined to create ideas and feelings. You can use the following elements in your own poems or other writing to appeal to your reader's senses.

Alliteration

Alliteration is the repetition of consonant sounds at the beginning of words.

Claudia crunched her caramel corn.

Assonance

Assonance is the repetition of vowel sounds.

Shake the rain from your wavy hair
And face this dreary day.

Onomatopoeia

Onomatopoeia is the use of a word whose sound refers to its meaning. Onomatopoeia captures the sound of actions such as *crash, gurgle, zap, buzz, smack,* and *boom.*

The tired team huffed and puffed their way to the locker room.

End Rhyme

End rhyme is the use of rhyming words at the ends of lines in a poem.

Oh, little light, so fair and fine,
Burn long, burn bright, and shine—shine!

Try It

Which of the above techniques are used in the following lines?
Clucking, cackling, pecking corn,
Chickens wake to another morn.

Internal Rhyme

Internal rhyme is the use of rhyming words within a line of poetry. This kind of rhyme contributes to the patterns and rhythm of a poem.

Mary, Mary, quite <u>contrary</u>,
How does your garden grow?
With silver <u>bells</u> and cockle <u>shells</u>
And pretty maids all in a row.

Repetition

Repetition repeats words and phrases. This technique is used to emphasize ideas in many kinds of writing, including speeches, stories, and poetry. In his famous "I Have a Dream" speech, Dr. Martin Luther King, Jr., used repetition for a powerful effect on his listeners. Here's an excerpt:

So let freedom ring from the prodigious hilltops of New
   Hampshire.
Let freedom ring from the mighty mountains of New York.
Let freedom ring from the heightening Alleghenies of
   Pennsylvania.
Let freedom ring from the snowcapped Rockies of Colorado.
Let freedom ring from the curvaceous slopes of California.
But not only that.
Let freedom ring from Stone Mountain of Georgia.
Let freedom ring from Lookout Mountain of Tennessee.
Let freedom ring from every hill and molehill of Mississippi,
   from every mountainside, let freedom ring.

Rhythm

The **rhythm,** or meter, of a poem is its pattern of stressed and unstressed syllables. In the following line, every other syllable is stressed.

Twìnkle, twìnkle, lìttle stàr

Ways to Develop Expository Text

Expository text refers to nonfiction writing that is written to inform or explain. Expository writing is different from narrative writing, which is used to tell fictional stories, because it is always based on facts. While expository writing can be entertaining, its main purpose is to provide information. Research papers, science reports, newspaper and magazine articles, and textbooks are all examples of expository writing.

Expository writing is usually associated with research; however, writers don't always have to look in other sources for facts. You already have a lot of knowledge based on your own experiences, and this information can be used in expository writing. For example, if you enjoy photography, you could write an expository essay explaining the process of taking a picture.

Elements of Expository Text

▶ Expository text is written to give a reader information about a subject. Its purpose is to tell about someone or something.

▶ The information presented is factual. It may be about real events or real people, or it may be instructional.

▶ The information is presented in a straightforward way.

▶ The events are presented in the order in which they occurred, or the steps are written in the order in which they should be done.

▶ The writing may be organized according to topics.

▶ Diagrams, photographs, maps, or other illustrations may be included to help the reader better understand the subject.

▶ The factual information can often be checked by using reference sources such as books or newspapers. For example, reference books can be used to check facts in science or history articles, while newspapers might provide information for checking details of recent events.

Expository text can be developed in a variety of ways. The method you choose should be based on the information you present and your purpose for writing. The following pages contain models for some of the ways you might organize information in expository text.

Compare and Contrast

Comparing means explaining how two or more people or things are alike. **Contrasting** means explaining how two or more people or things are different. When writing expository text, you will sometimes want to explain how people or things are alike or different. By comparing and contrasting, you can help readers understand more about each person or thing in your report and make your writing more meaningful.

Some words you might use in making comparisons are *both, same, like, as, just as, also, too, neither/nor, not only/but also*, and *resembles*. When contrasting, you might use the terms *different, but, unlike, than, although, instead of, rather than*, and *differs*. Using these words gives readers a signal that you are comparing items or describing how items are different. Including signals can be helpful when comparing and contrasting, but you don't always have to use them.

Take a Look

These paragraphs show how to write a comparison/contrast with signal words and without.

> Soccer and football are **both** popular sports. **Like** soccer, football is played on a large field. The football field is **different** from the soccer field because it is marked with lines called "yard lines." At the ends of the football field there are goalposts **instead of** goal cages, which are used in soccer.

> Soccer and football are sports in which two teams compete against one another. Soccer players and football players wear team uniforms. Soccer uniforms consist of light clothing, with shin guards as the only protective equipment. Football uniforms include heavy padding for the shoulders, hips, and thighs and a helmet to protect players' heads.

Try It

Identify the similarities and differences presented in the second sample paragraph.

Cause and Effect

Cause and effect is a technique writers often use for developing expository text that explains why things happen or why things are the way they are. **Causes** tell what makes something happen, and **effects** tell what happens as a result of the cause.

You might write about one cause leading to several effects, or several causes that result in one effect. In either case, presenting the cause or causes first then the effect or effects is the logical way to organize this kind of writing. The signal words *since*, *because*, *therefore*, and *so* point out to readers the connection between causes and effects.

Take a Look

The first paragraph explains several effects resulting from one cause, while the second paragraph explains how several causes result in one effect.

> The lack of oxygen at high elevations on Mt. Everest has resulted in both mental and physical challenges for climbers. Many climbers have described an inability to think clearly. They are able to answer questions correctly, but it takes them much longer to process information. This condition is made worse by their inability to achieve a deep sleep. Other physical effects climbers experience include loss of coordination and speech, severe headache, and double vision.

Cause

Effects

> The climbers found themselves trapped in a violent storm. They struggled against temperatures as low as –40 degrees Fahrenheit and winds as strong as 125 miles per hour. Their tent was torn, and they were extremely hungry. Because they faced so many obstacles, the crew was forced to pack up and return to their base camp.

Causes

Effect

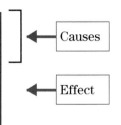

Questions and Answers

Another way to organize and present information is to form questions and answer them. This approach can be very useful for writing a research paper or science report.

The question-and-answer format also helps readers. It is easier for them to follow the writer's thoughts by thinking about the question, possible answers, and what was found through research.

Here are some steps to follow for including questions and answers in your writing:

▶ Include a question you or one of your readers might have about your subject.

▶ Write possible answers to your question.

▶ Use an encyclopedia or other reference book to research answers to your question. Include in your report the information you find, and explain whether it supports or disproves the possible answers you had written.

Take a Look

Here's an example of the question-and-answer approach to organizing and presenting information.

What causes an earthquake? I used to think earthquakes were caused by a kind of explosion under the ground. Now I know that earthquakes happen when the plates that make up the crust of the earth try to slide past each other. As they slide, their jagged edges rub against each other. The rough spots catch onto each other and then break away, making the land shake. These plates are moving all the time, but usually we can't feel the movement. When the tension between the rocks builds, the plates move quickly and violently, and an earthquake occurs.

Problem and Solution

Presenting expository text as a problem and solution is similar to using the question-and-answer format. First, you state a problem then present one or more solutions. Within a single paragraph, you can state the problem in the topic sentence and use supporting sentences to present the solution. However, in longer papers, you might want to use separate paragraphs for the problem and each of the solutions. Using the problem-and-solution method to organize your thoughts creates a logical structure for your writing.

In the following excerpt from *The Wright Brothers: How They Invented the Airplane* by Russell Freedman, the first paragraph states the problem, and the second paragraph presents solutions.

> The experiments that Wilbur and Orville had carried out with their latest glider in 1901 were far from encouraging. Reflecting on their problems, Wilbur observed: "We saw that the calculations upon which all flying machines had been based were unreliable, and that all were simply groping in the dark. Having set out with absolute faith in the existing scientific data, we were driven to doubt one thing after another, till finally, after two years of experiment, we cast it all aside, and decided to rely entirely on our own investigations."
>
> In the gaslit workroom behind their bicycle shop, Wilbur and Orville began to compile their own data. They wanted to test different types of wing surfaces and obtain accurate air-pressure tables. To do this, they built a wind tunnel—a wooden box 6 feet long with a glass viewing window on top and a fan at one end. It wasn't the world's first wind tunnel, but it would be the first to yield valuable results for the construction of a practical airplane.

Before and After

Before and after is a technique for ordering information in chronological, or time, order. Like cause and effect, this type of organization is useful for showing a relationship between events. A writer explains or describes a condition that existed before a certain event then explains or describes how the condition changed after the event.

Take a Look

In the following paragraphs, the writer uses the before-and-after method to describe changes that resulted from an invention.

Before digital cameras were invented, pictures took much longer to process. Although Polaroid cameras provided images fairly quickly, their quality was not as good as most standard cameras. People had to drop off film at a processing center, then go back hours or even days later to get their pictures.

Now that pictures can be digitized, people are able to have instant, high-quality images. Also, there is no need to wait for the mail to deliver pictures to relatives far away. With a digital camera, you can send pictures in minutes using the Internet.

Reading Your Writing

The purpose of expository text is to inform the reader. Expository text includes factual information about people or events or explains how to do something. There are many ways to present information in expository writing; choose a method that is appropriate for your purpose and subject. Carefully planning your expository writing will help you create a well-organized report or essay that is easy for readers to follow.

Ways to Develop Persuasive Writing

Persuasive writing is used to convince readers to think, feel, or act a certain way. Because this is not an easy task, it is especially important that you have a clear purpose and defined audience when writing to persuade. Once you have decided these two things, you should think about the best way to present your argument.

There are two techniques for influencing the reader. One approach is to support your opinion with facts and reasons. The second method is to appeal to readers' interests or emotions. Choose the technique that is most appropriate for your audience.

The organization of your persuasive writing is another important factor to consider. One option is a question-and-answer format. This type of persuasive writing begins with a question. The answers that follow it contain the persuasive points of your argument. Another way to organize persuasive writing is by presenting your reasons in order of importance. Order your reasons from least to most important. This leaves readers with your most convincing point fresh in their minds.

Take a Look

In the following persuasive paragraph, the writer's opinion is supported with facts and reasons.

> Start with a question.

> State an opinion.

Why should our school serve breakfast? They should do it because of all the positive effects it will have on students. If students could eat breakfast at school, they would be better able to concentrate and learn. Studies have shown that students who eat breakfast score better on tests. Serving breakfast at school would also help students eat more healthfully. Often, students grab a doughnut or other quick snack at home. These foods are high in fat and calories. If the school served breakfast, the dietician would make sure that students were offered nutritious meals. Finally, teachers would also benefit from students eating a good breakfast. Schools that serve breakfast report that students are less likely to be tardy or absent, and they have better behavior.

> Support the opinion with facts.

Appealing to readers' interests and emotions is a persuasive technique used by many advertisers. This kind of persuasive writing uses words that are likely to affect or to change the mind of the reader.

Take a Look

The writer of this persuasive paragraph hopes to convince readers of the benefits of working as a newspaper carrier.

If you like to meet people, be outdoors, and make money, we have the perfect job for you! Call the distribution office today to begin your exciting career delivering newspapers. With a paper route, your work is done early in the day, leaving evenings free for other activities. You can meet the interesting people in your town as you travel through new neighborhoods but also enjoy the freedom and independence of working alone. Improve your health with plenty of fresh air and exercise. Believe it or not, you get paid for all of this! Not only will you receive an attractive salary from the newspaper but you get to keep all the tips you receive from our generous customers.

State a purpose.

Begin with the weakest reason.

End with the strongest reason.

Try It

Identify words and phrases in the sample paragraph that appeal to readers' interests or emotions.

Reading Your Writing

The two techniques for persuasive writing are using facts and reasons to support an opinion and appealing to readers' interests and emotions. Identify your purpose and audience to decide how to best present your argument. Using a question-and-answer format or organizing your reasons by order of importance are effective ways to persuade readers.

Ingredients for Writing a Story

There are many different kinds of stories and stories about many different subjects. However, successful stories all have some things in common. They include interesting characters, an entertaining plot, a vivid setting, and an appropriate point of view. Learning how to develop and combine these elements will help you create effective stories.

Characterization

Characterization is a writer's way of showing what the characters in a story are like by telling what they do, say, think, and feel. Strong characters help readers connect with your story. If your audience cares about what happens to your characters, they will want to keep reading.

A story usually has at least one main character and one or more supporting characters. The characters might be real or imaginary, and they should have distinct personalities. Writers often use dialogue to make characters more realistic by showing how they speak, what they think or feel, and how they interact with each other.

One way to develop a character in the prewriting stage is to create a word web. Write the character's name in the center of the web, and write his or her traits in the surrounding spaces. You might also include information about the character's past, plans for the future, and relationships with other characters.

Take a Look

This web shows some features of one of the main characters in the story "The Frog Prince."

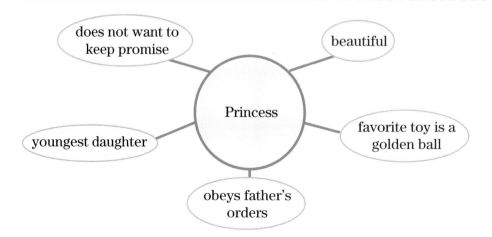

- does not want to keep promise
- beautiful
- Princess
- favorite toy is a golden ball
- youngest daughter
- obeys father's orders

Plot

The **plot** is the chain of events in a story. A plot usually consists of a problem and actions the characters take to solve it. The events of a story—including a beginning, middle, and end—are the story's **plot line.**

Certain things usually happen in each part of a story. In the beginning of a story, the characters, setting, and problem are introduced. In the middle of a story, the characters experience one or more **conflicts** as they try to solve the problem. Excitement occurs when the conflicts take place. The highest point of interest, called the **climax,** takes place when the problem begins to be resolved. The end, or conclusion, of a story finishes telling how the problem was solved.

Take a Look

Here is a diagram showing the plot of "The Frog Prince."

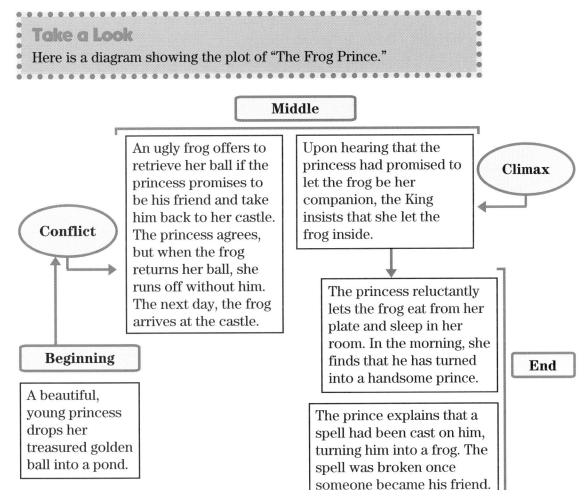

Middle

An ugly frog offers to retrieve her ball if the princess promises to be his friend and take him back to her castle. The princess agrees, but when the frog returns her ball, she runs off without him. The next day, the frog arrives at the castle.

Upon hearing that the princess had promised to let the frog be her companion, the King insists that she let the frog inside.

Climax

Conflict

Beginning

A beautiful, young princess drops her treasured golden ball into a pond.

The princess reluctantly lets the frog eat from her plate and sleep in her room. In the morning, she finds that he has turned into a handsome prince.

End

The prince explains that a spell had been cast on him, turning him into a frog. The spell was broken once someone became his friend.

Setting

The **setting** of a story is the time and place in which the events occur. A good story includes plenty of details that create a vivid setting for the reader. Interesting settings will help hold your reader's attention. There are several things a writer should consider when planning the setting.

▶ The setting of a story is *when* the events take place. A story can be set in the past, the present, or the future. Writers must decide how specific their references to time will be. Sometimes it is important to specify the year in which a story occurs. Sometimes the writer will establish the season of the year, the day of the week, or the time of day.

▶ The setting of a story is also *where* the events take place. The setting may be general, such as a state or country, or specific, such as a pond in the forest behind the king's castle.

▶ A story may have more than one setting. Each new setting should be described carefully so that the reader understands the change in time and place. To add order to your story and avoid confusing readers, limit the number of settings you use. If the action is occurring in too many locations, readers might get lost.

▶ Make the setting interesting by using details that appeal to the reader's senses. Describe how a place looks, sounds, feels, and smells.

Take a Look

One morning long ago, in a forest behind the king's great castle, a beautiful young princess went out to play. The princess breathed in the scent of spring flowers as she skipped toward a pond at the center of the forest. In her delicate hands she held a smooth, glistening, golden ball that was her most precious possession. When she reached the peaceful pond, still covered with morning mist, the ball slipped from her hands and into the cool water.

Try It

Look at the above paragraph. What words does the writer use to create a vivid setting for the story?

Point of View

Point of view is the position of the storyteller, or narrator, in relation to the story. The narrator might be a character in the story or an outside observer who is not part of the action. It is important for writers to use a point of view that is appropriate for a particular story. Most stories are written from either a first-person or third-person point of view.

First-Person Point of View

▶ The story is told by a character in the story.

▶ The narrator uses the first-person pronouns *I*, *me*, *my*, *we*, *us*, and *our*.

▶ The story gives the thoughts and feelings of only one character—the one who is narrating the story.

> I couldn't believe that frog was calling for me outside our castle. I tried to pretend I didn't notice, but my father said, "Don't you hear someone calling your name?" Then I had no choice but to open the door.

Third-Person Point of View

▶ The story is told by an observer who is not part of the action of the story.

▶ The narrator uses the third-person pronouns *he*, *she*, *they*, *him*, *her*, *them*, and *their*.

▶ The narrator may tell about the thoughts and feelings of the characters or simply report what the characters say and do.

> The princess became nervous as she heard the frog calling her name. She pretended not to notice. The king, who was irritated by the shouting, said to his daughter, "Don't you hear someone calling your name?" Then the princess had no choice but to open the door.

The point of view a writer uses in a story controls the kind of information readers will get. Do you want to describe all of the characters' thoughts and feelings, or only those of the narrator? Use only one point of view throughout the story.

Reading Your Writing

Characterization, plot, setting, and point of view are the elements that every good writer must consider when writing a story. Combining these ingredients with skill will help you write a story that is interesting and memorable to readers.

Using Dialogue

Dialogue is written conversation between two or more characters in a story, and it is a powerful tool for writers who know how to use it well. Dialogue can make stories more natural and characters more real and interesting. It also keeps a story moving at a nice pace. Instead of getting bogged down in long descriptions about what characters are thinking or feeling, writers can express it in dialogue. Here are some other reasons to use dialogue in your writing.

Purposes of Dialogue

▶ Dialogue makes the characters seem more believable by showing readers what they think and feel.

> "I could have died of embarrassment," Molly wailed.

▶ Dialogue makes stories seem realistic.

> Parker asked, "Did anybody notice?"

▶ Dialogue keeps readers interested in the story.

> "Only everybody in my health class. They all turned and stared right at me," cried Molly.

▶ Dialogue keeps the story action moving along.

> "Well, I'm sure they've all heard a stomach growl before. Come on, it's time for us to go meet David," Parker replied as he turned to leave.

It is important for writers to know and use proper mechanics for dialogue, such as quotation marks and indenting. Without these conventions of writing dialogue, readers might become confused about who is saying what.

Dialogue adds interest to your writing, but you can make your dialogue more interesting as well by using a variety of verbs in the speaker tags. (A speaker tag comes before or after the quotation and includes the name of the person speaking.) Instead of using the word *said* all the time, use words like *announced, responded, wondered, answered, suggested, sighed, laughed,* and *remarked*.

Sometimes a line of dialogue does not need a speaker tag because the speaker is clear, as in the following example:

"Why can't Austin spend the night?" asked Ryan.
"I told you, your sister already asked to have a friend over," answered Mother.
"That isn't fair."
"I'm sorry, but you know the rules."

While dialogue is interesting, you don't want to use too much of it at once. Remember to break up dialogue with descriptions and action. For example, tell what the characters are doing while they are speaking.

The following excerpt from the fiction book *School Spirit* by Johanna Hurwitz includes a nice balance of dialogue and text.

> "That's not our garbage," Lucas complained. "People waiting at the bus stop on the corner by the school are the ones who throw a lot of that stuff in the yard."
> "We still should clean it up," said Zoe. "If someone from the school board comes by, they don't know whose junk it is. They just see it's in our school yard. It looks like we don't care."
> "Sometimes there's garbage inside the school too," said Julio, feeling guilty. Just this morning he had kicked a crumpled ball of paper from one end of the hallway to the other without picking it up.

Try It

What can you tell about the three characters in the above example based on their dialogue?

Reading Your Writing

Dialogue is written conversation between characters in a story. When you write stories with more than one character, you will probably use dialogue. Try to write dialogue that tells readers about the characters, keeps the readers interested, and moves the story along.

Vocabulary

If you made a list of every word you know and use, that would be your vocabulary. As a writer, you need to keep adding to that list, no matter how long it is. The more words you know, the better chance you have of communicating exactly what you want to say to your readers.

Compound Words

A **compound word** is a word that is made by joining two or more smaller words. The words in a compound word may be nouns, a noun and another kind of word, or two words that are not nouns. A compound word may be written in one of three ways: *closed*, *hyphenated*, or *open*. A closed compound has no space between the words. An open compound does. In a hyphenated compound, a hyphen separates the words.

Closed	Open	Hyphenated
classmate	tape recorder	baby-sit
grandfather	sea bass	self-confident
barefoot	ozone layer	home-cooked
landscape	post office	far-fetched
somewhat	home run	hand-me-down

Fun Fact

The word *compound* is itself a part of several different compound words, including *compound fracture*, *compound interest*, and *compound microscope*.

How do you know when a compound word should be closed, open, or hyphenated? There are no clear rules, so if you aren't sure, look up the word in the dictionary.

Often, you can tell the meaning of a compound word by studying its smaller words.

I ate a *home-cooked* meal. *home + cooked = cooked* at *home*

The new cars were in the *showroom*. *show + room = room* where cars are *shown*

He wore an *overcoat*. *coat* worn *over* clothes

Sometimes, you can't figure out a compound word's meaning based on the words that make it up. For example, *outstanding* doesn't mean "*standing out*side"; it means "excellent."

Try It

Lifeguard, *midnight*, and *rainbow* are common compound words. What are the complete definitions of these words?

Writing Connection

Using compound words allows you to be specific in your writing without using unnecessary words. For example, it's much clearer and easier to write "I stood at one edge of the waterfall," rather than "I stood at the edge of the place where the water was falling over the rocks."

Antonyms

Antonyms are words with opposite, or nearly opposite, meanings. The following are pairs of antonyms.

night, day	fast, slow	friend, enemy
cheerful, depressed	tie, loosen	innocent, guilty
greedy, generous	spend, earn	often, seldom

Some words have more than one meaning, and therefore they have more than one antonym.

lost, found	dull, clever
lost, won	dull, interesting
	dull, sharp

Antonyms can be used in writing to contrast people, things, or ideas. Notice how antonyms are used below to contrast two brothers.

The two brothers were different in every way. Whereas John was cautious and timid, Jake was careless and bold. John was polite and neat; Jake was rude and messy. John found it difficult to talk to people, but it was easy for Jake to talk to anyone. John usually agreed with every opinion he heard; Jake, on the other hand, argued with everyone.

If you're having trouble finding an antonym for a word, use a thesaurus. Many thesauruses include antonyms as well as synonyms. Most computer word processing programs also include an electronic thesaurus. Keep in mind that many words do not have antonyms, for example, *desk, gasoline, decide, camp,* and *picture.*

Try It

Replace the underlined words with antonyms to express the opposite meaning. The <u>shallow</u> lake gleamed brightly in the <u>sunlight</u>.

Synonyms

Synonyms are words that have the same or nearly the same meaning. For example, *frighten* and *scare* are synonyms because they have the same or almost the same meanings. Here are some more groups of synonyms.

grateful, appreciative, thankful   stop, halt, end
trash, waste, garbage   live, dwell, reside
boring, tiresome, tedious   disaster, calamity, catastrophe
weak, feeble, frail   tiny, wee, small

When writing, it's important to use words that are precise. That is, they are exactly the right words to communicate your thoughts. Read the paragraphs below. Notice how the second paragraph uses more exact words to communicate.

When Mount Vesuvius erupted, hot ash and gas <u>came out</u> of the top. The hot ash and gas <u>came down</u> the mountain as fast as 70 miles per hour. Then, thick sheets of <u>hot</u> magma <u>came down</u> the mountain.

When Mount Vesuvius erupted, fiery ash and gas <u>spewed out</u> of the summit. The burning ash and gas <u>raced down</u> the slope as rapidly as 70 miles per hour. Then, thick sheets of <u>glowing</u> magma <u>rumbled down</u> the mountain.

Some words have meanings that are similar, but not exactly the same. You must decide which word expresses your thoughts exactly. For example, some words that have nearly the same meaning as <u>walk</u> include <u>stroll</u>, <u>stride</u>, <u>trudge</u>, and <u>pace</u>. However, because these words have slightly different meanings from <u>walk</u>, they can't be substituted for one another.

Fun Fact

Can you think of a one-word synonym for the word *synonym*? Believe it or not, there are no synonyms for *synonym*!

Try It

How could you use synonyms to make the following sentence clearer and more exact?
▶ *The girl ran up to the ball and kicked it into the goal.*

Analogies

An **analogy** contains two pairs of words that are related to each other in the same way. There are many ways that words in analogies can be related to one another. Some of these are described in this lesson.

Synonyms The relationship between the words in the pairs below is that they mean the same, or almost the same.

> *begin* is to *start* as *shout* is to *yell*

Antonyms The relationship between the words in the pairs below is that they are opposites or almost opposites.

> *build* is to *destroy* as *awake* is to *sleep*

Part to Whole The relationship between the words in each of these pairs is that the first word names a *part* of the second word, which names the *whole*.

> *toe* is to *foot* as *page* is to *book*

Object to Group The relationship between the words in each of these pairs is that the first word names an *object* that belongs to a larger *group*, or *class*, of objects.

> *broccoli* is to *vegetable* as *green* is to *color*

Object to Use The relationship between the words in each of these pairs is that the first word names an *object* whose *use* is described by the second word.

> *pot* is to *cook* as *phone* is to *talk*

Connotations

Would you rather be called "smart" or "brainy"? "Funny" or "clownish"? You likely would choose one word over the other because of its connotation. **Connotation** is the feeling a word creates in the reader, or a word's suggested meaning. The words *clever* and *crafty*, for example, both have the general meaning of "smart." But *clever* has a positive connotation. A *clever* person is someone who knows how to solve problems. *Crafty*, on the other hand, has a negative connotation. A *crafty* person might be someone who is dishonest or has a hidden motive.

Here are some words with similar meanings but different connotations: positive, negative, and neutral.

Positive	Negative	Neutral
scent	odor	smell
slender	bony	thin
delicate	weak	breakable
observant	calculating	careful
thrifty	cheap	frugal
chat	gossip	talk

When you write or speak, you often choose a word from among a group of synonyms because of its connotation. For example, consider the sentence below. Because of the surrounding words, or context, one word makes more sense than the other in the sentence.

The (trip/trek) through the desert took its toll on the survivors. Although both *trip* and *trek* have the basic meaning of "journey," *trip* suggests a casual and even a fun journey. *Trek* suggests a difficult and maybe even dangerous journey.

Try It
Which word would you choose for the sentence below, based on the context?
▶ *The teacher asked for (silence, tranquility) during the test.*

Writers use the connotations of words to produce positive, negative, and neutral images in their readers' minds. For example, if a writer wants his or her readers to like a certain character, the writer will use words with positive connotations to describe that character. If you read that a character is kind, generous, and patient, you probably will like that character.

Below are two paragraphs that present the same basic information. Because some of the words chosen have different connotations, the tone and meaning of each paragraph is different.

The proud parents gazed at the performance on the stage. Their tiny child, dressed in a rose-colored tutu, tiptoed out from behind the curtain. The parents leaned forward eagerly, their faces radiant with happiness.

The haughty parents watched the presentation on the stage. Their tiny child, dressed in a pink tutu, stepped out from behind the curtain. The parents bent forward anxiously, their faces shining with satisfaction.

Try It

Look at the pair of sentences below. How do the underlined words affect the tone and meaning of the sentences?

▶ *The couple <u>looked</u> at the other diners as they <u>ate</u> their meals.*

▶ *The couple <u>glared</u> at the other diners as they <u>gobbled</u> their meals.*

Writing Connection

Knowing the connotations of words helps you choose words that fit the context of what you are writing. By choosing the words that have exactly the right shade of meaning, you make your writing accurate and precise. In addition, you create a certain tone, sending your readers the exact message that you intend.

Homophones

Homophones are two or more words that sound the same but have different meanings and spellings. *To*, *too*, and *two* are examples of homophones. Because homophones sound the same, it is easy to write one word—for example, *too*—when you mean another—*to*.

Here are some common homophones.

to/too/two
Frank bicycled to the store.
His house is too far away.
He bought two comic books.

by/buy
The baseball fan walked by the concession stand.
She decided to buy some popcorn for a dollar.

hole/whole
The bagel has a hole in the middle.
I ate the whole bagel.

pair/pare/pear
I need a clean pair of socks.
Grandpa can pare an apple in ten seconds.
This pear is ripe and juicy.

whether/weather
Mrs. Gonzalez doesn't know whether she'll come with us.
What's the weather going to be like for our field trip?

their/there/they're
Their dog is sick.
They're going to take him to the vet.
The dog doesn't like to go there.

your/you're
Your bus is leaving!
Hurry, or you're going to miss it!

its/it's
The monkey lost its toy.
Oh, it's over there!

hear/here
Do you hear that beautiful music?
Sit over here and listen to it.

aloud/allowed
The writer read the story aloud.
Skateboarding on the sidewalk is not allowed.

altar/alter
The priest stood before the altar.
The architect decided to alter the plan.

base/bass
The base of the trophy was inscribed with her name.
The singer's bass voice filled the room.

More Homophones

knight/night
The armor in the museum once belonged to a knight.
My dad goes to bed late at night.

rain/reign/rein
The rain is pouring down.
The queen will reign for many years.
The horseback rider let go of the rein.

aisle/I'll/isle
The father walked his daughter down the aisle.
I'll bring the cake and candles.
The isle was in the middle of the Pacific Ocean.

carat/caret/carrot
Her engagement ring held a diamond of one carat.
The editor used a caret to insert text.
Did you feed the rabbit carrots?

for/fore/four
I picked some flowers for my mother
The captain surveyed the fore part of the ship.
Four comes after three.

son/sun
Our teacher has one son and two daughters.
The sun shines brightly.

Try It

Which homophones correctly complete the sentence?
▶ *Did you (here/hear) that she (died, dyed) her hair green on St. Patrick's Day?*

Writing Connection

Because homophones sound the same, it's easy to make a mistake by writing one homophone when you really mean another. By learning the different meanings of words that sound alike, you can avoid misspellings, which distract readers.

Homographs

Homographs are words that are spelled the same but have different meanings and different origins. For example, the word *rest* has two meanings: "relax" and "the remainder."

The homographs in each group of sentences below are pronounced the same.

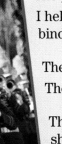

The <u>band</u> began to play a song. (group of musicians)

I held the papers together with a rubber <u>band</u>. (a thin strip used for binding)

The birch tree's <u>bark</u> is smooth and silvery. (covering of a tree)

The watchdog began to <u>bark</u>. (sound a dog makes)

The <u>cobbler</u> repaired my shoes. (person who makes or mends shoes)

That cherry <u>cobbler</u> was delicious! (fruit pie with a top crust only)

The <u>compound</u> was guarded by dogs. (an enclosed yard)

That sentence has a <u>compound</u> subject. (having more than one part)

I made a sandwich on the <u>counter</u>. (long table in a kitchen or store)

Her argument was so sound that I could not <u>counter</u> it. (oppose)

I chose to use the blue <u>counter</u> for the board game. (metal or plastic piece used in counting or games)

The judge reviewed the <u>file</u> that the lawyer handed him. (folder in which papers are kept)

The groomer used a <u>file</u> to flatten the dog's claws. (steel tool)

The sweater was made of <u>fine</u> wool. (high quality)

The library charges a <u>fine</u> for overdue books. (money paid as punishment)

My mother works for an accounting <u>firm</u>. (company)

The cake will be finished when the middle is <u>firm</u>. (solid; not weak)

The dogs were led by a <u>husky</u>. (sled dog)

Sled dogs need to be <u>husky</u>. (big and strong)

Some homographs are pronounced differently. Some of these words, which have only one syllable, are shown below.

Please <u>close</u> the door. (shut)
Make sure that no one is standing <u>close</u> to it. (near)

A single <u>tear</u> slid down her cheek. (drop of liquid from the eye)
Can your <u>tear</u> that sheet of paper in half? (rip)

Other homographs are pronounced differently because the accent shifts. For example, the word *present* may mean "gift" or "give," depending on which syllable is accented. More words with more than one syllable that are spelled the same but pronounced differently are shown below.

Snow must be <u>compact</u> to form a snowball. (tightly packed)
The members made a <u>compact</u> to keep their club a secret. (agreement)

I had to <u>console</u> my little sister when she hurt her knee. (comfort)
The CDs are in the <u>console</u> with the stereo. (cabinet)

We came in the house through the side <u>entrance</u>. (place of entry)
The singer's voice will <u>entrance</u> you. (fill with delight or wonder)

I'll be out in a <u>minute</u>. (sixty seconds)
There was only a <u>minute</u> difference between the two paintings. (very small)

A sphere is a solid <u>object</u>. (thing)
I <u>object</u> to not getting dessert! (protest)

Wasn't that album produced as a <u>record</u> before it was a CD? (musical disk)
We will <u>record</u> the statistics of the baseball game. (write down)

Fun Fact

Words with multiple meanings are often used in writing for a humorous effect. For example, most puns are plays on words that have the same sounds but different meanings.

Try It

How is the word *record* pronounced in each use below?
▶ *Did you record the lyrics of the song from the record?*

Greek and Latin Roots

Many English words have Greek and Latin roots. Often, when you know the meaning of a word's root or roots you can figure out the word's general meaning.

Greek Roots

Study the Greek roots and their meanings given below.

Root	Meaning	Sample Word and Definition
bio	life	**bio**graphy: the story of a person's life
geo	earth	**geo**logy: the study of the earth
gram	letter; written	tele**gram**: written message
graph	write	auto**graph**: person's signature
mech	machine	**mech**anic: person who works on machines
meter	measure	baro**meter**: instrument that measures pressure of the atmosphere
phon	sound	**phon**ics: study of sounds
photo	light	**photo**graphy: process of producing images on film using light
therm	heat	**therm**ometer: instrument that measures temperature

In your reading, be alert for words that have the roots described in this lesson. Try to figure out the meanings of these words based on their roots.

Try It

What do you think *geothermal* energy is? Even if you're never heard the term, you can figure it out based on the meanings of its roots.

Latin Roots

Study the Latin roots and their meanings given below.

Root	Meaning	Sample Words and Definition
aqua	water	*aquatic:* growing or living in water
aud	hear	*inaudible:* not able to be heard
dic	speak	*dictate:* to say something aloud to be recorded
form	shape	*transform:* to change the shape or appearance of
ject	throw	*eject:* to throw out; cause to leave
ped	foot	*pedal:* a lever worked by the foot
pop	people	*popular:* liked by many people
port	carry	*portable:* capable of being carried
struct	build	*structure:* building; anything that is built
vac	empty	*vacant:* empty

Fun Fact

The English vocabulary is estimated to consist of more than 1 million words—more than any other language in the world.

Keep in mind that a few roots have the same spelling but mean different things. For example, the Greek root **ped** means "child," whereas the Latin root **ped** means "foot." Also, different roots can mean the same thing; the Greek root **pod** also means "foot," as in "podiatrist."

Try It

The prefix *bi-* means "two." What is a *biped*?

Writing Connection

Knowing root words is a valuable tool. You can figure out the meanings of unfamiliar words that include root words that you know. In addition, your knowledge of root words will help you use words precisely and increase your vocabulary, which will add variety to your writing.

Prefixes

A **prefix** is one or more letters added to the beginning of a root or base word that changes the word's meaning. Some prefixes have the same or similar meanings. Knowing the meanings of prefixes will help you figure out the meanings of unfamiliar words. Study the list of prefixes below. Notice how each prefix changes the meaning of the base word.

Prefix	Meaning	Sample Words
anti-	against	antigravity, antisocial
auto-	self	autobiography, automobile
bi-	two	bicycle, biplane
dis-	not; opposite	discontinue, disappear
en-	in; into	enlist, engrave
fore-	in front of; occurring earlier	forehand, foremost
il-	not	illogical, illegal
im-	not	immobile, impatient
in-	not	insane, inactive
inter-	among; between	intersection, intercontinental
intra-	within	intramural, intrastate
ir-	not	irresponsible, irregular
mid-	middle	midyear, midnight
mis-	not; wrong	misbehave, misfortune
non-	not	nonfiction, nonsense
over-	too much	overpriced, overdo
pre-	before	prepay, preheat
re-	again	rewrite, remake
semi-	half	semicircle, semiannual
tri-	three	triplet, tricycle
un-	not; the opposite of	unwilling; untie

Here are some words with prefixes used in sentences. Notice how each prefix changes the meaning of the word and the meaning of the sentence.

Jaywalking is <u>illegal</u> in our city.
Gandhi believed in <u>nonviolent</u> demonstrations to bring about change.
The theater showed five <u>previews</u> before the feature presentation.
The executive was fired for <u>irresponsible</u> behavior.
The writer <u>enclosed</u> a stamped, self-addressed envelope.
The center fielder made an <u>unbelievable</u> catch.
The diners thought the four-star restaurant was <u>overrated</u>.

Keep in mind that you can't add a prefix to any word you choose and make a new word. For example, although you might want to combine the prefix *dis-* with the word *speak* to form *disspeak*, meaning "speak incorrectly," it is not a word.

If you are unsure about adding a prefix to a word, look it up in the dictionary. Most dictionaries have lists of words that begin with the same prefix.

In some cases, even if you know the meaning of a word's prefix, you might not be able to figure out the word's meaning. This often happens because the root also has an ending and the root itself may not be obvious. Other times, you may not know the meaning of the base word. You must then look up the meaning of the base word or the word with its prefix in the dictionary. Study the words with prefixes below. Which words' meanings could you figure out if you separated the base word from its ending?

Word	Prefix	Base Word	Meaning
illegible	*il-*	legible	not readable
distrustful	*dis-*	trustful	not trusting
irreparable	*ir-*	reparable	not fixable
nonresistant	*non-*	resistant	not fighting back or opposing
interchangeable	*inter-*	changeable	able to change places with another

Try It

Which word in parentheses best completes the sentence below? Why?

▶ *The shortstop (overacted/reacted) expertly to the ball hit sharply to her left.*

Writing Connection

By learning the meanings of prefixes, you will understand how they change the meanings of words, which in turn will increase your vocabulary. The more words you know, the better you will be able to express yourself in writing.

Suffixes

A **suffix** is one or more letters added to the end of a root or base word that changes the word's meaning. A suffix can also change the part of speech of a word. For example, adding **-ful** to the noun *fear* makes the word *fearful,* an adjective.

Some suffixes have the same or similar meanings. Knowing the meanings of suffixes will help you figure out the meanings of unfamiliar words. Study the list of suffixes below. Notice how each suffix changes the meaning of the base word.

Suffix	Meaning	Sample Words
-able/-ible	is, able to be	preventable, digestible
-er/-or	one who	painter, actor
-ful	full of	faithful, helpful
-ious	state or quality of	rebellious, gracious
-ish	relating to	selfish, childish
-ist	one who performs or practices	violinist, biologist
-less	without	childless, hopeless
-ly	like; resembling	grandmotherly, friendly
-ous	full of	perilous, joyous
-ion	state or quality of	depression, attention
-ment	state or condition of	resentment, excitement
-ness	state; condition; quality of	darkness, kindness
-ure	action; process	failure, exposure
-ward	direction	westward, homeward
-y	being or having	chewy, rainy

Here are some words with suffixes used in sentences. Notice how each suffix changes the meaning of the word.

The spread of the virus is <u>preventable</u>.
There will be no more <u>discussion</u> on the topic.
The doctor reassured the patient that the <u>procedure</u> was <u>painless</u>.
The older child was <u>helpful</u> with the new baby.
The weather was warm and <u>cloudy</u>.

Rules for Adding Suffixes

When you add suffixes to base words, follow the rules below.

1. If a suffix begins with a vowel and the base word ends with a silent *e,* drop the *e* before adding the suffix.

   desire + able = desirable
   space + ious = spacious
   flute + ist = flutist

2. If a base word ends with a *y,* change the *y* to *i* before adding the suffix—unless the suffix begins with an *i.*

   plenty + ful = plentiful
   rely + able = reliable
   fifty + ish = fiftyish

Keep in mind that you can't add a suffix to any word you choose and make a new word. For example, although you might want to create a word from the base word *pretty* and the suffix *-ish*, which means "like," *prettyish* is not a word. If you are unsure about adding a suffix to a word or root, look it up in the dictionary.

In some cases, even if you know the meaning of a word's suffix, you might not be able to figure out the word's meaning because you don't know the meaning of the base word. For example, you may come across the word *guileless.* Even though you know that the suffix *-less* means "without," if you don't know what the base word *guile* means, then you won't be able to define the word. In this case, you must look up the meaning of the base word or the word with its suffix in the dictionary.

Try It

What are the differences among the words *quiet, quietly,* and *quietness*?

Writing Connection

By learning the meanings of suffixes, you will understand how they change the meanings of words, which in turn will increase your vocabulary. The more words you know, the better you will be able to express yourself in writing.

Context Clues

What do you do when you come across an unfamiliar word in your reading, and you don't have a dictionary handy? You probably try to figure out the meaning of the word by looking at the context. The **context** is the words and sentences that surround the unfamiliar word. The context usually gives you clues about the meaning of the unfamiliar word.

Tips for Using Context Clues to Figure Out the Meanings of Words

▶ In a *definition*, the writer provides the meaning of the word within the sentence or surrounding sentences. Look for clue words such as *or*, *that is*, and *in other words*. These all point to a definition.

> The *curator*, or person responsible for a museum's collections and exhibits, loved her job.

▶ Some writers *compare* or *contrast* the unfamiliar word with another word that you might know. Look for comparison and contrast words, such as *also*, *like*, *too*, *but*, *unlike*, and *on the other hand*.

> The *peregrine's* body, like those of other predatory birds, is well adapted for hunting.

▶ *Cause-and-effect* relationships are indicated by words such as *because*, *as a result*, and *therefore*.

> Because my father is an *optimistic* man, he tends to see the brighter side of a situation.

▶ Often, an unfamiliar word appears in a *series*. You can sometimes figure out the meaning of the word based on the other words.

> Dung beetles, burying beetles, and *nut weevils* all lay eggs.

▶ Sometimes, you just have to use the general context to figure out the meaning of a word. There are no specific clues available for you to use.

> Smoking is known to be a *detriment* to good health.

How could you use context clues to figure out the meaning of *fickle* in the passage below?

Fiona is the most *fickle* person I know. Her twin sister Felisha, on the other hand, never changes her mind.

The first sentence doesn't provide any context clues about the meaning of *fickle;* all we know about Fiona is that she is fickle. However, the words "on the other hand," in the second sentence, signal that a contrast between the sisters is being described. Felisha never changes her mind. Therefore, a fickle person must be one who always changes his or her mind.

Words with More Than One Meaning

In some cases, you might come across a word that has more than one meaning. You can use the context clues on the previous page to help you figure out which meaning of the word the author intended. Knowing what part of speech the unfamiliar word is can also help you figure out its meaning. For example, the word *fair* can be a noun or an adjective, and it has many different meanings: "unbiased or just," "a temporary amusement park," "attractive," and "clear." How can you tell which meaning fits the sentence below?

The festival planners were hoping for *fair* weather during the weekend.

First, you can determine that *fair* is used as an adjective because it modifies the word *weather.* Thus, in this sentence, *fair* does not mean "a temporary amusement park." By then studying the word's context, you can determine that in this sentence, *fair* means "clear."

Fun Fact

The word *context* comes from the Latin word *contexere,* which means "to weave together." Indeed, when you write, you weave together words, providing your readers with a context full of meaning.

Try It

Use the context clues in the sentence below to figure out the meaning of *acrophobia.* What type of context clue did you use?

▶ *People with acrophobia, or a fear of heights, should stay away from the Empire State Building.*

Across-the-Curriculum Words

In school, you use vocabulary words that are related to each subject that you study.

Math

consecutive: following one right after the other in sequence
convert: to change from one unit to another
expression: a symbol or combination of symbols and signs that represents a quantity or operation
finite: having a limited number
formula: a rule or principle stated as an equation
graph: an equation plotted on coordinate axes
integer: a natural number (such as 1 and 2), the negative of a natural number, or 0
numeral: a symbol representing a number, such as 10
profit: the difference between the cost to produce an item and the amount it sells for
rate: the amount of one thing compared to the amount of another
ratio: the proportional relationship between two numbers
sequence: an ordered set of numbers

Science

acid precipitation: rain, snow, or fog that is polluted with acidic chemicals
amphibian: a cold-blooded animal that lives near water
atmosphere: air that surrounds Earth
atom: the smallest unit of a chemical element that has properties of that element
buoyancy: the ability to float in water or gas
cell: the basic unit of living organisms
constellation: a group of stars
evaporation: the change from a liquid or solid state into vapor
habitat: the place where an animal or plant naturally lives
larva: an insect in a wormlike stage of growth
membrane: a thin layer of tissue lining or covering a body surface
nucleus: the central part of an atom
optical: relating to vision
sedimentary: a type of rock made from particles of rock or soil
smog: a combination of smoke and fog

Social Studies

amendment: a change to the U.S. Constitution

Capitol: the building in which U.S. Congress meets in Washington, D.C.

civil rights: individual rights of citizens guaranteed by the U.S. Constitution

currency: money

export: to sell or carry goods to other countries

frontier: an imaginary line that marks the division between settled and unexplored territory, as during the settlement of the United States

inflation: the rise in the average prices of goods and services

natural resource: a material found in nature that is useful to humans

province: a political division of a country, similar to states

ratify: to formally approve, as constitutional amendments

secede: to withdraw as in a state *seceding* from the Union

veto: to refuse to approve a bill or a proposed law

Health

allergy: a strong reaction to certain substances

cardiac: relating to the heart

chronic: long-lasting or recurring, as an illness

contagious: easily spread from one person to another

diagnosis: the identification of a disease based on symptoms

diet: the food and drink consumed by a person

epidemic: a rapid spread of a disease in an area

hygiene: practices contributing to good health, such as brushing teeth

symptom: a change in normal body functions that indicates disease

toxin: a poison produced by animal or plant cells

virus: a microscopic agent that causes disease in humans, animals, and plants

Try It

Choose a word from one of the lists in this lesson. Define the word using your own words.

Adjectives and Adverbs

Have you ever taken a photograph that's out of focus? It's hard to tell whether people are smiling or frowning, or exactly what they are wearing. When you don't choose precise adjectives and adverbs, your writing can be as fuzzy as a photo that is out of focus. Your readers are faced with the chore of trying to make sense out of cloudy ideas and blurry images.

Adjectives and adverbs describe, or modify, other words. Adjectives modify nouns. Adverbs modify verbs, adjectives, and other adverbs. Using modifiers that appeal to the senses can help make your writing more specific, vivid, and interesting.

As modifiers, adjectives and adverbs limit the meanings of the words they describe or, in other words, make the meanings more specific. Read the two sentences below.

> The dog barked.
> The tiny, snow-white dog barked shrilly.

In the first sentence, the noun *dog* could mean any kind of dog—a huge dog, a small dog, a white dog, a hunting dog, and so on. Also, the verb *bark* could mean any kind of bark—high-pitched, deep, continuous, frantic, and so on. Because the words *dog* and *bark* are so general, and because there are no modifiers to limit their meanings, the reader comes away with a fuzzy image after reading this sentence.

In the second sentence, the meaning of the general noun *dog* is limited to mean only a dog that is tiny and snow-white. The general verb *bark* is limited by the adverb *shrilly*. These modifiers also appeal to the senses, giving the reader a much clearer and more accurate picture of the scene.

When you select a modifier, you should base your selection on the specific kind of information that you want to give your readers. What exactly do you want your readers to visualize? What point do you want to get across?

The noun and verb in each group of sentences below are the same, but the modifiers are different. Notice how the different modifiers limit the meanings of the words they modify and communicate different ideas.

The rain fell.
The soft, misty rain fell silently to the ground.
The hard, pelting rain fell forcefully to the ground.

The doctor closed the door.
The angry, red-faced doctor closed the door sharply.
The pale, somber doctor closed the door quietly.

Try to avoid using adjectives and adverbs that are overused, especially those that don't appeal to the senses. Adjectives such as *nice, good, pretty, bad,* and *smart* are used so often that they don't express much meaning. In addition, they aren't specific or vivid; therefore, they don't give the reader a clear image. The same is true of overused adverbs, such as *very* and *really.*

Sometimes, you choose between two modifiers that are similar in meaning based on what *feeling* is connected with each one. This feeling is called the word's **connotation.** (See page 314 for more on connotation.) By choosing words that have certain feelings associated with them, you can relay these feelings to your reader. For example, although *tattle* and *report* both have the general meaning of "tell," *tattle* has a negative connotation, while *report* has a positive connotation.

Try It

What adverbs and adjectives could you add to the sentence below to convey a positive image? A negative image?
▶ *The truck climbed the slope of the hill.*

Writing Connection

When you use vivid and accurate adjectives and adverbs in your writing, you give your readers a clear image of what you are describing. You can convey positive, negative, or neutral images simply by choosing precise adjectives and adverbs to modify more general words. Vivid, specific modifiers also make your writing more interesting and enjoyable for your readers.

Using Precise Verbs

When you write, it is important to use words that are precise—including *verbs*. Verbs express action. They tell what is going on. Therefore, the verb is the word in a sentence that usually communicates the most meaning, so you should be especially careful in choosing verbs. Choosing the right verbs allows you to accurately represent actions in your writing.

You should base your selection of a verb on the kind of information that you want to give your readers. What exactly do you want your readers to visualize? What exact point do you want to get across?

Look at the verbs below. Notice how each group of verbs has a slightly different meaning. As you read each group, visualize each action. Notice the different image each verb brings to your mind.

leave	flee	abandon
sleep	snooze	doze
catch	grab	seize
like	adore	cherish
hate	detest	despise
eat	gobble	munch
run	sprint	jog
hold	grasp	clutch

Read each description below. Notice how the choice of verbs affects your idea of what's going on. The first description communicates fatigue. The second suggests illness or injury.

The field laborer walked to the truck. He got into the truck bed. He sat down, breathing heavily.

The field laborer limped to the truck. He struggled to climb into the truck bed. He collapsed, moaning.

Verbs and Connotation

Sometimes, you choose between two verbs that are similar in meaning based on what *feeling* is connected with each. This feeling is called the verb's **connotation.** (See page 314 for more on connotation.) By choosing verbs that have certain feelings associated with them, you can relay these feelings to your reader. What feeling is associated with the verb in each sentence?

The man <u>smirked</u> at the politician's comments.

The man <u>smiled</u> at the politician's comments.

The man <u>snickered</u> at the politician's comments.

The man <u>beamed</u> at the politician's comments.

The word *smirked* has a negative connotation. The reader gets the feeling that the man is ridiculing the politician. The same is true of *snickered. Smiled* has a positive connotation: the man probably agrees with the politician. *Beamed* also has a positive connotation. The reader gets the idea that the man is smiling happily and appreciatively.

Try It

How do the verbs in the following sentences affect their meaning? What kind of image or feelings does each sentence produce for you?

▶ *The woman seized her child's hand and dragged him out of the store.*

▶ *The woman held her child's hand and guided him out of the store.*

Writing Connection

When you choose precise verbs in your writing, you can convey to your readers exactly the type of information that you intend. Even without additional modifiers, vivid and precise verbs can themselves create strong images in a reader's mind.

Rules for Writing: Grammar, Usage, and Mechanics

You know about rules. When you know and follow the rules of a game, you're better at the game. It's the same with writing. Knowing the rules and following them will make you a better writer.

Grammar

Grammar is about how language is organized. Parts of speech, such as nouns and verbs, are grammar. The names for different parts of a sentence, such as subject and predicate, are grammar. The names for different types of sentences, such as simple, compound, and complex, are grammar. Knowing about grammar helps you understand how to build sentences that make sense to your readers.

Nouns

Besides starting with *m*, what do the words *millionaire, mall, mountain,* and *maturity* have in common? They are all nouns! Nouns name everything. For example, nouns name persons, places, things, and ideas.

Kinds of Nouns

There are many different kinds of nouns. Nouns that name things in general are called **common nouns**—*millionaire,* for example, is a common noun. Nouns that name *specific* things are called **proper nouns.** The important words in a proper noun are capitalized. The proper noun *Mall of America* is a specific mall.

If you can see or touch a noun, then it's a **concrete noun,** like *penny.* If you *can't* see or touch it, then it's an **abstract noun,** like *charity.*

Compound nouns are made of more than one word, and they may be concrete or abstract. There may or may not be hyphens or spaces between the words: *father-in-law, lampshade,* and *elementary school.*

Singular and Plural Nouns

A noun that names one person, place, thing, or idea is a **singular noun.** A noun that names more than one person, place, thing, or idea is a **plural noun.** Most singular nouns become plural by adding **-s,** but note the exceptions below.

Noun Ending	To Form Plural	Example
s, z, ch, sh, x	Add *-es*	scratch/scratches
o preceded by a vowel	Add *-s*	radio/radios
o preceded by a consonant	Usually add *-es* Sometimes add *-s*	hero/heroes piano/pianos
y preceded by a vowel	Add *-s*	key/keys
y preceded by a consonant	Usually change *y* to *i* and add *-es*	city/cities
f or *fe*	Usually change *f* to *v* and add *-s* or *-es*	life/lives

For **compound nouns** that are hyphenated or written as more than one word, make the main noun plural: *time clocks, ladies-in-waiting.*

Possessive Nouns

A **possessive noun** shows ownership or possession of things or characteristics.

To form the possessive of all singular nouns, and plural nouns that *do not* end in *-s,* add an apostrophe and *-s: dog's collar, children's books.*

To form the possessive of all plural nouns ending in *-s,* add just an apostrophe: *wolves' habitat, the Smiths' house.*

Collective Nouns

A **collective noun** names groups, or collections, of people, animals, or things. *Family, audience,* and *herd* are examples of collective nouns.

A collective noun that is the subject of a sentence can take a singular or plural verb, depending on how it is used.

> The **audience whisper** loudly to each other during a shocking scene.
> The **family shares** its season tickets with the neighbors.

In the first sentence, the verb is plural because each audience member acts separately. You can add the plural word *members* after *audience,* and the sentence makes sense. In the second sentence, the family acts as one. Look for other words that give clues. *Each other* in the first sentence tells you that the audience members are acting separately. The singular word *its* in the second sentence tells you that the verb should be singular.

Try It

▶ *The army squad take their positions.*

▶ *The chorus performs its yearly holiday show.*

Do you see the clue words that tell you if the verb should be singular or plural?

Writing Connection

Most collective nouns *sound* singular because they don't end in the plural *-s.* So when you write one as a subject of a sentence, remember to first decide how you are using it—as a singular noun or a plural noun.

Pronouns

A **pronoun** is a word that is used in place of a noun or nouns.

Personal Pronouns

Personal pronouns refer to people or things. Some personal pronouns are subject pronouns: *I, you, he, she, it, we,* and *they.* A **subject pronoun** serves as the subject of the sentence. When it is used like a predicate noun, it is called a **predicate pronoun.**

> **They** built an aviary for more than 150 birds. (subject pronoun)
>
> The most popular exhibit was **it.** (predicate pronoun)

Object pronouns are *me, you, him, her, it, us,* and *them.* A pronoun used as a **direct object** follows an action verb. It answers the question *Whom?* or *What?* A pronoun used as an **indirect object** answers the question *For Whom?* or *To Whom?* or *To What?* Object pronouns may also be used as the object of a preposition.

> The penguin habitat amuses **me.** (direct object)
>
> The zookeeper promised **them** an exciting time. (indirect object)
>
> Didn't I give my camera to **you?** (object of a preposition)

Be sure to use *subject* pronouns in compound *subjects.*

> **He** and Ray played the piano together. (not *Him* and Ray)

Use *object* pronouns in compound *objects.*

> Mr. Pit treated Ray and **me** like family. (not Ray and *I*)

If you can't decide whether to use a subject or object pronoun, try writing the sentence with only the pronoun. You wouldn't say Mr. Pit treated *I* like family; you'd say Mr. Pit treated *me* like family.

First person pronouns *I, me, we,* and *us* should always come last in compound subjects and objects: *Tanya and* I *listen to jazz music.*

Possessive Pronouns

A **possessive pronoun** shows possession—it tells who or what has something. Use possessive pronouns to take the place of possessive nouns. Do not use apostrophes with possessive pronouns. Some possessive pronouns can be used alone.

> the **anthropologist's** tools   **her** tools
>
> I brought my tools. Did you bring **yours**?

Reflexive, Intensive, and Demonstrative Pronouns

A **reflexive pronoun** ends with -*self* or -*selves*. It directs the action of the verb back to the subject.

Paula pushed **herself** to the limit.

An **intensive pronoun** is formed the same way as a reflexive pronoun. It adds *intensity*—force or emphasis—to a noun or pronoun already named.

The official solved the problem **himself.**

The reflexive and intensive pronouns are *myself, yourself, himself, herself, itself, ourselves, yourselves*, and *themselves*.

A **demonstrative pronoun** *demonstrates* by indicating or pointing out something. *This, that, these*, and *those* are demonstrative pronouns.

This was once a breathtaking palace.

Indefinite, Relative, and Interrogative Pronouns

An **indefinite pronoun** does not refer to any *definite* or specific person, place, or thing. Singular indefinite pronouns include *anybody, anyone, anything, each, either, everyone, everything, much, neither, nobody, no one, nothing, somebody*, and *something*. Plural indefinite pronouns include *both, few, many, others*, and *several. All, any, most, none*, and *some* may be singular or plural, depending on what follows them.

All of the trees are birches. (plural)

All of the pie is gone. (singular)

A **relative pronoun** introduces an adjective clause. It connects the adjective clause to the main clause and *relates* back to the sentence's main clause. Some relative pronouns are *that, which, who, whom*, and *whose.*

The man **who** teaches the class is Mr. Flores.

An **interrogative pronoun** introduces an interrogative sentence. Use *who* for the subject of the sentence, and *whom* for an object in the sentence. Both refer to people. Use *which* and *what* for things and ideas, and *whose* to show possession.

Whom did the newspaper reporter call? (direct object)

What can we do to keep the school open? (subject)

Whose idea is it to close down the school? (possessive)

Try It

Can you identify the three types of pronouns in this sentence?

▶ *Everyone who buys this is a satisfied customer.*

Verbs

It's time to take some action and talk about verbs. A **verb** is a word that expresses an action or a state of being. An **action verb** expresses a mental or physical action.

> The Wright Brothers **built** a flying machine. (physical)
>
> Orville **thought** about the problem. (mental)

The words *have*, *has*, and *had* may be used as action verbs when they tell what the subject is holding or owns.

> The Wright brothers **had** a bicycle shop in Dayton, Ohio.

A state-of-being verb expresses what a subject is or is like.

> The first airplane flight **was** in 1903.
> That day, the weather **grew** colder.

Linking Verbs

A **linking verb** does just what it says—it *links*, or connects, the subject to a noun or adjective in the predicate. A **predicate noun** follows a linking verb. It renames or identifies the subject of the sentence.

> Orville Wright **was** the **pilot.** (linking verb, predicate noun)

A **predicate adjective** also follows a linking verb, but it describes the subject.

> The Wright brothers **were elated** and **exhausted.** (linking verb, predicate adjectives)

The verb *be* is one of the most common linking verbs. Other linking verbs include *seem, appear, taste, turn, feel, smell, grow, become, look, remain,* and *sound.* You can also use most of these verbs as action verbs.

> The passenger **felt** afraid. (linking verb)
> The passenger **felt** sweat dripping down her face. (action verb)

Helping Verbs

A **helping verb** *helps* the main verb express an action or make a statement. The most common helping verbs are forms of *be, have,* and *do.* Other helping verbs include *may, might, must, can, could, will, shall, would,* and *should.*

It **should work** this time.
We **will try** to fly again.

Verbals: Gerunds and Participles

A **verbal** is a verb form that is used as a noun, adjective, or adverb.

A **gerund** is a kind of verbal that ends in *-ing.* It is used as a noun. It may be a subject, a predicate noun, a direct object, or the object of a preposition.

Flying is my passion. (subject)
Many people researched **flying**. (direct object)

A **participle** is a verb form that ends in *-ing* or *-ed.* It can be used as an adjective.

They used a **soldering** iron to make wings out of tin.
The **soldered** metal was quite strong.

Active and Passive Voice

When a verb is in the **active voice,** the subject performs the action. In the **passive voice,** the subject receives the action of the verb.

The Wright brothers **built** the airplane. (active)
The airplane **was built** by the Wright brothers. (passive)

Writing Connection

To spice up your writing and keep the reader engaged, use the active voice most of the time. It is stronger and more direct. Use the passive voice to emphasize the receiver of the action or if you are unsure of who is performing the action.

Adjectives and Adverbs

Adjectives

An **adjective** is a word that describes a noun or pronoun. It tells *what kind, how many,* or *which one.* An adjective usually comes before the noun it modifies.

> **That** magician performed **three amazing** tricks.

Types of Adjectives

Predicate adjectives come *after* a linking verb in a sentence. They describe the subject of the sentence. (See page 342 for more on predicate adjectives and linking verbs.)

> The path was **rocky** and **steep.**

A, an, and **the** make up a group of words called **articles** that can act as adjectives. *A* and *an* are **indefinite articles**. They give only general information about a noun. *The* is a **definite article.** It identifies specific nouns.

> **A** snake bit **the** hiker.

Proper adjectives are formed from proper nouns. Some proper adjectives are spelled exactly like their noun counterparts. Others add an ending to the noun form.

> the culture of **South America** (proper noun)
>
> **South American** culture (proper adjective)
>
> legends from **Iowa** (proper noun)
>
> **Iowa** legends (proper adjective)

Some adjectives are made from two or more words joined together to describe a noun, such as **coal-black** *dog.* Most of the time, you should hyphenate these kinds of adjectives when they come before the noun. When they follow the noun, or are predicate adjectives, *don't* hyphenate them: *the dog is* **coal black.**

Writing Connection

In some cases, leaving out a hyphen in adjectives that appear before the noun might confuse readers. They might not know whether the last word of the compound is part of the adjective or part of the noun it modifies.

Adverbs

An **adverb** is a word that describes a verb, an adjective, or another adverb.

The windows rattled **loudly.** (describes the verb *rattled*)

Very tiny spiders hung from the ceiling. (describes the adjective *tiny*)

Visitors **almost** never came to the mansion. (describes the adverb *never*)

Adverbs that modify verbs tell *how* (quickly), *when* (soon), and *where* (there). They can appear in different places in a sentence, depending on what you want to stress—before or after the verb or at the beginning or end of a sentence.

The bakery **often** sells French pastries.

Often the bakery sells French pastries.

Adverbs that modify adjectives and other adverbs often tell *how, how much,* or *to what degree.* These adverbs usually come before the word they modify.

The butter tastes **unusually** sweet.

Very soon, the cheese will become moldy.

Most adverbs are formed by adding -*ly* to an adjective. Others do not end in -*ly*. Some of these include the words *already, always, even, forever, late, near, now, often, outside, sometimes, straight,* and *well.*

> **Fun Fact**
>
> The word *adjective* comes from the Latin word that means "to place beside." *Adverb* comes from the Latin word *ad,* which means "next to" and *verbum,* which means "word."

Try It

Does the adverb in the following sentence modify an adjective, adverb, or verb?

▶ *The soprano sang a breathtakingly beautiful song.*

Writing Connection

Adjectives and adverbs make your writing clearer, more interesting, and more vivid. Knowing how to use them correctly is a powerful tool to help you continue to improve your writing.

Prepositions

A **preposition** is a word that shows the relationship of a noun or pronoun to another word in a sentence.

The animals **near** the fire could not escape.

The preposition *near* shows the relationship between *fire* and *animals*.

Common Prepositions

about	before	except	of	through
above	behind	for	off	to
across	below	from	on	under
after	beside	in	onto	until
against	between	inside	out	up
along	but	instead of	outside	upon
among	by	into	over	with
around	down	like	past	without
at	during	near	since	

In a sentence, a preposition always has an object. The **object of the preposition** is the noun or pronoun that follows the preposition. The object may be compound. A **prepositional phrase** consists of the preposition, the object of the preposition, and any words that modify the object.

Terrified animals dashed **through the burning trees and grass.**
(prepositional phrase with a modified compound object)

Some words can function as either prepositions or adverbs.

I looked **up.** (adverb)   I looked **up** the stairs. (preposition)

Try It

Identify the preposition and object of the preposition:
▶ *A lightning bolt spiraled down a large tree trunk.*

Writing Connection

Pronouns also function as objects of prepositions. These pronouns, such as *me* and *him*, are known as object pronouns. Knowing that a pronoun is the object of a preposition will allow you to use the correct form of the pronoun.

Conjunctions and Interjections

Conjunctions

A **conjunction** connects words, phrases, or clauses in a sentence. A **coordinating conjunction** connects two or more elements in a sentence. *And, but, for, nor, so, yet*, and *or* are coordinating conjunctions.

> Edmund Hillary **and** Tenzing Norgay reached Mount Everest's peak. (*and* connects two equal nouns)

> Hillary checked his own equipment, **but** he found nothing wrong. (*but* connects two equal independent clauses)

Correlative conjunctions, such as *either/or* and *neither/nor*, are used in pairs to connect sentence parts.

> They **either** continue climbing **or** turn back.

When you join a compound subject with *or* or *nor*, the verb in the sentence should agree with the subject that is closest to it.

> **Neither** low oxygen **nor** icy gusts of wind cause them to turn back. (*cause* agrees with *gusts*)

Subordinating Conjunctions

A **subordinating conjunction** introduces a **dependent clause**—a clause that cannot stand alone as a sentence. *Although, after, as, because, before, until,* and *whenever* are some subordinating conjunctions.

> They hugged each other **before** they descended.

Interjections

An **interjection** expresses emotion. Interjections may stand alone if they express strong emotion, or appear as part of a sentence if they express milder emotion.

> **At last!** They spied the top of the mountain. (expresses excitement)

> **Oh,** if only it weren't just another peak. (expresses discouragement)

Subjects and Predicates

A **sentence** has a subject and a predicate. The **subject** names whom or what the sentence is about. The **predicate** says what the subject does, has, is, or is like.

Simple and Complete Subjects and Predicates

The **simple subject** is the main word or word group in the subject. The **simple predicate** is the main word or word group in the predicate. The **complete subject** includes the simple subject and all of the words that describe it. The **complete predicate** includes all of the words in the predicate.

simple subject	*simple predicate*
The **dragon**	**attacked.**
The **knight**	**rested.**
complete subject	*complete predicate*
The fierce dragon	**attacked the brave and daring knight.**
The tired knight	**rested in the cool water until sunrise.**

Try It

In the following sentence, identify the simple subject, complete subject, simple predicate, and complete predicate.

▶ *A good old hermit lived in a little house by himself.*

Writing Connection

Knowing how subjects and predicates work together to form a sentence helps you produce writing that readers take seriously. Coming across subjects without predicates and predicates without subjects is distracting and confusing to readers. They may lose confidence in the writer's abilities, and therefore in the writing itself.

Compound Subjects and Compound Predicates

A **compound subject** has more than one simple subject. The subjects may be joined by the conjunctions *and, or, both...and, neither...nor,* or *either...or.* The subjects have the same predicate.

The **boys and girls** laughed.

Use a plural verb with a compound subject that includes *and* or *both...and.* For subjects with *or, neither...nor,* or *either...or,* the verb should agree with the subject to which it is closest.

The king and queen **give** gifts.

Neither the children nor the queen **speaks** for a moment.

A **compound predicate** consists of two or more simple predicates that share the same subject. Both simple predicates, or verbs, agree with the subject.

The knight **charges** and **attacks** the dragon.

Try It

For each sentence, choose the correct form of the verb in parentheses. Then identify the subjects and predicates and tell whether they are simple or compound.

▶ *The king (embraces, embrace) and (kisses, kiss) his daughter.*

▶ *Neither the king nor the townspeople (was, were) afraid of the dragon anymore.*

▶ *The king and queen (waves, wave) and (departs, depart).*

Writing Connection

Using compound subjects and predicates in sentences allows you to connect ideas and make your sentences longer and more refined.

Fun Fact

Even though the word *predicate* functions as a noun in this lesson, it is also a verb that means "affirm" or "assert."

Objects and Subject Complements

A **direct object** *directly* receives the action of an action verb. It answers the question *whom?* or *what?* after the verb. A direct object is always a noun or pronoun.

Delia helps **Mama.**

An **indirect object** *indirectly* receives the action of a verb. It *accepts* the direct object and answers the question *to whom?* or *to what?*

Annie gave **Lila** a smile.

The direct object in the sentence is *smile.* It answers the question *what? Lila* is the indirect object. It answers the question *to whom?*

Direct and indirect objects may be compound. This means that there is more than one direct object or indirect object in a sentence.

Delia helps **Mama** and **Sheila.** (compound direct object)
Annie offered the **girl** and the **boy** tea. (compound indirect object)

In the sentence above, *offered* is a **transitive verb** because it transfers action to a direct object (tea). **Intransitive verbs** do not have direct objects: *Annie offered to make tea.*

Identifying indirect objects can be tricky. Keep in mind that an indirect object always appears between a verb and its direct object. Also, if you move the direct object to just after the verb, you can put the preposition *to* or *for* in front of the indirect object.

Mike handed **Lila** newspapers. (*Lila* is an indirect object)

Writing Connection

If the object of a preposition is too far away from the verb, then the reader may lose the train of thought.

▶ *Lila **gave** the piping-hot French bread and the mixed-greens salad with fresh tomatoes **to Annie.***

In this case, you can make your writing clearer by changing the object of a preposition to an indirect object.

▶ *Lila gave Annie the. . . .*

Predicate Nominatives and Predicate Adjectives

Predicate nominatives, also called predicate nouns, and predicate adjectives appear in sentences with linking verbs. A linking verb is different from an action verb. A **linking verb** *links*, or connects, a sentence's subject with a noun or adjective.

> Mike **was** a **newsboy**. (linking verb *was* connects *Mike* to *newsboy*)
>
> The papers **felt heavy**. (linking verb *felt* connects *papers* to *heavy*)

Predicate nominatives and predicate adjectives are called *subject complements* because they complement or add to the subject. The first sentence includes the predicate nominative *newsboy*. A **predicate nominative** is a noun or pronoun that follows a linking verb and renames or identifies the subject.

The second sentence includes the predicate adjective *heavy*. A **predicate adjective** follows a linking verb and describes the subject.

There can be more than one predicate nominative or predicate adjective in a sentence.

> Mike was a **hardworking son** and a **good salesman**. (compound predicate nominative)
>
> Lila was **happy** but **nervous**. (compound predicate adjective)

Try It

Identify the predicate nominative(s) or predicate adjective(s) in each sentence.

▶ *Katie Rose became a nanny during her teens.*

▶ *The babies were happy and active.*

Writing Connection

Armed with your knowledge of direct and indirect objects, predicate nominatives, and predicate adjectives, you can make your writing more interesting by varying the types of sentences you write.

Words and Phrases Used as Modifiers

A **modifier** is a word or phrase that describes, or *modifies*, another word or phrase. Adjectives and adverbs are modifiers. An **adjective** modifies a noun or pronoun. An **adverb** modifies a verb, an adjective, or another adverb.

Participles may also act as adjectives. A **present participle** is formed by adding *-ing* to a verb. A **past participle** is usually formed by adding a *-d* or *-ed* to a verb.

> his **riding** skill   a **disappointed** boy

A **participial phrase** is a phrase that begins with a participle. It may include a present participle or a past participle. It can function as an adjective.

> **Aching with envy,** we watched Rollie buy cards. (present participial phrase modifies *we*)
>
> **Obsessed with the cards,** I stared in the window. (past participial phrase modifies *I*)
>
> Rollie, **smiling contentedly**, placed his cards in an album. (present participial phrase modifies *Rollie*)

A **prepositional phrase** begins with a preposition and ends with a noun or pronoun. It can function as an adjective or adverb.

> The baseball glove **in the window** was not for sale. (adjective phrase—describes *glove*)
>
> The President cards became popular **with the boys.** (adverb phrase—describes adjective *popular*)

Appositives and appositive phrases act as adjectives. An **appositive** is a noun that appears next to another noun that it modifies or renames.

> My youngest brother, **Brian,** collects baseball cards. (appositive—modifies *brother*)

An **appositive phrase** includes the appositive plus the words that modify it.

> Rollie, **the richest boy in town**, could buy as many cards as he wanted. (appositive phrase—modifies *Rollie*)

Words and Phrases Used as Nouns: Gerunds

Is bicycling a favorite activity of yours? Do you enjoy running or skating? If so, then you like *gerunds!* A **gerund** is a verb form that ends in *-ing* and is used as a noun.

> **Inventing** is hard work.

A gerund can function in the same ways as other nouns. It may be a subject, a predicate noun, a direct object, or the object of a preposition.

> **Listening** is an important skill. (subject)
>
> Midori's favorite activity is **playing.** (predicate noun)
>
> Some people enjoy **singing.** (direct object)
>
> What are the benefits of **practicing?** (object of a preposition)

A gerund may also be modified by adverbs or a prepositional phrase. In this case, it is a **gerund phrase.**

> Midori enjoys **playing quickly.**
>
> Midori likes **playing for an audience.**

A gerund may also have a direct object.

> Many people enjoy **playing a musical instrument.**

Fun Fact

The word *gerund* comes from the Latin word *gerere*, which means "to do" or "to carry on."

Try It

How does the gerund function in the following sentence? What part of speech modifies the gerund?

▶ *Working hard is second nature to Midori.*

Writing Connection

Using gerunds correctly in your writing adds variety to your sentences. Try using gerunds in all four of the ways described above.

Clauses

All complete sentences contain a clause. A **clause** is a group of words that has a subject and a predicate. It may be used as a sentence or as part of a sentence.

There are different kinds of clauses. A **main clause** has a subject and a predicate *and* can stand alone as a sentence.

> **The cats hiss loudly.** (main clause)

Some sentences include a main clause and one or more subordinate, or dependent, clauses. A **subordinate clause** has a subject and a predicate, but cannot stand alone as a sentence. It must be combined with a main clause.

> The cats hiss loudly **when they meet.** (subordinate clause)

Adjective Clauses

An **adjective clause** is a kind of subordinate clause. It modifies a noun or pronoun in the sentence's main clause and usually begins with a relative pronoun. *That, which, who, whom*, and *whose* are relative pronouns. An adjective clause may also begin with *where* or *when*.

> Are you the person **who studies archaeology?** (adjective clause modifies the noun *person*)

Often, a relative pronoun that begins an adjective clause acts as the subject of the clause.

> The scientists discovered skeletons **that are fifteen hundred years old.** (adjective clause modifies the noun *skeletons*, and *that* is the subject of the clause)

Writing Connection

Do *not* use commas around an adjective clause that is necessary to the meaning of the sentence.

> The volcano **that erupted thousands of years ago** destroyed whole cities. (adjective clause specifies which volcano erupted)

Do use commas to set off an adjective clause that is not key to the meaning of the sentence.

> The volcano, **which is silent now,** destroyed whole cities. (adjective clause adds nonessential information to the sentence)

Adverb Clauses

An **adverb clause** is a subordinate clause that modifies the verb in a sentence's main clause. It tells *how, why, where, when,* and *under what conditions* the action of the verb takes place.

> **After she found the skeleton,** she paused. (adverb clause modifies the verb *paused*—it tells *when* she paused)
>
> The skeleton was named the Ring Lady **because she wore two gold rings.** (adverb clause modifies the verb *was named*—it tells *why* she was so named)

Subordinate clauses also modify state-of-being verbs.

> The skeleton should be here **when you return tomorrow.** (adverb clause modifies the verb *should be*—it tells *when* the skeleton will be there)

A subordinating conjunction introduces an adverb clause.

Some Subordinating Conjunctions

after	before	until	where
although	if	unless	whereas
as	since	when	wherever
as if	than	whenever	while

Fun Fact

Subordinate is based on the Latin word that means "to place in a lower order or rank." In the military, *subordinates* are those who are lower in rank.

***

Try It

Can you see the main clause and the subordinate clause in each of the following sentences? Does the subordinate clause work as an adjective or adverb?

▶ *As I entered the chamber, I could barely see.*

▶ *We found the carpenter's tool, which had been slung on his back.*

***

Writing Connection

Knowing that subordinate clauses cannot stand alone will make you less likely to write sentences that are incomplete and confusing to the reader. Combined with main clauses, however, subordinate clauses can add a lot of detail to your writing, making it more exact and easier to follow.

Types of Sentences

Simple Sentences

A **simple sentence** has only one complete subject and one complete predicate. The subject, predicate, or both may be simple or compound.

Complete Subject	Complete Predicate
He	ran. (simple subject, one simple predicate)
His nickname	was J.C. (simple subject, one simple predicate)
J.C. and his brothers and sisters	lived in an old house. (compound subject, simple predicate)
Jesse Owens	swept floors and delivered groceries. (simple subject, compound predicate)

Compound Sentences

A **compound sentence** contains two or more *simple sentences*, which are called **main clauses.** To connect the main clauses in a compound sentence, use a comma or semicolon plus a conjunction or a conjunctive adverb. Some conjunctive adverbs are *besides, furthermore, however, nevertheless, therefore, thus, likewise,* and *similarly.*

Jesse's whole family was working, **but** they still didn't have enough money. (comma plus coordinating conjunction connects two main clauses)

Some people didn't believe Jesse could become a great athlete; **however,** he proved them wrong. (semicolon plus conjunctive adverb connects two main clauses)

Sometimes all you need is a semicolon.

Some athletes like to train alone; others like to train with fellow athletes. (semicolon connects two main clauses)

Complex Sentences

Here's where things get a little complex! **Complex sentences** include a main clause and one or more subordinate clauses. A **subordinate clause** has a subject and a predicate but does not stand alone as a sentence and must be combined with a main clause. Subordinate clauses may act as adjectives, adverbs, or nouns. (Pages 354–355 explain clauses in more detail.)

> The athletes traveled to Germany **where the Olympics were being held.** (main clause followed by subordinate adjective clause beginning with *where*)
>
> **When Jessie came back from the Olympics,** he received a ticker-tape parade. (subordinate adverb clause begins with *when*, followed by main clause)

A subordinate clause *depends* on the main clause to form a complete sentence. It is therefore also known as a *dependent clause.*

Compound-Complex Sentences

A **compound-complex sentence** contains more than one main clause and one or more subordinate clauses.

> Jesse set several high school and college records, and he won four gold medals at the Olympics, where he set a new world record. (two main clauses followed by subordinate adjective clause beginning with *where*)

Try It

Can you identify the three clauses in the following sentence? What type of sentence is it?

▶ *Jesse Owens attended The Ohio State University, where he set three world records, and he went to the Olympics a year later.*

Writing Connection

Knowing how to use main clauses and subordinate clauses will help you create different kinds of sentences. With this knowledge, you can vary the length of your sentences, as well as the types of sentences you use, making your writing more interesting and lively.

Problems with Sentences

Fragments

A **fragment** is an incomplete sentence. Some fragments are missing a **subject**—the part that tells whom or what the sentence is about. Other fragments are missing a **predicate**—the part that tells what the subject does or has, is or is like. Still others are missing both the subject and the predicate. The way to fix them is to add what is missing.

Fragment	What's Missing?	Complete Sentence
The black wolf.	a predicate	The black wolf **stared at Miyax.** (predicate added)
Flicked their tails.	a subject	**The Arctic ground squirrels** flicked their tails. (subject added)
Near a wolf den.	a subject and predicate	**Her father camped** near a wolf den. (subject and predicate added)

Run-on Sentences

A **run-on sentence** is two or more complete sentences written as though they are one sentence. To fix run-on sentences, correctly combine the sentences included in the run-on, or write them separately.

Run-on Sentences	Corrected Sentences
Miyax was hungry she was lost. Miyax was hungry, she was lost.	Miyax was hungry, **and** she was lost. Miyax was hungry. **S**he was lost. Miyax was hungry**;** she was lost.

Writing Connection

Double-check your writing for fragments. If a sentence begins with a capital letter and ends with a period, it should have a subject and a predicate.

Rambling Sentences

Some sentences go on and on, expressing many different ideas and they include a lot of conjunctions and they don't seem to ever end and they are so long that the reader can't follow the train of thought.

As the previous sentence illustrates, a **rambling sentence** is a sentence that goes on and on, and usually includes many conjunctions. To fix a rambling sentence, break it up into smaller, more manageable sentences. Here is the corrected version of the rambling sentence presented above.

Some sentences go on and on, expressing many different ideas. They include a lot of conjunctions, and they don't ever seem to end. They are so long that the reader can't follow the train of thought.

Try It

How would you fix this rambling sentence?

▶ *There are many different kinds of music and rock music, which is also known as "rock 'n' roll" music started in the 1950s and some famous rock musicians include Elvis Presley, The Beatles, and The Rolling Stones.*

Awkward Sentences

An **awkward sentence** is a sentence whose meaning is unclear. Often, awkward sentences are hard to understand because certain words and clauses are poorly placed:

> A common type of music with a strong rhythm created in inner cities is called rap music.

In the example awkward sentence above, the subject is too long, making the verb too far away from the beginning of the sentence. Also, because there are too many modifiers in the subject, it is hard to tell whether the *music* or the *rhythm* was created in inner cities. To correct the sentence, change the order of modifiers so they don't appear one right after the other, and shorten the subject to make it nearer to the verb.

> Created in inner cities, rap music has a strong rhythm and is a common type of music.

Try It

How would you fix the following awkward sentence?

▶ *The music based on work songs and religious songs sung by African Americans is called the blues.*

Redundant Words and Phrases

A word or phrase that is redundant repeats what has already been stated in a sentence. It can be cut out of the sentence without losing any meaning.

Sentence with Redundant Words

The famous rock musician Elvis Presley was famous and very well known. (*famous* appears twice and means about the same thing as *well known*)

Corrected Sentence

The rock musician Elvis Presley was very famous.

Misplaced Modifiers

A **misplaced modifier** modifies the wrong word or appears to modify more than one word in a sentence. Be sure to place a modifier as close as possible to the word or phrase it modifies.

Sentences with Misplaced Modifiers

Powerful and moving, the audience reacted strongly to the opera. (modifier *powerful and moving* appears to describe *the audience*, when it should describe *the opera*)

She took a program into the theater filled with names and descriptions of the singers. (seems as though the theater is *filled with names and descriptions* rather than the program)

Corrected Sentences

The audience reacted strongly to the powerful and moving opera.

She took a program, which was filled with names and descriptions of the singers, into the theater.

Writing Connection

Sentences with misplaced modifiers can confuse readers. Correct a misplaced modifier by revising the sentence. Rephrase the sentence by moving the modifier closer to the word being modified.

Kinds of Sentences

A **declarative sentence** makes a statement. It ends with a period. The subject in a declarative sentence usually comes before the verb: *I ate a bologna sandwich.*

Look at this **imperative sentence.** It makes a request or gives a command. Most imperative sentences end with a period, but some strong imperative sentences take an exclamation point. The subject in an imperative sentence most often is the *implied* "you." In the example, the subject is understood to be "you": *You look at this imperative sentence.*

What kind of sentence is this? Why, it's an **interrogative sentence,** which is a sentence that asks a question. As you might guess, it ends with a question mark. The subject of the sentence is often an interrogative pronoun that appears at the beginning. In other cases, the interrogative pronoun may act as an object, with the subject appearing in the middle of the sentence.

> ***What*** *is the most exciting sport?* (*What* is the subject.)
>
> ***Whom*** *did the pitcher strike out?* (*Whom* is the object; *the pitcher* is the subject.)

You better watch out for this sentence! It's an **exclamatory sentence,** which expresses strong emotion. It ends with an exclamation point. The subject in an exclamatory sentence usually appears before the verb: ***He*** *hit a grand slam!* (*He* is the subject.)

Try It

Can you tell whether the following sentence is declarative, imperative, interrogative, or exclamatory?

▶ *Consider the career of Mickey Mantle.*

Writing Connection

The kinds of sentences you use in your writing depend on the purpose of your writing. For example, if you're writing an essay for school, you will likely use mostly declarative sentences. If you're writing an instruction manual, you would use a lot of imperative sentences. In most kinds of writing, however, interrogative and exclamatory sentences are used sparingly.

Usage

Usage is about how we use language when we speak and write. For example, the rules of usage tell you when to use *was* and when to use *were*. They tell you when to use *broke* and when to use *broken*. They tell you when to use *smaller* and when to use *smallest*. Learning and using the rules of usage will make it easier for people to understand what you say and what you write.

Using Verbs

Verb Tenses

Verb tenses are forms of verbs that help show whether the action of the sentence happened in the past, present, or future. In English, a verb form indicates the past (sailed), and another form indicates the present (sail). Unlike other languages, there is no special form of verbs to indicate the future. The words *will* or *shall* are used with verbs to tell what will happen in the future.

Present Tense

The **present tense** expresses an action or condition that is repeated or that happens regularly.

> They **compete** in the Olympics every four years.

The present tense can also express a general truth.

> The gold medal **is** the highest medal available.

Except with the verb *be*, the present tense is the base form of the verb: *I **walk**, you **walk**, we **walk**, they **walk**.*

The exception is the third person singular (he, she, it) to which you add an *-s* or *-es: He, she, or it **walks**.*

Past Tense

The **past tense** expresses an action or condition that began and ended in the past. In regular verbs, the past tense is formed by adding *-d* or *-ed* to the base forms. **Irregular verbs** form the past tense in different ways.

> Women **competed** in the Olympics for the first time in 1900. (regular verb)

> The skater **won** a medal in the 1998 Olympics. (irregular verb)

Future Tense

The **future tense** expresses an action or condition that will occur in the future. Form the future tense by adding the word *will* or *shall* to the base form of the verb.

> Athletes **will** always **travel** far to attend the Olympics.

Perfect Tenses of Verbs

The present perfect, past perfect, and future perfect tenses all use helping verbs. A helping verb, also called an **auxiliary verb,** appears with the main verb in the perfect tenses. It *helps* the main verb to express action or to state something. The auxiliary verbs used in the perfect tenses are *have, has,* and *had.*

The Present Perfect Tense

The **present perfect tense** expresses an action or condition that took place at an undetermined time in the *past.* It can also be used to show that an action began in the past and continues in the present. It is called the *present* perfect because the auxiliary verb is in the present tense. The present perfect is made of *has* or *have* and the past participle of the main verb.

> Carl Lewis **has retired** from Olympic competition. (undetermined time in past)

> The ice skaters **have practiced every day** since the world championships. (began in past, continues in present)

The Past Perfect Tense

The **past perfect tense** expresses an action or condition that began and ended before another event in the past. It is made of *had* and the past participle of the main verb. The past perfect is often used in sentences that include a past tense verb in another part of the sentence.

> The ice skater **had fallen** twice by the time her program *ended.*

The Future Perfect Tense

Use the **future perfect tense** to express an action or condition that will begin *and* end before another future event begins. It is made of *will have* or *shall have* and the past participle of the verb.

> By the time the skier competes, he **will have skied** for more than half his life.

Writing Connection

Choose your verb tenses carefully when writing. Only switch tenses when you need to indicate a change in time. An unnecessary shift in verb tense may distract or confuse the reader.

Irregular Verbs

The past and past participle forms of some verbs are formed irregularly.

Pattern	Base Form	Past	Past Participle
One vowel changes to form the past and past participle.	begin	began	begun
	drink	drank	drunk
	ring	rang	rung
	shrink	shrank *or* shrunk	shrunk
	sing	sang	sung
	sink	sank	sunk
	spring	sprang *or* sprung	sprung
	swim	swam	swum

Pattern	Base Form	Past	Past Participle
The past and the past participle are the same.	bring	brought	brought
	build	built	built
	buy	bought	bought
	catch	caught	caught
	creep	crept	crept
	feel	felt	felt
	fight	fought	fought
	find	found	found
	get	got	got
	have	had	had
	hold	held	held
	keep	kept	kept
	lay	laid	laid
	lead	led	led
	leave	left	left
	lend	lent	lent
	lose	lost	lost
	make	made	made
	meet	met	met
	pay	paid	paid
	say	said	said
	seek	sought	sought
	sell	sold	sold
	send	sent	sent
	sit	sat	sat
	sleep	slept	slept
	spend	spent	spent
	spin	spun	spun
	stand	stood	stood
	sting	stung	stung
	swing	swung	swung
	teach	taught	taught
	tell	told	told
	think	thought	thought
	win	won	won

More Irregular Verbs

Pattern	Base Form	Past	Past Participle
The base form and the past participle are the same.	become	became	become
	come	came	come
	run	ran	run

Pattern	Base Form	Past	Past Participle
The past ends in *ew*, and the past participle ends in *wn*.	blow	blew	blown
	draw	drew	drawn
	fly	flew	flown
	grow	grew	grown
	know	knew	known
	throw	threw	thrown

Pattern	Base Form	Past	Past Participle
The past participle ends in *en*.	bite	bit	bitten *or* bit
	break	broke	broken
	choose	chose	chosen
	drive	drove	driven
	eat	ate	eaten
	fall	fell	fallen
	freeze	froze	frozen
	give	gave	given
	ride	rode	ridden
	rise	rose	risen
	see	saw	seen
	shake	shook	shaken
	speak	spoke	spoken
	steal	stole	stolen
	take	took	taken
	write	wrote	written

Pattern	Base Form	Past	Past Participle
The past and the past participle don't follow any pattern.	do	did	done
	tear	tore	torn
	wear	wore	worn

Pattern	Base Form	Past	Past Participle
The base form, the past, and the past participle are the same.	burst	burst	burst
	cost	cost	cost
	cut	cut	cut
	hit	hit	hit
	hurt	hurt	hurt
	let	let	let
	put	put	put
	read	read	read
	set	set	set
	spread	spread	spread

Subject-Verb Agreement

One definition of the word *agree* is "to be in harmony with; match." When a subject and verb *agree* in number, they match. A singular subject has a singular verb, and a plural subject has a plural verb.

> The president serves a four-year term. (singular subject and verb)

> Representatives serve a two-year term. (plural subject, plural verb)

In the above examples, the verb directly follows the subject. Sometimes, though, a prepositional phrase comes between the subject and verb. This makes it harder to find the subject of the sentence.

> The **justices** of the Supreme Court **review** federal laws.
> (plural subject agrees with plural verb, *not* with singular object of preposition—*Supreme Court*)

The subject is also sometimes hard to find in an **inverted sentence,** in which the subject follows the verb. Many inverted sentences begin with a prepositional phrase. Sentences that begin with *Here* or *There* often are inverted. *Here* or *There* is never the subject of a sentence.

> Across the street **is** the **White House.** (inverted sentence beginning with a prepositional phrase)

> Here **is** the **building** where Congress meets. (inverted sentence)

In some interrogative sentences, the subject appears between the auxiliary verb and the main verb.

> **Does** this plan **work?**

Writing Connection

When you are revising your writing, you can check subject-verb agreement in an inverted sentence or an interrogative sentence by rearranging the sentence so the subject comes first: The **White House is** across the street. This **plan does work.**

Agreement Between Indefinite Pronouns and Verbs

Indefinite pronouns also make agreement tricky. An **indefinite pronoun** is a pronoun that does not refer to a specific person, place, or thing. Some indefinite pronouns are always singular and some are always plural. Others may be singular or plural, depending on what follows them.

Some Indefinite Pronouns			
Singular		**Plural**	**Singular or Plural**
another	neither	both	all
anybody	no one	few	any
anyone	nothing	many	most
anything	somebody	others	none
each	someone	several	some
either	something		
everybody			
everyone			
everything			
much			

Neither of the Congressional branches **is** now in session.

Many senators **serve** more than one term in office.

Agreement with Compound Subjects

Compound subjects compound the task of making sure subjects and verbs agree. A **compound subject** contains at least two simple subjects that have the same verb. A compound subject may take a singular or plural verb, depending on the words used to join them.

Both senators **and** representatives **belong** to Congress.

Wyoming **and** Vermont **have** just one representative each.

When a compound subject is joined by *and* or *both...and,* the verb should be plural. Sometimes, *and* is used to join words that belong to one unit or refer to the same thing. Then the subject and verb are singular.

The president and commander-in-chief **is** Franklin D. Roosevelt.

Some compound subjects are joined by *or, either...or,* or *neither...nor.* In these cases, the verb agrees with the subject that is closest to it.

Neither the chief justice **nor** the other justices **run** in an election.

Pronoun Agreement

A **pronoun** is a word used in place of a noun or nouns. An **antecedent** is the noun to which the pronoun refers. Pronouns must agree with their antecedents not only in number but also in gender.

> When I asked Hillary where the United Nations headquarters is located, **she** said **it** is in New York.

> *(She is singular and feminine, agreeing with the antecedent Hillary. It is singular and neuter, agreeing with the antecedent headquarters.)*

Indefinite Pronouns and Agreement

A verb should agree in number with an indefinite pronoun that appears as the subject of a sentence. This can be tricky—some indefinite pronouns are always singular, some are always plural, and others are singular or plural depending on what follows. See page 341 for more on indefinite pronouns.

> **Each** of the members **listens** intently.

The prepositional phrase has a plural noun, but the subject *Each* is singular, so the verb must be singular as well.

When an indefinite pronoun is the antecedent of a possessive pronoun, the pronouns must agree in number.

> **Everyone** took **his or her** job seriously.

Even though the antecedent *Everyone* sounds as if it should be plural, it is always singular. Therefore, the possessive pronouns that refer to it should be singular as well.

Unless you know for sure that *everybody* or *everyone* refers to males or females only, then you should use *his or her* as the possessive pronoun. This leads to another problem. To avoid the awkward repetition of *his or her*, rewrite the sentence. One way to do this is to change the elements from singular to plural:

> **They all** took **their** jobs seriously.

Another way is to simply take out the pronoun or pronouns in question:

> **Everyone** took **the** job seriously.
> *(his or her is replaced by the)*

Agreement with Demonstrative and Interrogative Pronouns

The **demonstrative pronouns** *this*, *that*, *these*, and *those* point out something. They must also agree with their antecedents.

> **These** are the **members** of the United Nations. (demonstrative pronoun *These* agrees in number with plural antecedent *members*)
>
> **That** is a **building** used by United Nations members. (demonstrative pronoun *That* agrees in number with singular antecedent *building*)

The **interrogative pronouns** *who*, *whom*, *whose*, *which*, and *what* are used to introduce an interrogative sentence. *Who* is used as the subject of the sentence. *Whom* is used as an object in a sentence. *Whose* shows possession.

> **Who** takes part in the Security Council? (subject)
>
> **Whom** did the General Assembly appoint as Secretary-General? (direct object)
>
> That idea is interesting. **Whose** is it? (possessive)

All of the interrogative pronouns can be singular or plural. Therefore, they always agree in number with their antecedents.

> The Security Council is made up of five countries. **What** are they? (*What* refers to plural antecedent *countries* and takes the plural verb *are*.)
>
> One city is the headquarters for the United Nations. **Which** is it? (*Which* refers to the singular antecedent *city* and takes the singular verb *is*.)

Fun Fact

British prime minister Winston Churchill provides a good example of the use of indefinite pronouns. In referring to the Battle of Britain in World War II, he said, "Never in the field of human conflict was so much owed by so many to so few."

Try It

Choose the word in parentheses that correctly completes the following sentence.

▶ *(Who, Whom) (is, are) the delegates to the Security Council?*

Forms of Adjectives and Adverbs

Adjectives and adverbs are **modifiers** because they describe, or *modify*, other words. The **comparative form** of a modifier compares one person or thing with another (adjective), or one action with another action (adverb). The **superlative form** compares one person, thing, or action with several others.

For most short adjectives and adverbs add **-er** to form the comparative and **-est** to form the superlative. For most longer modifiers, form the comparative by adding *more* and the superlative by adding *most*. To form the negative comparative and superlative, use *less* and *least*. Don't use *more, most, less,* or *least* with words that already end in **-er** or **-est**—"the **most** fast**est** falcon." This is known as a double comparison and is incorrect.

Some adjectives and adverbs have irregular comparative and superlative forms and use completely different words for these forms.

Adjective	Adverb	Comparative	Superlative
good, well	well	better	best
bad	badly	worse	worst
many, much	much	more	most
little	little	less	least

Some adjectives and adverbs have similar meanings and are easily confused, such as *good* and *well* and *bad* and *badly*. *Good* and *bad*, including their comparative and superlative forms, are adjectives that are used before nouns and with linking verbs.

> The scientist felt **good** about the results of the experiment.
> (*good* is used after linking verb—describes *scientist*)

Well and *badly* are adverbs. Use them, and their comparative and superlative forms, to modify verbs, adjectives, and other adverbs.

> The scientist works **well** with others. *(well* modifies verb *works)*

Well can also be used as an adjective but only to mean "healthy."

The demonstrative pronouns *this, that, these,* and *those* can also be used as adjectives. They tell *which one* or *ones*. They should agree in number with the noun they modify.

> **This** chick looks healthy.

Double Negatives

A **double negative** includes two negative words that express the same idea. Avoid using double negatives in your writing (and speech!). Use only one negative word to express a negative idea.

The adverb *not* is a negative word. It appears as *n't* when in a contraction, such as *doesn't*. Because the *not* is not spelled out but rather "hides" in a contraction, it's easy to make the mistake of adding another *not*.

Other negative words are in the chart, which also includes affirmative words. **Affirmative words** are the opposite of negative words. They express a positive idea.

Negative	Affirmative
never, hardly, barely	always, ever
nobody	everybody, anybody
no, none	all, one, any, some
no one	anyone, everyone, one
nothing	anything, something
nowhere	anywhere, somewhere

Fun Fact

In some languages, it is correct to use two negative words to express a negative idea. In French, for example, the negative words *ne* and *pas* are used before and after the verb to express a negative thought. *Je ne comprends pas* means "I do not understand."

You can correct a double negative by removing one of the negative words. Or, you can change a negative word to a positive word.

Double Negative	He did**n't** have **no** money for the subway.
Corrected	He did**n't** have money for the subway.
	He didn't have **any** money for the subway.

Try It

How would you correct the double negative in the following sentence?

▶ *Nobody didn't get a Medal of Honor before 1863.*

Misused Words

Do you *lay* down or *lie* down? Do you *rise* or *raise* your hand in class? *Lie* and *lay* and *rise* and *raise* are two of the many pairs of words that are commonly misused.

Lay and Lie

Lie means "to place oneself in a reclining position," or "to be placed." *Lay* means "to put" or "to place."

	Lie	Lay
Present	lie, lies	lay, lays
Present Participle	lying	laying
Past	lay	laid
Past Participle	lain	laid

Remember this rule to figure out which verb to use: *Lie* is *never* followed by a direct object, and *lay* is almost *always* followed by a direct object.

The players **lay** their helmets on the bench.
(direct object; present tense of *lay*)

The players **lie** on the grass to do sit-ups.
(no direct object; present tense of *lie*)

Sit, Set

Sit means "to place oneself in a seated position." *Set* means "to put or place." *Sit* does not take a direct object. *Set* usually does.

	Sit	Set
Present	sit, sits	set, sets
Present Participle	sitting	setting
Past	sat	set
Past Participle	sat	set

The coach **sat** down to watch the game.

The kicker **set** the tee on the ground.

Rise, Raise

Rise means "to move upward." *Raise* means "to cause to move upward," or "to bring up." *Rise* does not take a direct object, whereas *raise* usually does.

	Rise	Raise
Present	rise, rises	raise, raises
Present Participle	rising	raising
Past	rose	raised
Past Participle	risen	raised

He **raised** his hand to signal the other players.
The coach **rose** from the bench.

Lead and Led

Lead and *led* sound alike—both rhyme with *head*. *Lead* is a metallic element. *Led* is the past tense of the verb *lead*, which means "in the front position."

	Lead
Present	lead, leads
Present Participle	leading
Past	led
Past Participle	led

She **led** the team to victory.

Lead poisoning has many symptoms.

Its and It's

Its and *it's* are easily confused because they sound exactly the same. However, *its* is a possessive pronoun and *it's* is a contraction of *it is* or *it has*.

The baseball bat had a mind of **its** own.

It's been a long game.

Try It

Why is this sentence incorrect?
▶ *The crowd raises to it's feet.*

Mechanics

The rules of mechanics are very important in writing. Imagine a paragraph with no capital letters at the beginnings of sentences and no punctuation at the ends of sentences. How confusing would that be? Of course, there is a lot more to mechanics than capitalizing the first word of a sentence and using end marks. The following lessons will give you what you need to know to understand and use the rules of mechanics to improve your writing.

Periods

Ending Sentences

▶ Use a period at the end of a declarative sentence. A declarative sentence makes a statement or asserts a fact.

> **I picked the last daffodil for you.**
> **Daffodils are native to Northern Europe.**

▶ An imperative sentence—one that expresses a command or request (when the request is not a question)—also ends with a period.

> **Evelyn, please take out the garbage.**
> **Let me take you to the Smithsonian Institution.**
> **See the new exhibit when it opens.**

▶ Do not use a period to end a sentence that is set in parentheses within another sentence.

> **Miguel Vasquez (he is my best friend) is going to be a lifeguard.**

▶ Place a period *outside* the parentheses at the end of a sentence if the words in parentheses are part of the entire sentence.

> **Miguel Vasquez is going to be a lifeguard (at the Brentwood Swim Club).**

▶ Place a period *inside* the parentheses at the end of a sentence if the words in parentheses form their own sentence.

> **Miguel Vasquez is going to be a lifeguard. (He finally finished his certification requirements.)**

Abbreviations

▶ Use a period after an initial that substitutes for a person's first or middle name.

Jan C. Sorenson   **P.G. Pappas**

▶ Use a period after an abbreviation of a personal title. Also abbreviate professional or academic degrees that follow a person's name.

Ms. Sue Myers   **Chris Piper, D.D.S.**

▶ Use a period after abbreviations in addresses. Do not, however, use a period after two-letter state postal abbreviations.

Ms. Jane Simpson
234 Cambridge St.
Hoboken, NJ 11122

Mr. Rick Rhoades
1567 Jackson Ave.
Santa Cruz, CA 99111

▶ Use periods with abbreviations that refer to times, dates, or units of measure (except for metric units).

a.m.   p.m.   A.D.   B.C.   oz.   ft.   lb.   in.

▶ Do not add an extra period after an abbreviation at the end of a sentence. However, use a period after an abbreviation and before a question mark or an exclamation point.

Many tourists go to Washington, D.C.
Would you like to go to Washington, D.C.?

More Abbreviations

▶ Some abbreviations do not use periods. Do not use periods for abbreviations that are pronounced letter by letter or as words (acronyms). The names of organizations or government agencies often are written as acronyms.

> NASA   IRS   CIA   YMCA

▶ Do not use periods when abbreviating metric units.

> cm   kg   ml   l   km

▶ Do not use periods when abbreviating most computer terms.

> WWW   CPR   e-mail   DVD

Decimals

▶ Use a period between the whole number and the fractional parts of a number:

> 32.5 mi.   1.75 km   109.26 lb.

▶ Use a period between numbers indicating dollars and cents.

> $4.50 $13.85

Outlines

▶ Use a period after a number or letter used in the first four levels of the outline numbering system.

> I. Plants
>   A. Common garden plants
>   1. Tomatoes
>   a. Roma tomatoes

Writing Connection

Abbreviations are shortened versions of longer words. They should be used sparingly in most types of writing.

Other End Marks

Question Marks

▶ Use a question mark at the end of interrogative sentences.

> **When was the French Revolution?**

▶ Use a question mark at the end of a question in the parentheses within another sentence.

> **Jose Rodriguez (don't you know him?) applied for the job.**

▶ Do not use a question mark in indirect questions.

> **Monica asked for the location of the bank.**

Exclamation Points

▶ Use an exclamation point at the end of a sentence that shows strong feeling or indicates a forceful command.

> **What an amazing movie!**
> **Let go of my hat!**

Interjections

▶ Use an exclamation point when an interjection expresses strong emotion.

> **Wow!**   **Yes!**   **Ouch!**   **Ha!**

> ### Writing Connection
> Be careful not to overuse exclamation points in your writing. Too many exclamation points will distract or annoy your reader.

# Commas

Commas separate ideas or items in a list, organize information, or show a pause or a change in thought.

Dates

▶ Use a comma within a date to separate the day from the year, but not the *month* from the year.

> **September 14, 1942**   **September 1942**

▶ When writing a date within a sentence, use another comma after the year (unless the date appears at the end of a sentence).

Series

▶ Use a comma after each item before the conjunction in a series of three or more words, phrases, or clauses.

> **Alaska, Vermont, and New York are my favorite states.** (words)
>
> **We can either sail to Alaska, drive to Vermont, or fly to New York.** (phrases)
>
> **Ian was reading his book before he boarded the plane, while he was flying, and after he arrived.** (clauses)

▶ Use a comma between two or more adjectives that equally modify the same noun.

> **I thought I heard a big, hungry bear stomping around outside our tent.**

▶ Do not use commas between two adjectives when the adjective nearest the noun it modifies sounds like it is part of the noun.

> **The baby played with a blue plastic toy.** (no commas needed between *blue* and *plastic* because *plastic toy* sounds like one thing)

Parts of a Letter

▶ In a friendly letter, use a comma after the greeting and the closing.

Dear Matthew,   Yours truly,

▶ In a formal business letter, use a comma only after the closing.

To Whom It May Concern: Sincerely,

Dialogue and Quotations

▶ Use a comma before or after a speaker tag in a direct quote to set it apart from the rest of the sentence.

Lee asked, "What time do you think it is?"

▶ When the speaker tag is at the end of the sentence, set the comma inside the quotation marks.

"I know it is after two o'clock," Gita answered.

▶ When the speaker tag is in the middle of the quotation, use a comma both before and after it. Place the comma inside the quotation marks before the speaker tag.

"Wait," Todd said, "my watch says two-thirty."

▶ When directly addressing a person, use a comma or commas to set off the person's name.

Sean, did you find your notebook?
Yes, Anna, I found it in the desk drawer.

Commas in Addresses

▶ Use a comma to set off the name of a state or country that follows the name of a city.

I've never been to Carson City, Nevada.

▶ Within a sentence, use a comma after the last word of a place name (unless it is at the end of a sentence).

Hebron, Newfoundland, Canada, borders the Labrador Sea.

Commas with Interjections

▶ Use a comma with an interjection when an exclamation point would be too strong. Some mild interjections include *oh, ah, well,* and *why*.

Oh, where did I leave my coat?

▶ Use a comma after *yes* or *no* when they are used as mild interjections.

Yes, you may go.

Interrupters

▶ Use a comma both before and after an interrupter—a word, clause, or phrase that interrupts the main thought of a sentence. There are two rules to help you decide whether an item is an interrupter.
1. It can be left out without changing the meaning of a sentence.
2. It could be placed nearly anywhere in the sentence without changing the meaning of the sentence.

Frank, as you know, told Rosa that Janet was right.
Minnesota, for example, did not become a state until 1858.

Try It
How many different places in this sentence could you put the interrupter *on the other hand?*
▶ *Sarah spent most of her day with her father.*

Compound Sentences

▷ Use a comma between the independent clauses of a compound sentence when they are joined by a coordinating conjunction.

Sharifa was waiting for us, but we didn't know it.

> **Exceptions**
> ▷ A comma is not necessary when the independent clauses are short and closely connected in thought.
>
> **I stayed but he left.**
>
> ▷ If the independent clauses are long and have commas within them, use a semicolon instead of a comma.
>
> **At the end of our trip, I stayed in Cincinnati, Ohio; but he went on to Pittsburgh, Pennsylvania.**
>
> ▷ If the independent clauses are not joined with a conjunction, use a semicolon instead of a comma.
>
> **I stayed in Cincinnati, Ohio; he left for Pittsburgh.**

Clauses and Phrases

▷ Commas should be used to set off a nonessential adjective clause in a sentence. If the clause simply gives more information and is not necessary to the basic meaning of the sentence, it is nonessential.

South Dakota, which is home to Mount Rushmore, became a state on November 2, 1889.

An essential adjective clause is necessary to the meaning of a sentence and should not be set off with a comma.

The dog that lives down the street barks constantly.

▷ Use commas to set off an appositive that is not essential to the meaning of the sentence. An appositive is a noun that is placed next to another noun to identify it or add information to it.

My oldest sister, Starla, bought a new car.

▷ Set off an adverb clause at the beginning of a sentence that comes before the main clause. An adverb clause begins with a subordinating conjunction, such as *after*, *because*, *before*, *if*, *since*, and *where*.

Because I overslept, I missed the bus.

▷ Set off two or more prepositional phrases, or a single long prepositional phrase, at the beginning of a sentence.

In the spring of 1985, my brother graduated from high school.

Colons and Semicolons

▶ Use a colon to introduce a list of items in a sentence. In the sentence before the list, include a word or phrase such as *these*, *the following*, or *as follows*.

> **These are my favorite dog breeds: the Italian greyhound, the Pekingese, and the cocker spaniel.**

▶ Use a colon to introduce an important quote.

> **Before crossing the Delaware River, George Washington said this to General Knox: "The fate of an empire depends upon this night."**

▶ Use a colon after the greeting in a formal business letter.

▶ Use a colon between the hour and minute of the exact time.

Semicolons

▶ Use a semicolon when the independent clauses in a compound sentence are not joined with a coordinating conjunction.

> **Richard wants to find a new job; he is a good manager.**

▶ Use a semicolon to separate the items in a series when they already contain commas.

> **The game show contestants were Samantha, an accountant; Rajesh, a software engineer; and Lydia, an airline pilot.**

Writing Connection

It is a good idea to use semicolons sparingly. Overuse could result in longer, more complicated sentences when shorter ones will do.

Quotation Marks, Underlining, and Apostrophes

Quotation Marks

▶ Use quotation marks to enclose the titles of short stories, poems, magazine or newspaper articles, songs, book chapters, and works of art.

"Eleven" (short story)   **"Safety First"** (article)

▶ Use quotation marks to set off the exact words that have been spoken or written by someone. Quotation marks go *outside* periods, commas, and other end punctuation marks.

"My favorite place to visit is Cape Cod," Ada said.
Jess said, "My favorite place to visit is New York."

▶ Use quotation marks to enclose a direct quote from a source.

Herman Melville's novel *Moby Dick* begins with these words: "Call me Ishmael."

Underlining

▶ Underline or italicize the titles of books, movies, magazines, and newspapers.

Prairie Songs (book)   *National Geographic* (magazine)

Apostrophes

▶ **Contractions:** Use an apostrophe to replace letters that have been left out to form a contraction.

would have = would've   did not = didn't   let us = let's

▶ **Possessives:** For a singular noun and some plural nouns, use an apostrophe and an *s* to show possession.

Please help me find the children's shoes.

For plural nouns that end in *s*, use an apostrophe alone.

I found the boys' coats, but *not* their shoes.

Parentheses, Hyphens, Dashes, and Ellipses

Parentheses

▶ Use parentheses to add extra information to a sentence.

This scrapbook (my favorite) is from my vacation in New Zealand.

The map (see figure 15) shows the location of the rain forest.

▶ Use parentheses to indicate a person's birth and death dates.

Abraham Lincoln (1809–1865)

Hyphens and Dashes

▶ Use a hyphen to divide a word at the end of a line, between syllables.

▶ Use a hyphen to make certain compound words. Check your dictionary to see if the compound word requires a hyphen.

high-pitched   attorney-at-law   vice president

▶ Use a hyphen to create a compound adjective when the adjective comes before the word it modifies.

a blue-green parrot   the well-to-do businesswoman

▶ Use a hyphen to write out numbers in a fraction.

two-thirds of the class   one-fourth cup of sugar

▶ Use a hyphen to write out compound numbers.

ninety-nine red balloons   twenty-two trombones

▶ Use dashes to indicate a break in a sentence or a change in thought.

The best part—well, the second best part—is that it was summer in New Zealand in December.

Ellipses

▶ Use an ellipsis (three spaced periods) to show that words have been left out of a direct quotation.

"There are several large cities . . . in New Zealand."

Capitalization

Sentences

▶ Capitalize the first word of a sentence.

The Iberian Peninsula includes all of Spain and Portugal.

▶ Capitalize the first word of a sentence in a direct quotation.

Esther said, "We have many pictures of our vacation."

Letters

▶ Capitalize the first word in the greeting and closing of a letter. Also capitalize the title and name of the person addressed.

Dear Frank,   **Dear Ms. Winstead,**

Yours truly,   **Sincerely,**

Personal Pronoun, *I*

▶ Capitalize the personal pronoun *I*.

My sister and I are going to leave tomorrow.

Words Used as Names

▶ Capitalize common nouns used as names, such as words showing family relationship.

When I talked to Mom yesterday, I could tell she was tired.

Proper Nouns and Adjectives

▶ Capitalize all proper nouns and adjectives created from them.

Spain, Spanish rice   **Florida, Florida oranges**

People

▶ Capitalize names of people, including their titles and initials. Also capitalize pet names.

President Abraham Lincoln   **Ms. Kazuko H. Kitamura**

my cat Mystic   **J.D. Salinger**

Titles

▶ Capitalize the first, last, and important words in titles of written works, such as books, newspapers, magazines, poems, plays, articles, and short stories.

National Geographic   *Tuck Everlasting*

▶ In running text, do not capitalize an article at the beginning of a title.

My mother reads the *New York Times* every day of the week.

▶ Follow the same rules of capitalization for titles of musical compositions and works of art.

"Torna a Surriento" (song)   *Mother and Child* **(painting)**

Geography

▶ Capitalize the names of natural geographic features, such as bodies of water, continents, and landforms.

Atlantic Ocean   South America   Rocky Mountains

▶ Capitalize compass direction words when they are used to refer to a specific region of a country.

the South   the Midwest   the North

▶ Do not capitalize compass direction words used in other ways.

There are beautiful lakes in northern Minnesota.

▶ Capitalize the names of planets and other astronomical bodies.

Earth   the Big Dipper   Haley's Comet

Places

▶ Capitalize the names of countries, provinces, states, cities, counties, and continents.

Bolivia   British Columbia   California   La Paz

▶ Capitalize the names of public areas.

Hawaii Volcanoes National Park   Times Square

▶ Capitalize the names of public buildings, bridges, roads, and streets.

the White House   Golden Gate Bridge   Foxtrot Street

Nationalities

▶ Capitalize nationalities, ethnic groups, or races of people.

French   African-American   Indonesian   Korean

Languages

▶ Capitalize the names of languages.

Sanskrit   English   Portuguese   Arabic

Religions

▶ Capitalize the names of deities and sacred documents of religions.

Islam   Christianity   Shiva   the Koran

Dates

▶ Capitalize the names of months, days, and holidays.

November Wednesday   Martin Luther King Day

Historical Importance

▶ Capitalize the important words in the names of historical periods, events, buildings, monuments, and documents.

World War II   the Capitol   Magna Carta
Vietnam War Memorial   The Great Depression

Organizations

▶ Capitalize the names and abbreviations of organizations, agencies, teams, and associations.

Girl Scouts of America   Bureau of Motor Vehicles

Product Names

▶ Capitalize the names of specific products.

Cannit Cola   Everspring Tea

Outlines

▶ Capitalize every word in a main heading and the first word in each subheading of an outline. Also use capital letters to indicate additional subheadings.

II. Traffic Rules
   A. Street signs
      1. Stop
      2. Yield

Glossary

A

abstract noun   a noun that names ideas, qualities, and feelings

acronym   the short form of several words, usually as in the name of an organization, such as NASA for National Aeronautics and Space Administration

across-the-curriculum words   vocabulary words that are specific to different subjects studied in school, such as words commonly used in math, science, social studies, and health

action verb   a verb that expresses a mental or physical action or tells what a subject is holding or owns

active voice   when the subject performs the verb's action

adjective clause   a dependent clause that modifies a noun or pronoun in the main clause of a sentence

adverb clause   a dependent clause that modifies the verb in the main clause of a sentence

affirmative word   a word that expresses a positive idea, such as *always*, *anybody*, and *everyone*; the opposite of a negative word

alliteration   the repetition of the consonant sounds at the beginning of words

anachronism   something in a work of historical fiction that is wrong for the time period

analogy   a comparison of two words based on how the two words are related

antecedent   a word referred to or replaced by a pronoun

appositive   a noun that follows another noun to modify or rename it

appositive phrase   includes an appositive and the words that modify it

assonance   the repetition of vowel sounds in words

auxiliary verb   a helping verb that helps the main verb show action or express a state of being

B

ballad   a poem that tells a dramatic or exciting story

bibliography   a list of research materials used and referred to in the preparation of an article or report

byline   the place where a reporter writes his or her name in a news story

C

caricatures   exaggerated illustrations of people, often used in editorial cartoons to make a point

cause and effect diagram (or organizer)   a type of graphic organizer that shows the effects of a particular cause

chain of events map   a type of graphic organizer in which the steps of a process are written in the order in which they happen or the events in a story's plot

character analysis   looking closely at a piece of writing to learn as much as you can about a character

chronological order   an organizational pattern that tracks events in time order

cinquain   a poem that has five lines and follows a special pattern

clause   a group of words that has a subject and a verb

closed compound word   a compound word that has no space between the words

closed couplet   a poem that is made of just one couplet

collecting grid   a type of graphic organizer used to record information gathered from many different sources

collective noun   a noun that names groups, or collections, of people, animals, or things, such as *family*, *audience*, and *herd*

common noun   a noun that names any person, place, thing, or idea and starts with a lowercase letter

comparative form   the form of an adjective or adverb that compares two of something

compare/contrast essay   a type of expository writing in which two subjects are compared and contrasted

complete predicate   includes all the words in the predicate of a sentence

complete subject   includes the simple subject and all the words that describe it

complex sentence   a type of sentence that is made of an independent clause and one or more dependent clauses

compound noun   a noun made of more than one word, such as *father-in-law*, *gaslight*, and *elementary school*

compound predicate   two or more simple predicates joined by a conjunction that share the same subject

compound sentence   two or more simple sentences joined by a conjunction

compound subject   two or more simple subjects connected by a conjunction that share the same verb

compound-complex sentence   a sentence that has two or more independent clauses and at least one dependent clause

concrete nouns   words that name things you can see, touch, hear, smell, or taste

conjunction   a word used to connect words, phrases, or clauses in a sentence

connotation   the feeling a word creates in the reader

context clue   words or sentences that surround an unknown word that give the reader clues about the meaning of the unknown word

conventions   the mechanics of writing that include spelling, punctuation, grammar, capitalization, and indentation

coordinating conjunction   a word that connects two or more elements in a sentence that have equal importance such as *and, but,* and *or*

correlative conjunction   words that work in pairs to join words and groups of words, such as *either/or* and *neither/nor*

couplet   a type of poetry that has two lines that rhyme

D

declarative sentence   a sentence that makes a statement and ends with a period

definite article   the article *the* that identifies specific people, places, things, or ideas

demonstrative pronoun   points out something. *This, that, these,* and *those* are demonstrative pronouns when they take the place of a noun.

dependent clause   part of a sentence containing a subject and verb that cannot stand alone as a sentence

dialogue journal   a type of journal in which two people write back and forth about a subject as if they were having a conversation

diamante   a five or seven-line poem that follows a pattern of a certain number of words in each line, which is how it gets its "diamond" shape

direct object   a noun or pronoun that receives the action of the verb

double negative   when two negative words are used to express a single idea

drafting   the second stage, or phase, in the writing process in which the writer starts writing

E

editing/proofreading   the fourth stage, or phase, in the writing process in which the writer makes corrections in spelling, grammar, usage, capitalization, and punctuation

editorial   a type of newspaper article that states an opinion about a current topic of interest

editorial cartoon   an editorial in the form of a cartoon that uses images and a few words to express an opinion

end rhyme   rhyming words at the end of two or more lines of poetry

exclamatory sentence   a sentence that expresses strong emotion and ends with an exclamation point

expository diagram   a type of graphic organizer that helps you sort information into topics and subtopics; also called *informational organizer*

expository writing   a form of writing that explains or gives information, such as newspaper and magazine articles, textbooks, and biographies

F

fantasy   a story that has characters, places, or events that could not exist in the real world

figurative language   words or groups of words that stand for more than their literal meaning, such as similes, metaphors, and personification

first-person point of view   the narrator tells the story and uses the words *I, me, my, we, us,* and *our*

5 Ws chart   a type of graphic organizer used to organize information that answers the questions *who? what? when? where?* and *why?*

focal point   a method of ordering details according to where they are located in reference to the main object in a scene

fragment   a group of words that does not express a complete thought and is missing a subject, a predicate, or both

free verse   a type of poetry that doesn't follow any specific form and usually does not rhyme

freewriting   a type of prewriting in which the writer lets his or her ideas flow freely onto the page in the form of sentences

future perfect tense   an action or condition that will begin and end before another future event begins

future tense   expresses an action or condition that will happen in the future

G

gerund   a kind of verbal that ends in *-ing* and is used as a noun

H

haiku   a three-line poem about nature that has a specific number of syllables for each line

helping verb   a verb that helps the main verb express action or make a statement; also called an *auxiliary verb*

historical fiction   a story that takes place in an actual time and place in the past. The story gives lots of details about the period in which the events took place.

homographs   words that are spelled the same but have different meanings and origins

homophones   words that sound the same but have different meanings and spellings

hyperbole   an extreme exaggeration often used for humorous effect

I

idea book   a journal used to keep ideas that a writer may wish to use in a piece of writing

idiom   a word or group of words that cannot be understood by knowing only the literal meaning, such as *lost your temper*

imagery   the use of words to create images or pictures in the mind of the reader

imperative sentence   a sentence that gives a command or makes a request and ends with a period or exclamation point

indefinite article   the articles *a* and *an* that refer to a general group of people, places, things, or ideas

indefinite pronoun   a pronoun that does not refer to a specific person, place, thing, or idea

independent clause   a group of words that has a subject and a predicate and can stand alone as a sentence

indirect object   a noun or pronoun for whom or to whom something is done

informal writing   casual writing, used for friendly letters, stories, and note taking

informational organizer   a type of graphic organizer in which major topics and subtopics are organized; also called *expository diagram*

intensive pronoun a pronoun that ends with *-self* or *-selves* and emphasizes a noun or pronoun already mentioned

internal rhyme words that rhyme in the middle of a line of poetry

interrogative pronoun a pronoun that asks a question, such as *whose*

interrogative sentence a sentence that asks a question and ends with a question mark

interrupter a word or phrase that interrupts the central idea of a sentence

inverted sentence a sentence in which the subject follows the verb, often beginning with a prepositional phrase

irregular verb a verb that does not follow the rule for adding *-ed* to form the past tense

L

lead the first paragraph of a news story that answers the five W's

learning log where you write about something you are studying, such as a science experiment

linking verb a state-of-being verb that links the subject of the sentence with a word in the predicate

lyric a type of poem that expresses strong personal emotions and has a rhythmic sound pattern

M

main clause a clause that has a subject and a predicate and can stand alone as a sentence

memo (memorandum) a short message that communicates something to a person or group of people

metaphor a figure of speech that compares two unlike things without using the words *like* or *as*

meter the rhythmic pattern of a poem

minutes the official notes of a meeting used to keep an organized record of the people present and the issues discussed

misplaced modifier a group of words that modifies the wrong word, or appears to modify more than one word in a sentence

modifier a word or phrase that describes another word or phrase

mood the feeling one gets when reading a particular piece of writing

N

narrative writing   a form of writing that tells a story or gives an account of an event

O

object of the preposition   the noun or pronoun that follows the preposition in a prepositional phrase

object pronoun   a pronoun used as a direct object or indirect object, such as *him* or *us*

onomatopoeia   a word that imitates the sound made by or connected with the thing to which you refer, such as the *pitter-patter* of rain

open compound word   a compound word that has a space between the two smaller words

outline   a type of graphic organizer used to show main topics and subtopics. An outline uses Roman numerals, capital letters, and lowercase letters to label these ideas.

P

parallelism   using words and phrases in the same way within a sentence

paraphrase   using one's own words to summarize all the ideas in another piece of writing

participial phrase   includes a participle and other words that complete its meaning. A participial phrase always functions as an adjective.

passive voice   when the subject receives the verb's action

past participle   a participle, acting as an adjective, formed by adding *-ed* to a verb

past perfect tense   expresses an action or conditon that began and ended before another event in the past

past tense   expresses an action or conditon that began and ended in the past

personal narrative   a story about something that happened in the writer's life

personal pronoun   a pronoun that refers to people or things

personification   a figure of speech in which an object or idea is given human qualities

persuasive report   a report that is written to change the thinking, feelings, or actions of the reader about a specific issue or get the reader to recognize the writer's point of view

persuasive writing a type of writing in which the writer tries to change the way the readers think or feel about a topic or to inspire action

phrase a group of words that does not have a subject or predicate

plagiarism the copying of someone's exact words and passing them off as your own

plot analysis identifying the problem, conflict or conflicts, climax, and conclusion of a story

point of view the position of the storyteller in relation to the story. Most stories are written from either first-person or third-person point of view.

portfolio a type of folder or notebook in which a writer keeps his/her pieces of writing

possessive nouns nouns that show who owns something

possessive pronoun a pronoun that shows who or what owns something

postscript (P.S.) a part added at the end of a letter that adds something the writer forgot to say in the main part of the letter

predicate the part of a sentence that tells what the subject does, has, is, or is like

predicate adjective an adjective that follows a linking verb and describes the subject

predicate nominative another name for predicate noun

predicate noun a noun or pronoun that follows a linking verb and renames or identifies the subject

prefix one or more letters added to the beginning of a root or base word that changes the word's meaning

preposition a word that shows position or direction

prepositional phrase a phrase that begins with a preposition and ends with a noun or pronoun

present participle a participle that is formed by adding *-ing* to a verb and acts as an adjective

present perfect tense expresses an action or condition that took place at an undetermined time in the past or that began in the past and continues in the present

present tense expresses an action or condition that is repeated or happens regularly

presentation how your writing looks in its final form

prewriting the first stage, or phase, of the writing process in which the writer thinks, brainstorms, and makes a list or web to write down thoughts he or she wants to include in a piece of writing

process   the step-by-step procedure one follows to do something, usually resulting in an end product

proofreading marks   a set of commonly agreed upon marks that is used to show where corrections are needed in a piece of writing

proper adjective   an adjective made from a proper noun that always starts with a capital letter

proper noun   noun that names a specific person, place, thing, or idea and always starts with a capital letter

prose   all types of writing, except poetry

public service ad   an advertisement that persuades the audience to do something in their best interest or in the best interest of the public as a whole

publishing   the final stage, or phase, of the writing process in which the writer makes a final and correct copy of the piece of writing and then shares it with the selected audience

purpose   the reason for writing something, usually to inform, to explain, to entertain, or to persuade

Q

quatrain   a four-line poem or a stanza of a longer poem that expresses one thought and has a variety of rhyming patterns

R

rambling sentence   a sentence that contains too many thoughts connected by conjunctions

realistic story   a story in which the characters, setting, and plot are made up but seem real

reflexive pronoun   a pronoun that ends with -*self* or -*selves* and refers back to the subject of the sentence

relative pronoun   a pronoun that introduces a word group called a dependent clause that modifies a noun or pronoun used in the main part of the sentence

research report   a report that gives information about real facts, ideas, or events

revising   the third stage, or phase, of the writing process in which the writer makes the writing better by adding, deleting, consolidating, rearranging, and/or clarifying material

rhythm   a pattern of accented and unaccented syllables in a poem

run-on sentence   two or more sentences incorrectly written as one

S

salutation   the greeting of a letter

science fiction   a form of writing that develops scientific or technological ideas into a fiction story

science observation report   an observation report written about a science experiment

sentence fluency   a quality of writing in which the sentences flow smoothly

signal words   words that tell the order in which things happen in a process, such as *first, next,* and *last;* also called *transition words*

simile   a figure of speech that compares two or more things that are not alike by using the word *like* or *as*

simple predicate   the main word or word group in the predicate in a sentence

simple sentence   has one subject and one predicate

simple subject   the main word or word group in the subject in a sentence

stanza   lines of poetry that are grouped together

state-of-being verb   a verb that does not show action but shows a condition or state of being

story map   a type of graphic organizer that is used to outline the events of a story

straight news story   a news story about a real event that has taken place recently that tells only the facts

subject   the part of a sentence that tells who or what the sentence is about

subject pronoun   a pronoun used as the subject of a sentence

subject-verb agreement   when the verb agrees with the subject of the sentence. They both must be singular or plural.

subordinate clause   another name for dependent clauses that are introduced by a subordinating conjunction

subordinating conjunction   word that introduces an adverb clause

subtopic   a subdivision of the main topic of a piece of writing

suffix   one or more letters added to the end of a root or base word that changes the word's meaning

superlative form   the form of an adjective or adverb that compares three or more of something

T

T-chart   a type of graphic organizer shaped like the letter *T* that is used to categorize information

tone   the attitude a writer expresses in a piece of writing

transitive verb   a verb that transfers action to a direct object

travel log   a record of observations made during a trip

triplet   a type of poetry that has three lines that are about the same length and rhythm and that form a complete thought

V

Venn diagram   a type of graphic organizer used to compare and contrast two subjects

verb tense   the time the action of the verb takes place such as present, past, or future

verbal   a verb form that is used as a noun, adjective, or adverb

voice   the tone or sound of a piece of writing

W

web   a type of graphic organizer that can be used to show characteristics of a person or thing or how ideas are related

writing process   a process used to develop writing. The stages, or phases, of the writing process are prewriting, drafting, revising, editing/proofreading, and publishing.

Index

The index is a list of words and page numbers. It lists the different things that are in the Handbook. The words are in alphabetical order. You look in the list for the word you want to find. Then you look at the page number of the Handbook where it can be found. The index is a good tool. Learn to use it. It can save you a lot of time.

R

rambling sentence, 251, 359
realistic story, 164–169
reasons, 300–301
redundant words, 360
reflexive pronoun, 341
relative pronoun, 341
repetition, 293
research, 27–28, 130, 136–143, 153,
     157–159, 171, 175
research report, 136–143
revising, 18–19, 38–43, 58–59, 83, 89, 91,
     93, 98, 107, 111, 116–117, 122–123, 129,
     135, 143, 151, 157, 163, 169, 175, 181,
     187, 195, 203, 209, 219, 223, 229, 237,
     241
revising checklist, 43
rhyme, 232
rhyming poetry, 232–237
rhythm, 232, 237, 293
run-on sentence, 46, 251, 358

S

salutation, 75, 77–78, 80–81, 84
science fiction, 176–181
science observation, 204–209
semicolons, 46, 386
sentence fluency, 10, 14, 43, 89, 91, 93,
     135, 143
sentence fragment, 250, 358
sentence problems, 250, 358–360
sentences, 10, 19, 43, 244–250, 348–349,
     356–359, 361
series, 382
setting, 100, 104–105, 107, 164, 168–169,
     174–176, 180–182, 186, 189, 195,
     304–305
setting analysis, 104–105
signal words, 118, 295
signature, 75, 77–78, 80–81, 84
simile, 233, 237, 241, 290
simple predicate, 348
simple sentence, 356

simple subject, 348
singular nouns, 338
solution, 216–219, 225, 228
sound of language, 292–293. See also,
     alliteration, 292
     assonance, 292
     end rhyme, 292
     internal rhyme, 293
     onomatopoeia,   292
     repetition, 293
     rhythm, 293
sources, 137–138
speaker tag, 306–307, 383
stage directions, 194–195
staging, 189
stanzas, 232
state-of-being verb, 342
story elements, 302–305
story map, 29, 35
straight news story, 124–125, 128
structures of writing, 242–265. See also,
     graphic organizers, 260–265
     paragraphs, 10, 19, 34, 43, 252–259
     sentences, 244–251
style guides, 46
subject, 244, 246, 249, 348–351, 358
subject pronoun, 340
subject/verb agreement, 46, 368
subordinate clause, 354, 356–357
subordinating conjunction, 248, 347, 355
subtopics, 24, 30, 34
suffixes, 324–325
summarizing words, 279
summary, 96–99, 112, 116, 138, 143, 213,
     253, 282
superlative form, 372
supporting details, 11, 34
supporting sentences, 252, 255
synonyms, 46, 284, 312–313

T

taking notes, 137, 143
task, 9, 19–21
T-chart, 108, 131

▶ Photo Credits: